Viewfinder

Viewfinder

A MEMOIR

AMOL PALEKAR

Published by Westland Books, a division of Nasadiya Technologies Private Limited, in 2024

First reprint, 2025

No. 269/2B, First Floor, 'Irai Arul', Vimalraj Street, Nethaji Nagar, Alapakkam Main Road, Maduravoyal, Chennai 600095

ISBN: 9789360455446

10 9 8 7 6 5 4 3 2

Concept, book design and curation: Sandhya Gokhale
Cover photo: © Mrunal Kalsekar
Cover design: Saurabh Garge
Endpaper and chapter illustrations: Narasimma Balaji
Typeset by Jojy Philip & Pratik Kalekar
QR code development: Srujan Deshpande

Printed at Parksons Graphics Pvt. Ltd

to those who believe
in the power of resistance...

About the QR Codes in the book

There comes a time when the desire for financial gain no longer drives every decision. For the past two decades, I've striven to make philanthropic pursuits, although embracing Gandhiji's aparigrah remains an ongoing aspiration. As a part of this journey and in celebration of our shared path, I've infused this memoir with my lesser-known works of art. It's a tribute to my audiences.

Credit for this visionary concept goes to Sandhya Gokhale who could not have realised it without unwavering support of Srijan Deshpande.

Although I don't hold the rights to all the films made available through this book, the rights holders responded graciously to my call, permitting these films to be freely shared online. Nearly all the films are National Award winners, due to which dedicated officials from the National Film Development Corporation/National Film Archive of India (NFDC/NFAI) have devoted months to digitise the content and then to upload it all. I owe each one of them my heartfelt gratitude.

Within this book, you will find QR codes connected to various posters, photos, films and audio-visual recordings. Each code is numbered, the list of which is provided as well. Simply scan the QR code with your mobile device, and you'll be directed to the relevant website (URL link). Clicking on it will allow you to immerse yourself in that particular work of art. To elevate the experience further, you can even cast it to your TV for a grander viewing.

I cherish this enduring connection that will forever tie us together.

Acknowledgements

Westland Books • Gautam Padmanabhan • Minakshi Thakur
• Saurabh Garge • Pallavi Mohan • Sharad Ashtekar
• Srujan Deshpande • Mrunal Kalsekar
• Ashok Shahane • R.J. Aniruddha • Prof. Milind Malashe
• Abhinav Kafre • Satish Naik • Pratik Kalekar
• Narasimma Balaji • Ganesh Natrajan • Uma Ganesh
• Sunil Khare • Sabina Sanghvi & Hemant Pachmiya
• Suhita Thatte • B. Balaji Rao & Amit Ropalekar • Osanja
• Unnati Kshirsagar • Ravindra Lakhe • Mangala Athlekar
• Shashi Vyas • Kishor Kadam • Sunil Shanbag • Sanjay Pethe
• NCPA Archives • Jasbir Singh Baidwan/Bhavesh Pratap Singh
(NFDC-NFAI)

• Samiha Dabholkar • Dr Girish Deshpande
• Sandhya Gokhale

Amidst the Clumsy Mess of Tossed Stubs…

The act of excavating one's own life and writing about it feels like an utterly undesirable enterprise. It feels as though I'm holding an enormous sack in my hands, a sack that keeps growing larger and larger, like yeasted dough, fermenting and distending shapelessly. Because of it being filled to the brim with a ceaseless stream of thoughts and ideas, countless events, heaps of people, familiar faces, hazy images, the uproar of emotions, good and bad tastes, myriad smells, loads of sorrow-pain-grief, and so much more that just doesn't seem to end. It's inescapable that I will cram into this sack details such as our cat purring and gnawing away at my earlobe, or the expectedly unique taste of every single pani-puri I've had over decades, or the sudden fear that grips me every time the curtain rises with that grinding sound in the theatre, or the way my face droops like a Modigliani portrait each time I look into the mirror… How much and what all should I pack into the sack?

What do I do with the trivial, scattered details? Like the first time a shirt stitched at Tardeo's Kachins touched my skin, the affection that overwhelmed me as I wiped the drool off my exhausted dog Junior's mouth, the twist in my gut as I packed the first canvas bought by the Tata Group… How are these not important? But they may not find a place within the physical confines of this book. Everything lived, endured, felt, preserved, created and accumulated—how will I decide what's disposable, what's essential and what isn't needed? Would I be unfair to those billions of lived moments that don't make it here?

Shall I just give up this effort? Why must I wrestle with doubts and dilemmas here when they don't assail me during the actual act of living? Living was easy in a way—putting one foot forward in zero gravity, then floating, flailing and reaching distant shores in default mode, sometimes gently and sometimes with a thud. But back then, did it ever feel effortless and smooth? The urge to peer into the darkness behind the curtain before the show stirs. To uncover the unseen driving 'reality' is a Kafkaesque conundrum, whether one has a front-row seat or is seated in the last row, farthest from the action. Every choice I made led to a fresh wave of dilemmas, except when impulse intervened, and then there was no dilemma at all. When I turned away a producer who came with cash in a bag, I didn't worry about how I would put bread on the table the next day, nor did I keep accepting the same roles just because I'd fallen in love with my own acting. Nor did I fear that I would lose Dubey's (Satyadev Dubey) support and friendship when I started accepting film offers. I hear also the echo of my daughter Shalmalee's words—'Dad, what have you done to yourself? Quit that cigarette'—the depth of her concern and my own self-neglect… How do I deal with such a maelstrom of emotions? The idea of stripping away all this entanglement from myself and leaving my vulnerabilities exposed to criticism and judgement—it's just too torturous.

But while I am at it, perhaps I could also drag out all the forgotten or deliberately buried things and events, and stuff them into this sack. The echoes of sighs, moans and sobs reverberating within me, the earthy taste of the crisp bellies of queen bees eaten in Bogota, the lousy cocktails at noisy parties, my breath stabilising at the oxygen-level of seventy, the farewell to the familiar walls of my house Chirebandi, the panic of forgetting lines while performing

Nakshatranche Dene (Debt of Stars) on stage, the enduring connection with *Ashwamedher Ghoda*, which got shelved after a four-day shoot, pieces of heart still lodged in completed yet never released films like *Paper Boats*, *Nirvaan, Kal, Ankush*, the tender touch of the script of *Kairee*, frayed and tattered after fourteen years of handling, being blindfolded while rehearsing for Divakar's unpublished short play *Andhale* and comprehending for the first time the world of the sightless, Sandhya's lingering whispers of 'hang in there'... Why allow this inner turmoil to disrupt the serenity of the present?

Even as I thrust memories into the sack, the chaos spills out, and a sea of scattered fragments surrounds me. How do I corral them all? It's like trying to collect forty years' worth of cigarette butts smoked daily, seventy-two a day, and the incessant smoke that was exhaled. Who knows where all the butts were tossed—in the depths of the Eiffel Tower, on the cobblestone streets of some small alley in Prague, in the Tasman Sea of Sydney, or in the filthy toilet of a cruise boat in Denmark. And in which direction do I walk to trace all the smoke left behind? It may be trapped in many chests; how will I ever find it? Can even Aladdin's genie find those lungs, some on the pyre, others beyond? Maybe artificial intelligence (AI) tools will do it—connecting some electrodes to the lungs, some to the brain, and the rest plugged into vast cloud databases. Even so, it will need my 'computer vision'. Otherwise, how will the machine interpret the significance of my digital footprint? So will this process, too, be circumscribed by my limitations? The machine will also ask me, 'How do you want it to be presented? Neatly, like your unwrinkled, starched shirts, or like a ramshackle snowman? Or like the overlayed strokes of oil paint on your canvas?' The machine's options will be countless, but the final call will still be mine to make.

'Every artiste has one's own class-characteristics,' my favourite poet-activist Namdeo Dhasal used to say. To me this was a tautologous claim; he was no exception, and neither am I. The contingencies of our existence will always be the constraints; my writing too will be tied to those. Should I then choose just the private endeavours, disregarding the broader socio-cultural reverberations of my existence and actions?

There's a precious trove of recollections that I have amassed over six decades:

> …the pleasure of honouring my friend Dinesh Thakur's last wish by bringing Dubey to his house; …the tears that welled up in my eyes when I read the headline, 'Amol and Utpal are the most popular romantic pair right now'; …the legendary painter Gaitonde's gentle praise when he paused in front of my artwork and whispered, 'I truly admire the painting'; …the conversation that ensued when the master filmmaker Satyajit Ray invited me to his residence after watching my film *Akriet*; …the surreal moment in which Sandhya said 'yes' to me; …the day I received my first Filmfare Award, having been nominated alongside stalwarts like Rajesh Khanna, Amitabh Bachchan and Sanjeev Kumar; …the memorable morning on which Kishori-tai invited me to join her for an early riyaz and gifted me with a soulful performance of Raga Lalit; …the triumphal silence after Hrishi-da declared his intention to make five films with me, as we sat together in his home; …the pat on my shoulder from Rajababu Barjatya, expressing gratitude for the film's success and my performance; …the twenty-five houseful shows of *Kusur* in which I played ACP Dandavate for eighty minutes at the age of seventy-five!

If I unearth such moments, I can easily construct a towering structure that touches the clouds. But then, why stuff all the painful, unavoidable, decisive moments as well into the sack? The sack will be shredded in no time given the cutting sharpness of my past. Maybe the storm will calm if the sack is ripped open. That's the moment to capture—when the sack's bottom tears… The contents, once packed tightly inside, now thrown up in the air, then slowly floating down like snowflakes, scattering gently on the ground. The shape that this scatter will form will be mine—like a blot of ultramarine blue ink spreading amorphously across blotting paper, abstract and moist. The motorcyclist riding round and round in the death-well, and the spectator engrossed in watching the rippling circles from outside—how starkly contrasting their experiences will be? Can the pace of those living through a gruelling ordeal ever truly align with the pace of those witnessing it from afar?

Coming back to the issue of keeping and discarding, can AI tools help me sort out my mess? One command can be easily executed: 'Computer, arrange before me the first hundred fragments that fall from the sack and hit the ground.' Such a random selection might turn out to be the naked truth! Let someone else decipher the heap then… maybe the publisher; let all the pieces that don't fit within the expected page count get shaved off. The ones with higher market value will likely be spared. Perhaps items such as 'what was left unsaid', 'things that remained undone' or 'the mistakes made' will have greater market worth, I suppose. My failure to create a more intense and immersive experience in the intimate scene of the play *Vasanakand*, the missed opportunities to tell several artistes that they were mediocre, my regret over not telling my mother before she passed that I forgave her, the missed chance to show B.R. Chopra a thumbs down after winning my case against him, the final glimpses of my mentors and many friends that I regretfully missed meeting before they passed away… who knows which regret will be more coveted, or which sorrow more sought after.

Do I have the necessary detachment for all this? Will this entire pursuit be genuine? Will I be truly honest? Most of all, after such a biopsy, will I, like Sisyphus, emerge unscathed? Marie Curie received her second Nobel Prize for discovering radium and polonium while researching uranium. But that same effort led to her death. She died of aplastic anaemia. It is said that her notebooks and research papers will continue to emit radiation for the next fifteen hundred years.

Why do these details come to my mind just now? This stream of consciousness, random, free-flowing, an absurd eruption…

What if someone finds the entirety of my eight decades trivial?

What expectations must others have from my quest to uncover the real person behind the actor? '*Ek Akela Is Sheher Mein*' in search of the real man behind the reel man—how can his search be straightforward and linear? I didn't have a target audience in mind before starting a film; the subject matter spoke to me, and the project took on a life of its own, attracting its own audience. Perhaps this book will unfold similarly, finding its own voice and attracting those whom it resonates with. I am more than just the hero of *Gol Maal*; reducing me to that single image overlooks the layers of my true identity. Despite the mismatch between who I truly am and how others see me, I've continued to evolve with my audiences, arriving at this momentous day.

I conclude my writing with René Magritte's words bolstering me: 'We must not fear daylight just because it almost always illuminates a miserable world.'

My catharsis is complete.

Everything has been resolved, like in the story of the Zen master who, after lifting a beautiful young woman from the middle of a stream and setting her down on the far side, simply moved on, unencumbered.

Just as we traditionally bid our film audiences 'Happy Viewing', I extend a warm welcome to readers, saying 'Happy Reading', as you begin to explore my world through this viewfinder.

Amol Palekar
Pune

The Hitch in the Double Role

I vividly remember the day I decided to dedicate my book to those who believe in the power of resistance.

It was 8 February 2019. I was set to inaugurate a retrospective of Prabhakar Barve's work *Inside the Empty Box* at the National Gallery of Modern Art (NGMA) in Mumbai. Sandhya and I reached a little early. We walked around looking at Barve's artistic oeuvre and his iconic diaries, meeting several artist friends along the way. Before we knew it, an hour had passed. It was time for the event, and the recently appointed director of the museum, Anita Rupavataram, arrived to lead us to it. On the way, she made a rather candid confession. 'Art is not my forte; honestly don't know much about visual arts. I have been transferred here from the Income Tax department.'

It was time for me to take the stage. To make sure I covered all my points quickly, I had prepared a short speech. I began by discussing the nuances of Barve's characteristic style and pictorial language. I especially touched on how his compositions transcended dimensional constraints and on the peculiarity of his colour scheme. Thereafter, I shared a personal memory of Barve. Normally, I avoid relating personal anecdotes in public, as they often come across as attempts to claim a close connection with a famous personality. But this incident underlined a rather rare quality of Barve's: his genuine admiration of younger artists.

In 1973, many artistes like Prabhakar Barve, Gaitonde, Prafulla Dahanukar, Pandit Jasraj and Jitendra Abhishekhi attended a show of my experimental play *Gochi* (Hitch). After the play, the customary 'fourth act' was convened in Vinod and Saryu Doshi's living room at their home on Pedder Road in Mumbai. 'While watching your experiment, I was constantly reminded of Salvador Dali's *Melting Time*. You have managed to intersect dimensions and spaces rather well in the presentation.' Barve's compliment took me by surprise. I didn't quiet grasp the sentences that followed, even though they reached my ears.

Further, in my speech, I cited an apt quote by René Magritte, as his influence on Barve was quite apparent in his narrative elements. 'Everything that is visible, hides something that is invisible.' Quoting that sentence, I moved on to my next point. The union government had recently issued two orders. The intention was clear: to tighten its grip on the affairs of NGMA, which for decades had freely exhibited thousands of works by many veteran as well as budding artists. Visiting the NGMA was sacred to many art lovers too. It was the prerogative of the gallery committee comprising local artists to decide whose work would be exhibited for what time frame, and so on. As per the government decree, the committee was abolished and an order was issued that going forward those decisions would be taken in Delhi. Also, the space in the gallery that exhibited the works of budding artists—even established ones occasionally—was to shrink significantly. It was announced that such works would be displayed only in one-sixth of the gallery space, i.e. they would be confined to the upper dome floor, and the selection of works that would be displayed in the rest of the gallery would be made by Delhi. Pursuant to these orders, the retrospectives of senior painter Sudhir Patwardhan and senior photographer Mehli Gobai, though confirmed earlier, were cancelled. It was yet another blow to artistic freedom. These 'fatwas' are often quietly swept under the rug, and those who are aware of them remain silent, either out of fear or to protect their own vested interests.

As I spoke about these orders, the director, Anita Rupavataram, interrupted me, questioning their relevance to the event. She asked me to refrain from talking about anything other than Barve. Sadly, veteran painter Suhas Bahulkar, the former president of the artists' local committee, seconded her: 'Don't violate propriety' were his words. Neither Sudhir Patwardhan nor any of the artists sitting in the audience protested. The entire gathering was a mute audience to the stifling silence. I felt disheartened to see the precarious state of artists. Why succumb to fear? Why relinquish your autonomy? Couldn't we muster some courage to stand tall, at least in the twilight of our lives? Wasn't there shame and disgrace in being powerless in the face of establishment? Are we really willing to sacrifice our dignity for a few assignments, grants, donations, houses under artists' quota, committee memberships and other accolades? The video of the incident went viral. Phone calls and messages of praise and solidarity poured in through the following week. Many who lacked the courage to publicly support me at the event later conveyed their appreciation. Despite it being a Sunday, the Ministry of Culture in Delhi immediately declared that the implementation of the notifications had been called off temporarily.

In recent times, we have seen the 'king's courtiers' resorting to extreme measures in their quest for 'royal favour'. Had my speech gone uninterrupted—without opposition—it would have been ignored and forgotten by all. Freedom of expression is being systematically restricted to disseminate anti-Muslim hatred and promote the Hindutva agenda. History is being distorted. In these troubling times, my failure to mitigate these challenges weighs heavily on me. When the opportunity to stand up against the ruler's arbitrariness presented itself, how could I have let it slip away? Since I was speaking at the very place that was being targeted, how could my actions be considered a 'violation of propriety' or a breach of protocol? The right time to speak up against tyranny is always *now*. My silence would have been deplorable. Defiance never came naturally to me, and it was noticeably absent in my childhood. I don't even recall grumbling against anything my parents and three sisters said, let alone getting into loud quarrels and fights. Even in my school life, I was always an obedient student and in complete awe of my teachers, Sohoni-bai, Rawale, Dugal, Malekar, Amrita, Savesar or Chitre guru-ji. At the school in Bordi, stealing raw chiku from the garden next to Sharadashram Hostel was about as far as my audacity went.

It must have been around 1958. I had completed ninth grade from Balmohan School in Shivaji Park when my parents decided to send me to a boarding school for two years. Perhaps they thought that this was how I would grow into a man. My elder sisters, Neelon-tai and Akka, came to bid me farewell at the Dadar train station. As Akka stood on the platform, she grew increasingly nervous. Neelon-tai noticed and asked her for the reason. After Akka whispered something in her ear, Neelon-tai stormed over to a man and slapped him. 'Is this how you treat a girl?' she shouted, hitting him again. This incident had a chilling effect on me.

Crises, challenges, dilemmas—whatever you might call them, something inside you triggers a response, compelling you to act. My first act of resistance, as far back as I can remember, was marrying Chitra Murdeshwar despite my mother's fierce opposition. Aai had two main reasons for her disapproval: one, Chitra's financial situation was better than ours; and two, she had recently undergone a surgery for a hole in her heart. I held my ground without getting into a quarrel, probably drawing strength from Neelon-tai's example, even though I was only twenty-two at the time.

Although I preferred a simple court marriage, I reluctantly agreed to a traditional wedding since both my mother and Chitra wanted it. My mother changed Chitra's name to Anuya. She and my father, Baba, attended the marriage rituals, but she didn't let Baba join us for the evening reception. After tying the knot, I embarked on a new journey of self-discovery and independence. Baba would visit Chitra and me in our small two-room house in Gavdevi, but my mother never came.

Perhaps having dealt with my mother's stern actions and bitterness, I could stand up to a tough autocrat like Satyadev Dubey later in life. He remained my revered guru regardless of his authoritarian nature. I vividly remember three instances when I committed the cardinal sin of opposing him.

It was in 1970 that I first co-directed a play with Satyadev Dubey. The play was *Vallabhpurchi Dantkatha* (originally *Ballabhpurer Rupkotha*, meaning The Legend of Vallabhpur) written by the iconic playwright Badal Sircar. I translated the original from Bengali to Marathi. Within a year, Dubey announced that he would direct Sircar's *Pagla Ghoda* (Wild Horse). I agreed to co-direct the play on the condition that Dubey wouldn't interfere with my rehearsals before the actual performance. One day Dubey suddenly arrived unannounced. After observing the rehearsal, he called me and my actors into the adjoining room.

'Do you understand the meaning of the dialogue you are delivering?' he asked my actor Gajanan Bangera.

'There is ridicule in the dialogue,' Bangera answered sheepishly.

Dubey could have gently suggested that he bring the sarcasm of the dialogue into his acting, but he didn't. Instead, he thundered. '*Toh phir lao na!*' (Then evoke it in your delivery).

Seeing Bangera nervous, I intervened. 'Dubey, please don't shake his confidence. Why did you visit after accepting my condition of zero interference?'

Govind Nihalani, who had accompanied him, mediated: 'What Amol is saying is right, let's get out of here.'

No one but I could talk back to Dubey in such a manner. He had granted me that privilege. My colleagues in Dubey's group Theatre Unit would often turn to me for help when they hit a roadblock with him.

The second time I confronted Dubey was when he started rehearsals for *Evam Indrajit* (And Indrajit). He cast Chitra in the play. One day, Dubey unexpectedly began rehearsing with an experienced actress Sulabha Deshpande, without informing Chitra. So I said to him, 'You may replace Chitra, but you owe her a justification or at least the reason for it.' Dubey hadn't anticipated such a confrontation. '*Isse cut karoji*' (Throw him out), he declared. After that, we didn't cross paths for a long time. I didn't have the maturity and insight then to comprehend the underlying politics in Dubey's various decisions and choices. It wasn't until many years later that I understood that his competition with the talented director Vijaya Mehta was the key factor.

The third time marked a point of no return. In the 1980s, Dubey was rehearsing his Hindi play *Sambhog Se Sanyas Tak* with Naseer (Naseeruddin Shah) and Ratna (Pathak). He asked me to produce the same play in Marathi with my theatre company, Aniket. I agreed, and the rehearsals commenced under his direction. One day, over drinks, I shared my opinion, saying, 'The script is quite poorly written.' Dubey felt I was overstepping boundaries. He accused me of having let stardom go to my head and demanded that I quit the play. I refused to comply, since my actors had put a lot of effort into it. I said that 'the play will be staged no matter what,' and we did exactly that. After that incident, Dubey blacklisted me.

By then, my thinking and ideological direction were well aligned. My approach to parenting, as Shalmalee was growing up, was also a carefully considered one. I made her aware of the existence of religion, caste and other social divisions, but taught her to adopt an inclusive perspective to life. I made sure I respected her autonomy, opinions and decisions. I was keen on inculcating in her an interest in Marathi literature, especially poetry, even though her medium of schooling was English. She attended our rehearsals and participated in artistic discussions. I especially remember an incident when she was in the eighth grade.

The principal of Jamnabai Narsee School in Juhu had called me.

'Your daughter called a teacher a male chauvinist today and is refusing to apologise,' she complained.

Shalmalee described the incident in great detail, telling me about the teacher's misogynistic position. 'If I had called him a male chauvinist "pig", it would have been an insult. But, Dad, I didn't say that.'

As the father of an intelligent daughter, I took immense pride in her. A few years later, she confided in me about her sexuality with complete openness. I have always been proud of her career choices and her personal decisions, including marrying her wonderful partner and giving birth to a beautiful son. There is no greater joy than raising a rational, independent daughter who forges her own path.

I inculcated in myself self-discipline so that I could engage in rational discourse rather than merely opposing ideas or individuals for the sake of an argument. Dubey's mentorship not only honed my craft but also gave me the confidence to express myself authentically. I admired his lucid thinking and candid nature. His passion for vibrant regional theatre, for exploring fresh texts and for finding newer ways of expression was unparalleled. Dubey's Theatre Unit led the way for the emergence of many other theatre groups such as the Indian National Theatre, Rangayan, Avishkaar, Pune's Progressive Dramatic Association (PDA) and Maharashtriya Kalopasak. Dubey demonstrated how diverse perspectives and interpretations could transform the same text into multiple narratives. Theatre Unit connected me with thespians from different cities like Kolkata, Delhi and Bengaluru, fostering artistic collaborations. Thanks to Dubey, I was able to transcend the prevalent boundaries of Marathi theatre and explore broader creative horizons.

In 1970–71, Dubey married a new entrant in the English publishing field Priya Adarkar. The marriage lasted only a few months, during which time we had merry get-togethers every Sunday. Artistes from all fields—musicians, painters, actors, writers, dancers—would gather in Dubey's spacious house. Engaging discussions on socio-political issues, script-reading sessions, poetry recitations and dance demonstrations would end with a hearty meal and beer.

One such Sunday was dedicated to our conversation with the renowned Hindi poet Bhawani Prasad Mishra. Some of Bhavani-ji's poems, especially the long poem *Geet Farosh*, were recited by Dubey in his unique style. Through his delivery, Dubey skilfully uncovered the vulnerability of the poet, his desperate struggle to meet the patron's expectations, and the helplessness he faces while selling his work. When I requested Bhavani-ji to read out the same poem himself, the tall poet in his crisp khadi dhoti burst into a hearty laughter. Then, patting his thigh, he recited the poem. In a strong, steady voice, he delivered every line without the slightest

Shall I write about birth or mourn the passing sky?
Or about the triumph or surrender?
This has the sheen of silk, and this is made of khadi,
One line is about acidity, the other about constipation!
I can offer more designs, this is intellectual,
This filmy one will allure the masses
The shadow of mortality haunts my lines,
My pen never rests, from dawn till dusk,
And creates verses of many a kind.

(Original Hin

जी, गीत जनम का लिखूं, मरण का लिखूं,
जी, गीत जीत का लिखूं, शरण का लिखूं,
यह रेशमी है, यह खादी का
यह गीत पित्तका है, यह बादी का!
कुछ डिज़ाइन और भी हैं, यह इल्मी
यह लीजे चलती चीज़, नई फ़िल्मी,
यह सोच-सोचकर मर जाने का गीत
यह दुकान से घर जाने का गीत।
मैं लिखता ही तो रहता हूं दिन-रात,
तो तरह-तरह के बन जाते हैं गीत।

hint of weakness. In fact, his tone carried an undertone of aggression as he challenged others to appreciate the depth of his work.

This was the time when I realised the value of fostering an environment conducive to respectful dissent, an environment for diverse perspectives to coexist and to unleash creative potential.

It was 1968, and the Tejpal Auditorium in Mumbai was packed for an evening of theatre. Dubey had directed Mohan Rakesh's Hindi play *Aadhe Adhure* (Halfway House). The packed theatre witnessed a powerful moment as the character Juneja's dialogue delivered a scathing critique of Savitri's character.

'While leaving, you had your whole life before you. But what have you returned with, other than sweat dripping from your quivering hands?' Savitri screamed frantically, 'Enough! All men are the same. The same heart beats beneath your varied facades. Your masks may differ, but the face remains constant.'

Juneja snapped back aggressively. 'Do you really believe you have the power to choose? Look around—do you see any choices you've made? Do you see any?'

A thunderous applause erupted in the auditorium. The audience responded predictably to the last assault on Savitri. As soon as the play ended, Dubey called all the actors to a corner. Amrish Puri, Jyotsna Karyekar, Bhakti Barve, Deepa Basrur and I went to him. Without praising our performance, he marched straight to Puri Saheb who had played a quartet of roles.

'Your portrayal of Juneja provoked an unwarranted ovation,' he began, firmly asserting that Savitri was at the heart of *Aadhe Adhure*. It was she who had subverted patriarchal traditions, and it was she who had borne the weight of supporting a family with a useless husband, a hopeless son, a drifting schoolgirl and an older daughter returning home after a failed marriage. 'The applause for Juneja,' he continued, 'only validates and celebrates latent masculinity.

As the director of this play, I refuse to endorse this antagonistic approach towards women. I want to celebrate Savitri. That applause is unacceptable to me.' His eloquence stunned everyone into silence. During rehearsal the next day, Dubey asked Puri Saheb to revise the tone of his dialogues. Dubey also introduced a few new lines into Savitri's part: 'So what if I didn't have a choice or even the option to choose? I have the right to explore my options.'

A few days later, Mohan Rakesh, the playwright, came from Delhi to see our production. That evening, the applause was for Savitri, not Juneja. Rakesh appreciated the improvisations generously. Once the play was over, following the tradition of the fourth act, Mohan Rakesh addressed two distinct and important issues. He resolutely opposed the new dialogues added by Dubey without his prior consent. 'Who gave you the right to put a patch on the carpet?' He also objected to the alterations that overtly—and, in Rakesh's opinion, unfairly—favoured Savitri's character in order for the audience to glorify and applaud her. It was clear that the male-centric narrative of Mohan Rakesh's original text was a conscious choice.

Dubey apologised for not seeking prior permission. However, he remained unwavering in his stand against patriarchy. He requested Mohan Rakesh to consider writing new dialogues for Savitri to convey his sentiments. A lengthy argument ensued, but eventually Mohan Rakesh graciously relented and acknowledged the director's right to differing creative interpretations. He allowed Dubey's alterations to continue. The insights from that debate had a profound impact on my young, impressionable mind and my artistic trajectory. That evening, a new avenue of understanding opened up to me, shaping my career in the performing arts.

In 1972, Surendra Verma's play *Surya Ki Antim Kiran Se Surya Ki Pahali Kiran Tak* (From the Last Ray of the Sunset to the First Ray of the Sunrise) reignited the debate about a director's right to creative liberties. The play's plot, which followed the tenth-century social custom of Niyoga, depicted Queen Sheelavati choosing her former lover for one night to produce an heir. During the rehearsals, as a director, I found the love triangle rather clichéd and boring, so I excluded her choice of the former lover and also the bedroom scene with him.

The play was performed with these alterations but without Surendra Verma's permission. At the time, I had felt it was my right as a director to edit the play without consulting the author. Today, however, I believe that I was wrong. Consent ought to be sought even before the rehearsals begin. In 2001, when we decided to make the film *Anaahat* based on Verma's script of the same play, my wife Sandhya Gokhale secured his consent in writing before we made any changes to the plot. Being a lawyer, she is vigilant and attentive to such details.

I helmed three distinct productions of Badal Sircar's *Pagla Ghoda* in 1970, 1992 and 2007, respectively. When I had gone to ask for his permission to change the script the first time, he had cheerfully said, 'I have written the way I wanted to; you follow your path as a director. If I don't like your version, I reserve the right to publicly criticise it and say that you killed my play.' When I edited the two-and-a-half-hour play down to ninety minutes, he admiringly said, 'Wow, I couldn't have done it in less than a hundred minutes.'

Dubey provided me with a solid grounding in theatre by teaching me the fundamentals. He also instilled confidence in me. At the same time, Badal-da encouraged me to venture into uncharted territories, to change the familiar grammar of theatre to find my own idiom. Eager to move beyond the traditional proscenium arch, Badal-da longed for an alternative space. I began my journey towards that goal with my play *Gochi*. My bond with Badal-da became more intimate and enduring with each successive year. I admired Mohan

Rakesh and Badal Sircar not only for their great playwriting skills but also for their humility and respect for the director.

Like these three stalwarts, Sadananda Rege, a respected poet in Marathi, also had a profound impact on my creative process. He was instrumental in my being able to identify alternative approaches. Around 1973, I read his play *Gochi*. He had written the play for the regular stage. However, I envisioned a surreal production. I revised the play significantly, trimmed it, while reordering the dialogues, and created a new narrative flow. The characters were reconstructed with a touch of abstraction. A small stage in Purandare Auditorium of the Sahitya Sangh in Mumbai was transformed into an intimate performance space, ready to envelop the audience into an immersive experience. Introducing the concept of intimate theatre to an era that had not yet experienced it, *Gochi* became a milestone and a turning point. We staged nearly sixty shows in this manner, performing not just in Pune and Mumbai but also in other cities, small and large villages, on lawns in front of bungalows, office canteens and once even in someone's garage!

Before each show, I would make a special announcement.

'You must have heard and read a lot about this production. We invite you to watch the play with an open mind, uninfluenced by any prior comments such as "this is not theatre", or by any adjectives such as "parallel" or "unfathomable". Moreover, no need to be serious while watching the play. Don't be afraid to laugh and enjoy.'

The first show earned me Rege's high praise and admiration for my unique interpretation, and I was commended for the overall excellence of the production. However, Rege's subsequent response left me utterly speechless. He insisted that my altered version of *Gochi* ought to be published in place of the original play. Though flattered, I declined. In my view, my interpretation should not become a limitation to the creative freedom of future directors. Future productions should not be tied down and be limited by my visualisation and realisation of Rege's original script. Rege then suggested printing both versions together in one volume. His proposal was, of course, rejected by the publisher, Ramdas Bhatkal of Popular Prakashan. 'As it is, the play is experimental—how many readers will buy the book? Printing both versions together will hike up the book's price, making it even more inaccessible.' Nonetheless, it was hugely fulfilling to see the creative synergy between a writer and director acknowledged and celebrated. *Gochi* remains very close to my heart to this day.

While rehearsing for *Gochi*, I began to notice the sonic effect of language and developed a keen interest in the auditory dimension of the written word. I naturally gravitated towards the rhythmic usage of nonsensical rhymes like *kapa, mapa, rapa, thapa, hapapa, gapapa* in the text. The soundscape of theatre intrigued me. I learnt to harness the hidden power of pauses and silences as theatrical tools to enhance performances. In films, we create different audio tracks for real-world sounds, off-screen audio and recorded background music. We take the story forward using dialogues and song montages. Such conventional sound techniques remain prevalent in contemporary theatre as well. For instance, pre-recorded sounds of crickets are used for night scenes and background music often underscores emotional tension. Against this backdrop, I felt that introducing live sound in *Gochi* could signify a shift in theatrical aesthetics and redefine the genre.

In 1975–76, Satyadev Dubey started rehearsals for Achyut Vaze's play *Sofa-cum-Bed*. But he decided to change the name of the play. He opted to portray the main character through a trio of actors, rather than using a single performer. That sparked Achyut's ire, prompting him to produce his own show. His decision ignited a heated debate within the experimental theatre circles. Two factions emerged. What was wrong with a writer directing and producing his own play if he didn't like the changes made by the director? Achyut's stand was backed by the celebrity actor-director Dr Shreeram Lagoo, and theatre critics, Pushpa-bai and Anantrao Bhave. The conflict took on an unfriendly tone. I presented two key points on behalf of Dubey at a meeting held at Pushpa-bai's house to discuss a possible resolution to the dispute.

'First, doesn't the director have any creative freedom to explore his own vision, interpretation of the text, even if it differs from the writer's original intention? Second, is it wise to split the already limited audience for experimental theatre by staging two parallel productions at the same time, based on the same script?'

Dr Lagoo and Anantarao continued supporting Achyut Vaze, but what upset me most was Pushpa-bai's silence. I raised yet another crucial issue. Dubey had contested the objections raised by the Maharashtra State Performance Scrutiny Board over certain dialogues in Achyut's script. Stressing that every word penned by an author is essential to his artistic vision and is, hence, indispensable, Dubey was determined to get the script cleared without a single cut. But while Achyut was championing the cause of writers' freedom, he had succumbed to the board's demands and agreed to the recommended cuts. Achyut's decision was unethical, but more than that, it was a huge setback to the fight for freedom of expression. Upon hearing my submission, an unsettling silence descended upon the room. Dr Lagoo then got up and left. Pushpa-bai's total silence, even with respect to my third point, troubled me more than Dr Lagoo's walking out. I included this incident in the foreword I wrote for a book on Pushpa-bai.

Sometime in 1976, I directed Mahesh Elkunchwar's play *Party*. By then, I had decided to use pre-recorded audio strictly when necessary and only for a compelling reason. Except for the ticking sound of a clock and sound of the telephone ringing, I did not use any other pre-recorded sounds in *Party*. Only the live audio generated by the actors' performances and their physical movements on the stage was used: the clinking of glasses, the crackling of ice cubes, the fizz and whoosh of a soda bottle being opened, the squeak of a chair breaking the awkward stillness, fingers tapping on a table, and so on. The aim was to underscore the tension and unease in the air.

At the visual level, my pursuit was to show changes in the atmosphere as the evening wore on. The house, meticulously decorated and tidy at the beginning of the party, starts to show signs of disarray as the party draws to a close. Similarly, as the attendees shed their inhibitions, the pretences of friendship and cordiality too fall away. The set design was conceived to metaphorically showcase these shifts.

I also decided to use the entire stage. The party spilled over into the entire house—while it began in the living room, it gradually spread to a corner bar, the kitchen, a cosy nook in the garden, and even, at one point, to a bedroom. All this movement happened simultaneously. While a scene unfolded between two characters in the bedroom, the other characters continued to mingle and socialise in the outer areas. The original plan was to illuminate the bedroom scene with a spotlight and keep the surrounding space dark, with only the characters in the bedroom acting and the rest remaining stationary. However, I chose a different approach. I asked all the characters to continue with their respective actions, using varying light intensities to mark the visual boundaries and to separate the spaces. This approach was more aligned with cinematic language, unfamiliar then to theatre practitioners.

The characters in the script were written in such a manner that they could be easily identified with real individuals. For instance, X was the prolific writer Vijay Tendulkar, Y was the distinguished playwright Vasant Kanetkar, Z was Mahesh himself, and the host of the party was the theatre scholar Kumudben Mehta. I felt that was gratuitous. In my opinion, Mahesh should have delved deeper into the artistic subtleties and complexities of the playwriting process.

To align with this perspective, I pruned the script to make it tighter and crisper, eliminating unnecessary verbosity. Naturally, Mahesh was not pleased.

By this point, we had already performed five or six shows. Mahesh, the prestigious publishing house Mauz Prakashan and I soon found ourselves in a heated debate. He argued, 'If the director wanted so many changes, he should have written the script himself.' This stance provoked me, and I shot back. 'If the director is expected to follow the writer's stage instructions to the letter, then the writer should direct the play himself.'

After the verbal tussle, I fired back an ultimatum: 'If you're so dissatisfied with this theatrical experimentation, then withdraw your permission.' My entire team of artistes and technicians was very upset with my ultimatum, given the significant resources and efforts we had invested in this play. Eventually, we decided to wind up *Party* as the joy had gone out of that endeavour. I informed Mahesh about my decision and closed that chapter.

Ironically, the matter didn't end there. Mauz Prakashan asked for my edited script in order to publish the play. Of course, I refused. But Anantrao Bhave gave his copy to the publisher. I later learnt that the version of the script edited by me and rejected by the writer had been published in book form. One interesting piece of trivia about *Party* is that Govind Nihalani later directed a film based on it. The film was criticised for being 'dramatic' and 'too theatrical'—the very elements Mahesh had opposed in the play for being 'too filmy'. On that occasion, I conveyed to Mahesh that a comprehensive analysis is needed to distinguish between 'cinematic' and 'dramatic' elements. With that message, *Party* finally came to an end for me.

Balancing theatricality and cinematic magic, indeed, requires a special tightrope walk. Once the pioneer of Konkani theatre, Machindra Kambli, and senior playwright Gangaram Gavankar approached me. They wanted me to adapt Gavankar's superhit play

Vastraharan (Disrobing) into a film. They had found a producer who was willing to invest in the movie. The play's unique selling points were its humorous dialogues, the witty banter between the characters on stage and their impeccable comic timing. I was of the firm opinion that the infectious energy and spontaneity of live-stage humour could not be replicated in cinema; the magic would be lost in editing and shot-breaking. After three or four meetings, I was able to dissuade them. A recent example that validates my point is the play *Alibaba and Chalishitale Chor* (Alibaba and the Thieves in their Forties) written by the creative playwright Vivek Bele. The script and dramatisation were stupendously effective but the film adaptation was equally unimpressive. The cinematic translation of the play suppressed its dramatic nature. In my opinion, the theatricality of a play gets truncated in a movie adaptation.

As I grew older, I realised the profound impact of an inspiring quote from Albert Camus's *The Myth of Sisyphus*, 'The only way to deal with an unfree world is to become so absolutely free that your very existence is an act of rebellion.' However, nonconformity comes at a cost; there's a price to pay for going against the tide. You always remain on the margins. You are never absorbed into the herd. When the opposition from the community becomes extreme, the intervention of police or law needs to be sought. In matters relating to the Marathi plays—*Gidhade* (Vultures), *Avadhya* (The Unvanquished), *Vasnakand* (Desire in the Rocks), *Sakharam Binder* (Sakharam the Binder), *Ghashiram Kotwal* (Ghashiram the Kotwal)—and the Marathi film, *Thaang* (Quest), that I directed, I witnessed up close the struggle with censorship. However, the fight for free expression and artistic liberty is a collective responsibility that requires active engagement on the part of the theatre community as well as the theatre-going audience. It is regrettable that the audience today doesn't feel compelled to stand up in support of free speech when it is under attack. With Sandhya's help, I have so far filed three public interest litigations (PILs) in the Mumbai high court and the

Supreme Court against censorship. I may not live to see the day when the judges deliver their verdict.

Only in two states, Maharashtra and Gujarat, is it mandatory for the script of any play to be certified by the State Performance Scrutiny Board before it is staged. If the board recommends any changes, the script must be revised accordingly. The text printed in a newspaper, literature published in a book, songs sung in a concert, works of art displayed in a visual art exhibition—none of these require prior approval. If these forms of expression are exempt from any scrutiny, it's unjust to censor theatre. If there is no law that requires religious and political leaders, who make provocative speeches in front of lakhs of people in public meetings, to get every word of their speech checked and obtain a pre-screening certificate, then it is unfair to treat the theatre differently. Moreover, what's the rationale behind certifying scripts in only Maharashtra and Gujarat when it is not done in all other states? No convincing answer that fits within the constitutional framework has been presented by the government in court so far. The objections routinely relate to the possibility of offending someone's feelings, morality or decency, or the possibility that it may trigger a law-and-order crisis. To ban or disallow the presentation of dissent, an objectionable thought or unpleasant language is the direct weapon of any authoritarian regime. The tyranny of the strong over the weak contravenes the basic tenets of democracy.

Government control is one thing, but now there's a more troubling tactic in play—the use of proxy groups to incite violence. This systematic brutality targets specific groups to spread fear among these communities and is used as a political weapon. In this climate, artistes often find themselves forced to retreat, especially when the theatre- or film-loving progressive audience doesn't stand by them in their fight against suppression. On 2 February 2024, students of Pune's Lalit Kala Kendra—an institute that has played an invaluable role in nurturing performing arts in the state—were attacked on charges of 'hurting religious sentiments'. When bullying occurs in plain sight, it's clear who is enabling the bullies. Another new trend is to file criminal complaints against the faculty and students after such incidents, rather than registering FIRs against the bullies. The same thing happened on 23 January 2024 at Pune's Film and Television Institute of India (FTII). An aggressive crowd entered its premises and damaged public property, attacking students too. But instead of protecting the students, the police first arrested a few of them and imposed non-bailable sections of the Indian Penal Code on them. The number of power brokers has grown so large that even the exploiters are now crying out to be exploited! The leaders make use of this cry for spreading fake news through social media. Acts of oppression or subjugation are used to deter the masses and to spread fear. Neither the public, nor the theatre community, not even artistes raise their voice against such methods.

Several years ago, some hooligans clamoured to change the name of the play *Marutichya Hati Champagne* (Champagne in Maruti's Hand) written by Vivek Bele. The objection was to the monkey god Maruti's name being linked to liquor. In the play, Maruti was the nickname of one of the characters. Why didn't all of us in the theatre community protest against such an unjust demand? Why did the name of the play have to be changed to *Makadachya Hati Champagne*? It has become alarmingly commonplace to hear about violent protests against films like *Bajirao Mastani* or attacks on filmmakers as in the case of *Padmaavat*, on the grounds of having distorted history.

In January 2017, extremists uprooted legendary playwright Ram Ganesh Gadkari's statue from Sambhaji Park in Pune. It was an attempt to discredit the veteran playwright by alleging that his century-old portrayal of Sambhaji Maharaj in his play *Rajsannyas* was offensive. Despite their passion for theatre, the Marathi community failed to speak out against this vandalism. Why didn't the fans take a stand against the insults hurled at theatre and its practitioners?

While that wound was still fresh, an invitation to renowned writer Nayantara Sehgal, to inaugurate the Akhil Marathi Sahitya Sammelan (the annual Marathi literary festival organised by the state) in early January 2019, was withdrawn. Rather than standing behind this outspoken non-Marathi critic of the ruling party, the majority of Marathi people chose to remain silent, thereby siding with the organisers of the festival. It was ironic that this occurred in Maharashtra, a state known for its progressive values. Indeed, the incident tarnished the state's image. I raised the flag of resistance to reassert civil liberties in this polluted cultural environment. I called upon like-minded writers, artistes and social activists to unite. On 29 January 2019, Bhalchandra Nemade, Pushpa Bhave, Jayant Pawar, Samina Dalwai, T.M. Krishna, Siddharth Varadarajan, Kishore Kadam, Praveen Bandekar, Yeshu Patil, Ashok Shahane, Nikhil Wagle and many others gathered to offer a symbolic apology on behalf of Maharashtra to Nayantara Sehgal, who was also present. This show of strength was necessary; a healthy democracy thrives only when people and communities are unwavering in their commitment to protect and preserve the rule of law and its protocols.

The fight for artistic freedom in Maharashtra has largely been waged by experimental-theatre practitioners. Very few people from the commercial theatre space have dared to speak out: one exception was the legendary artiste Dada Kondke. Dada had mastered the art of using humour to address adversities. In his films, he used unpolished language and double entendres that appealed to the movie-going masses. The Censor Board was flummoxed with him and had struggled to deal with his style of expression. 'Obscenity is a matter of personal interpretation. Any of the verbs in Marathi, like taking, carrying, sleeping, pushing, can be dismissed as obscene, if one so desires.' Giving such clever arguments, Dada had secured approval for the film title *Andheri Raat Mein Diya Tere Haath Mein.* But then in 2015, the BJP government announced a list of 'banned words in the space of performing arts and media' through its loyal chairman Pahlaj Nihalani. I have challenged this list as well in my ongoing petition in the Supreme Court.

Compared to this current climate of appeasement and conformity, the turmoil the experimental theatre community created in the 1970s and 1980s was revolutionary. Had a comprehensive chronicling of the parallel theatre movement of that time been done, it would have surely highlighted our triumphs against creative oppression. Of course, it is equally true that many co-fighters in that struggle have now become silent as they have compromised and accepted political patronage and government favours. Some organise film festivals funded by the government; some take jobs in media departments of colleges funded by politicians—different paths but the same purpose.

In the 1970s, Vijay Tendulkar's *Gidhade* ran into censorship problems. Satyadev Dubey was the producer and Dr Lagoo the director. Together, they waged a long battle over it. They accepted only one change, and forced the board to withdraw the remaining thirty-five cuts. Despite heavy rain, the first show of *Gidhade* at Tejpal Auditorium was packed. After the third bell, as the lights became dim and the credits were announced, a special instruction was heard. 'As per the mandate of the Censor Board, a red stain on the sari of the female protagonist will not be shown. The same has been replaced by a blue stain, but it should be considered red.' The audience erupted into laughter, whistles and applause. A triumphant hush followed, and the curtain rose. After that, many shows of the play were performed to a full house.

How many more instances shall I offer of those who championed artistic freedom and autonomy in that era?

In 1971–72, the debate over art being open to multiple interpretations took centre stage. This time the play in focus was *Avadhya* written by C.T. Khanolkar. One day, I received a call from Kumudben Mehta. She asked me to visit her that evening. When I reached, I found the eminent poet C.T. Khanolkar sitting in the veranda of her home. 'When I was at the J.J. School of Art, our teacher Sambhaji Kadam had cast me in the lead role in your one-act play *Jevha Aarsa Bolto* (When the Mirror Speaks),' I told him as my introduction. Khanolkar seemed restless at the beginning but eventually seemed to relax. Then he started reading the script of *Avadhya*. I was used to hearing powerful renditions by celebrated writers like P.L. Deshpande and Vijay Tendulkar, so Khanolkar's monotonous reading bored me. However, the play's subject piqued my interest as a director.

The scenes unfold inside a lodge in a small village. Through a peephole in the wall of the central character Gangadhar's room, two or three people spy on the courtship between a young man and a young woman in the neighbouring room. As the couple's growing intimacy becomes audible, Gangadhar's dual identities emerge. (The term 'schizophrenic' is not used in the play.) The dialogues reveal a compelling mix of raw emotions and lyrical finesse. Finally, Gangadhar commits suicide by thrusting a broken liquor bottle into his abdomen. Khanolkar's poetic language—he wrote poetry under the pen name 'Aarti Prabhu'—and his rough dialogues created a unique blend. The unfolding of events transcend reality, presenting shocking yet thought-provoking content. This was the first time that explicit words like lust and sex were used on stage—they had never been uttered on stage before, not only in Marathi but in other Indian languages as well.

My aim was to depict intimacy in a raw and authentic way, without resorting to either vulgarity or pretence. I started rehearsals with Deepa Basrur and Dilip Kolhatkar, along with Eknath Hattangadi, who was an amazing actor. Casting an actress who could emote with the body language required to perform silent romantic scenes sans dialogue proved to be challenging. My search ended with Jyoti Randive, a professor at the Elphinstone College. She was the perfect fit for the role.

Rumours circulated that the Maharashtra State Performance Scrutiny Board would ban the production, but I pressed on with the rehearsals. The Board's scrutiny yielded no evidence to support banning the show. It did not suggest any cuts and granted the play an 'Adults Only' certificate. Interestingly, all the Board members attended the opening night show, expecting something scandalous. The next day, acclaimed critic Madhav Manohar praised the play as 'the first Marathi coming-of-age play' in a two-page review. We also heard that the Board members' apprehensions had melted away after watching the show. Renowned dramatist, Vasant Kanetkar, lambasted the play. Despite his scathing review, the play was a runaway success, and it was staged numerous times, all the shows being sold out. The production's financial success was the cherry on top.

Following the tremendous success of this experimental play, a producer called Pramod Dhurat proposed that he would finance the play for mainstream theatre, casting renowned actors like Satish Dubhashi and Sulabha Deshpande. He asked me to direct his production as well. When it was finally staged, the shows were sold out. After one such full-house show, I expressed my disapproval to the actors for having deviated from the playwright's original dialogues and inserting their own lines. Satish didn't take my concerns seriously. I spoke with the playwright Khanolkar as well. He was willing to make concessions as long as the production paid his royalty in time, and so he chose to stay out of the conflict. I was taken aback by his self-serving, opportunistic attitude. My stance was clear: every playwright has a distinct style expressed through their dialogue—based on the choice of words, rhythm and tone used by them. Therefore, actors ought to deliver those dialogues exactly as written. Deviating from the script, to me, amounts to disrespect towards the playwright's craft and is an unprofessional practice. I formally requested the producer, in writing, that my name be removed from the credits as the director, putting the matter to rest.

Looking back, I wonder if the audiences were drawn to *Avadhya* because of their expectation of titillating content. If so, they might have been disappointed. Was our Marathi theatre so devoid of sexual and sensual themes that the starved audiences found the tiny hint of it in Khanolkar's play gratifying? Of course, we had never promoted *Avadhya* in the way the Marathi play *Kachecha Chandra* was publicised, insinuating a scandalous incestuous relationship between Prabhat Film Company's superstar Shanta Apte and her brother. I took pride in not having exploited *Avadhya*'s controversial theme to pull in audiences.

Unfortunately, the pursuit of artistic freedom also led to some undesirable deviations.

Around 1972, the Maharashtra State Performance Scrutiny Board objected to Vijay Tendulkar's *Sakharam Binder*. What was more concerning was that some individuals and groups started publicly opposing the play. Director Kamlakar Sarang organised a special private show for Shiv Sena chief Balasaheb Thackeray. When I learnt about the private show, I urgently called Kamlakar. I believed then and still do that under no circumstances should an artiste attempt to obtain political patronage for his/her art. I earnestly urged Kamlakar not to make this mistake, but to no avail. Balasaheb, who was an ardent theatre enthusiast himself, was captivated by the play! The Board members were at a loss.

In August 1974, for the first time, I knocked on the court's door against the ban on Mahesh Elkunchwar's Marathi play *Vasnakand* directed by me. After hearing Mahesh's reading of the powerful play at the dramatists' camp conducted by Satyadev Dubey in 1970, I decided to stage it, and submitted an application to the Board. As was anticipated, the Board rejected it. I decided to stage the play anyway. I managed to book Rabindra Natya Mandir at Prabhadevi for three consecutive dates—19, 20 and 21 August—paying the rent money in advance. I also put out a newspaper advertisement. The next day, a member of the Legislative Assembly raised the question: how could the play be staged despite the Board's refusal to grant certification, that too in a theatre owned by the government? On the Friday evening, that is, 16 August, the auditorium sent me a legal notice informing me about their decision to cancel our booking. The next day, we approached the Bombay high court and got an order that an 'urgent hearing' would be held on Monday morning, 19 August. Renowned lawyer Atul Setalvad argued brilliantly on my behalf that, 'Although the management has the authority to cancel our booking, they are obligated to provide a justification. Therefore, the management cannot cancel the shows arbitrarily.' The government argued that staging a play revolving around an immoral incestuous relationship could have a detrimental impact on society. It might even provoke an unsavoury reaction and lead to vandalism at the theatre, thereby creating a law and order situation. Since the government could not substantiate its claim, the Hon'ble judge gave us the green signal. Chitra and our team had been stationed at the theatre hall since morning; I called from the court and asked them to start the lighting and stage design. As the matter had become an ego issue for the government, they immediately filed an appeal against the order. However, since they weren't granted interim relief staying the presentation of the play, our show could go on as planned. The appeal would be heard and argued the next day.

I managed to get my hands on a copy of the order only around 5 p.m. I rushed from Fort to Prabhadevi, arriving just thirty minutes before the start of the performance. Chitra and I were the sole actors in the play. Putting aside stress and fatigue, I managed to muster the energy and washed my face with cold water. I stood in the wings, waiting for the third bell to ring. I still recall my friend Dilip Kulkarni saying that I should not stress about having skipped the grand rehearsal. After the show, I ran home without celebrating the 'fourth act'. I rushed to the high court the next morning. A two-judge bench rejected the government's argument in its entirety and the ban on *Vasnakand* was lifted.

In his judgment, Justice Chandrashekhar Dharmadhikari emphatically raised a point: it is the duty of the police and the government to protect artistes and works of art from subversive elements, and that the administration should not succumb to external pressures.

Many theatre practitioners like Rekha Sabnis, Vinay Apte, Achyut Vaze, Kamlakar Nadkarni, Hemu Adhikari, Dilip Kolhatkar, Bapu Limaye, Ashok Sathe, Bondre Dampatya, Jairam Hardikar and Subodh Gadgil were present at the auditorium to ensure that all three shows ran smoothly. Many experimental theatre organisations also contributed financially towards our expenses. All these troupes that otherwise competed against each other now stood united on the issue of artistic freedom. Such was the camaraderie in that era.

Indira Gandhi's Emergency was declared during this same period. It was time for us artistes to ignite the flame of resistance. The staging of *Julus* (The Procession) was my act of defiance against the Emergency.

Whether in sophisticated city theatres or rustic village theatres, there would always be a distance between the audience and the performers on stage. Theatre veteran Badal Sircar had challenged these conventional forms by introducing an alternative third theatre, 'Tisari Rangbhumi', in West Bengal. A copy of his play *Michhil* fell into my hands. Its structure did not conform to the conventional format. There was no hero or heroine, no love triangles or conflicts, no soliloquies or a memorable dialogue to be quoted for generations. Badal-da had already departed from the Ibsenian mould. This script only put forward a structural framework. He metaphorically unpacked the monotony of everyday life, revealing the emptiness within. He leveraged symbols of authority, like the police or religious leaders, in order to expose the suffering and vulnerabilities of the common people. That script left me fascinated, even mesmerised. I felt compelled to present the play in Marathi. Chitra did an excellent Marathi translation from the Hindi version of the original Bengali script. *Michhil* became *Julus*. As our rehearsals progressed, my vision for a performance, reliant solely on and expressed through the artistes' body language, gained clarity. Rehearsals carried on for two months.

Julus was first staged in the state drama competition in 1975. The performance radiated a captivating energy and rebellious vibe. The Leftist-scientist-thespian Hemu Adhikari and I were committed to staging an anti-establishment play on a government platform, and we succeeded. The show got sold out four to five days before the competition had even commenced. The 'House Full' sign outside the theatre was a symbol of our triumph and delight. On the opening night, the theatre was so crowded that even an ant couldn't have squeezed in! The sound of the third bell echoed off the walls. As the lights dimmed, actors sitting in the balcony and back seats began to move towards the stage, chanting and shouting slogans. A wave of collective unease went through the audience. The actors arrived on the stage and began to protest. Suddenly, all the lights went out, including those on the 'Exit' signs. Just then, a bright torch beam cut through the darkness, followed by a deep voice. 'Silence, nothing has happened. Everything is fine.' As the stage lights gradually returned, a khaki-uniformed policeman appeared, using his torch to guide the crowd off the stage. Only an old man and a young child remained. The play was so captivating that the audience did not miss having an intermission. At the end, the old man and the child along with the initial crowd came down from the stage and mingled with the audience. The audience joined in the 'julus', exhibiting their spontaneous support.

The play failed to enter the final round of the competition because of two objections raised by the examiners. First, the duration of the play was less than two hours, so it did not meet the minimum required time limit; second, they were unsure whether to classify the play as a drama. That failure had no significance for us. Our call against Emergency had reached thousands of viewers, and support for the cause increased over time. Social activist Mrinal Gore, as well as two or three leaders who had gone underground, had come in disguise to see the play and praised it tremendously. After that, almost 150 shows of *Julus* were performed in every corner of Maharashtra. At IIT-Powai, when we ended the performance in front of the mostly non-Marathi crowd, 1,500 students joined the final 'julus'—the procession. We also performed under the scorching sun in front of a thousand students at Delhi's Jawaharlal Nehru University (JNU). Additionally, there were performances staged in private garages, basements, playgrounds, open spaces of public swimming pools and in any other space where people could find a place to sit. Those were the most fulfilling moments of my life.

Regarding our performance of the play in Nashik, the prominent theatre reviewer Kamlakar Nadkarni, in his book *Nataki Nataka Chakoritli Aani Binchakoritli*, wrote,

> This happened in 1975, on the occasion of the one-day literature festival at Nashik. Speeches, seminars, discussions got over. A small board was erected on a pole in the playground in front of the main building.
>
> 'At eight o'clock tonight, the play produced
> by Bahurupi, *Julus.*
> Director: *Amol Palekar.*'
>
> It was six in the evening when we artistes gathered near the pole. But there were no spectators as the play had not been advertised. At 7 p.m., a policeman threw a torch beam across the ground. Gradually, an audience started collecting

> when they saw the name 'Amol' on the board. They were puzzled: why was there no stage, lights or actors in sight when the show was to start in an hour?
>
> Just then, a few young boys arrived, talking loudly. The policeman marched in too, his feet stomping heavily, and warned everyone to be silent. Slowly, people became absorbed in the performance. Scenes like the Ganapati immersion procession and the crowd entering the local train received a tremendous response. When the show ended, the audience realised to their surprise that what they had just witnessed was the actual play.
>
> The play contained political satire, provocative critiques of fraudulent spiritual gurus and discussions on oppression. Despite its anti-government stance, we were able to successfully perform *Julus* at public venues in many states without it getting banned. Doordarshan recorded the entire performance, and it was telecast all over Maharashtra during Emergency.

The widespread popularity of the play silenced the critics of experimental theatre. They used to denigrate the experimentalists as 'troupes doing calisthenics on stage'. *Julus* proved that by breaking free from the shackles of realism, a director could create a profoundly immersive and enriching theatrical experience.

In August 2004, I got yet another opportunity to direct *Julus*—with the vibrant energy and enthusiasm of young actors from Pune's Jagar Sanstha. I plugged into the play contemporary language, symbols, actions and incidents, creating a powerful, new-age 'procession'. It was a deeply moving experience for me, especially with Badal-da being present in the audience.

The suppression of democratic values is a natural consequence of power tussles in politics, lending us constant opportunities for opposition and rebellion. The rulers are often in different guises; they change their political symbols over the course of party politics. But their ultimate goal is always to control the masses. I am proud that, throughout my life, I have consistently exposed the ulterior motives of those in power, regardless of their party affiliation.

There are many who have received Padma awards and other accolades, despite their paltry, insignificant contributions. It is an open secret that awards are often managed through agents and secured by reciprocal favours and even dubious transactions. Despite fifty years of active work in three fields of the performing and visual arts, artiste Amol Palekar has not received a single award from the government; it is a testament—one may even call it a badge of honour—to the unyielding, rebellious spirit of Amol Palekar. When I, this rebel, stood in Lourmarin, on the burial ground in which Albert Camus rests, a deep sense of fulfilment permeated every cell of my being. Camus' words 'I rebel therefore I exist' whispered echoes in my heart.

In many countries around the world in the twenty-first century, dictatorship is being successfully implemented through democratic means. In El Salvador, in 2021, when Bukele's party won a majority in the parliament, the five judges of the top-most court were removed and laws were enacted fixing a retirement age, leading to the ouster of over 200 judges. In the next elections, the new judges of the Supreme Court of El Salvador ruled in favour of Bukele holding that his bid for re-election was not unconstitutional. Over a period of eighteen years, Recep Tayyip Erdoğan has established a wilful dictatorship in Turkey. Pro-government judges have been appointed in Poland since the Law and Justice Party came to power in 2015. Ultimately, in November 2021, the Polish Supreme Court passed a shocking ruling, 'the Polish government is not obliged to comply with the laws of the European Union', in a case against the persecution of refugees from Belarus. Hungary's Victor Orbán was apparently careful not to violate the constitutional framework while recruiting his supporters to the courts.

Even the electoral system is abused as if it is a right. Ahead of the 2021 presidential elections in Nicaragua, more than fifty civil society organisations were decertified, and seven opposition leaders were charged with treason and sent to prison. During the 2018 presidential elections in Venezuela, the public was openly threatened with withdrawal of food concessions if they didn't vote for Chávez. Recent elections in Bosnia, Lebanon, Northern Ireland, Sri Lanka, Zimbabwe and Belarus have shown that democracy has been in tatters for a while. The new form of dictatorship in India is apparent all over the world as 'dictatorship in the guise of democracy'.

Another observation in this context is the worrying trend of fascist movements from various nations increasingly providing support and solidarity to one another. Hungary's Orbán showed his support for Putin by imposing an arms embargo on Ukraine. Russia–China–Turkey offered billions in aid to Venezuela, despite economic sanctions imposed by the West against malfeasance in the 2018 elections. In 2020, the Russian police was sent in to quell an uprising to preserve democracy against the irregularities in the Belarus elections. Fugitive intellectuals and leaders of the Uyghur Muslim tribe from Northwest China used to seek political asylum in Turkey before 2019, but President Erdogan halted this policy, detaining many Uyghur citizens residing in Turkey in refugee camps.

Against this background, the changes in the Indian political landscape since 2014 stand out as well. It seems that the ruling party has succeeded in achieving the goal of using democratic means to run a dictatorship in a systematic manner. Currently, democracy is under threat due to the government's continuous, multi-pronged attack on the progressive, humanitarian, secular values of Indian culture. In a prejudiced, toxic environment, without any fear of repression, a young leader like Rahul Gandhi is once again trying to instil tolerance and brotherhood. His aspiration is to share the dream of a secular and inclusive society with the masses, with the ultimate aim of protecting and preserving India's constitutional values. He met the people of thirteen states by walking a distance of 3,500 km in 150 days. His efforts to spread the hope of a new consciousness were both necessary and praiseworthy. Sandhya and I joined his Bharat Jodo Yatra with the belief that the presence of a vast ocean of supporters would have the collective power to soothe the turbulent tide we have found ourselves caught in. Despite the possibility of being labelled a Congress supporter, I remain optimistic about the yatra.

My career in cinema also reflects my passion for autonomy. I have always opted for unconventional routes and have never shied away from taking risks. I chose opportunities that allowed me to maintain my creative freedom. This, despite the fact that the film industry's commercial profit-oriented approach, prioritising collections over principles, has little tolerance for a different set of values. Nonconformity comes at a personal cost. I survived in the industry for five decades and emerged wiser. Challenges have risen and passed, but I have relished every moment of success as well as failure. I have never felt drained, lost or purposeless; that, to my mind, is my ultimate reward.

In the early days of my career, I worked on a film called *Chitchor*. A set was erected at Rajkamal Studio of Bombay for shooting a few scenes and a short sequence of a song. On my very first day of shooting, I heard a knock on my make-up room door. Outside, to my surprise, stood 'chocolate boy' hero Shashi Kapoor. His face was lit up with a charming smile capable of sweeping countless women off their feet. 'I am Shashi Kapoor,' he said. 'I heard that you were shooting here. I just wanted to drop by and offer my sincere congratulations and also a warm welcome to the world of cinema.'

Protesting against the murder of Narendra Dabholkar, with Baba Adhav, Naseeruddin Shah, Bhai Vaidya, Mukta Manohar and other like-minded folks

Bharat Jodo Yatra (20 November 2022), with Rahul Gandhi and Sandhya Gokhale

I was initially surprised that he was aware of my engagement with theatre, but then looking at his lifelong dedication to nurturing the theatre culture at Prithvi, along with his wife Jennifer and later his daughter Sanjana, it only seemed natural that he knew about my work. After that first meeting, he and I developed a special bond. I also painted his portrait at a special function organised on the sesquicentennial anniversary of the J.J. School of Art.

Once, I visited Shashi to seek guidance on some concerns I had about certain film industry practices. That day, I discovered his impressive business acumen. The conversation went something like this:

> Shashi: I hear you have been rejecting film offers one after the other. You shouldn't do that.
>
> I: I am not interested in taking up only comedies or playing monotonous characters. There are many subjects beyond light-hearted stories. I don't want the industry to typecast me.
>
> Shashi: But your popular image is your currency. That's exactly the leverage you need to establish yourself as a hero. Don't ask the producer to select a story other than what he has offered.
>
> I: But why can't we try? Recently, I signed a film called *Agar*. The producer initially wanted to make a comedy with the successful star cast of *Chitchor*. On my insistence, he is going to make a murder mystery.

Shashi earnestly explained the dynamics of the industry to me. His mantra was simple: accept at least ten films based on the success of one hit; your 'star value' will be measured accordingly. He told me that typically, three-fourths of the ten signed movies remain incomplete, with only a few getting finished. If any of them becomes a hit, you must continue the cycle in the same way. Stay in the game by being a player, not just a pawn, he said.

I never quite endorsed Shashi's pattern of accepting films. I couldn't be a typical 'filmy' hero or a star, conforming to the stereotypical traits of an industry insider. I rarely attended premiers or parties and didn't socialise or follow social protocol. During the Diwali season, when endless sessions of drinking and gambling were the norm in booked suites of five-star hotels, I found it all boring. I also avoided making the rounds of the offices of producers, and buttering them up to secure new roles, or sending gift boxes to distributors in the Naaz Cinema Building at Tardeo. I felt no pressing need to have many films in hand at once; also, I didn't feel the need to assimilate, so I never tried to fit in. Courtesy all these 'nays', I remained an outsider, maintaining that status all along.

The way stars were pampered, especially in the Hindi film industry, always saddened me. Sometimes, it would be the case that the shift would begin at 9 a.m., the star would arrive on set only by 4 p.m. They would sit in the make-up room for hours even after coming late to the studio, call other producers to the set to discuss new offers, thereby holding up the entire unit. These were all unforgivable practices in my view. I considered it grossly unprofessional to waste the producer's money and time.

Another poor practice in the industry was the producers not paying the pre-decided remuneration even after completing the shoot. I took on a massive challenge on this count. I had signed a film called *Agni Pareeksha* under the grand banner of BR Films, with co-actors Rameshwari and Parikshit Sahani. The first schedule of shooting ended in 1981. After that, Rameshwari had an accident during the shooting of a different film produced by Rajshri Pictures, in which she injured her eye. As she was recovering, Parikshit got hurt while shooting for the role of Shivaji in a film by a renowned director Ram Gabale. Everyone's dates had to be rescheduled. Finally, the much-delayed shooting of *Agni Pareeksha* was somehow completed. Even after the film was entirely ready, the last instalment of my remuneration hadn't been paid to me. I called Chopra Saheb and told him that I had completed my dubbing and asked him to give me a guarantee letter from the laboratory that no print would be released till my dues were paid, which was the industry practice in such circumstances. My request really upset him. 'How dare you ask me for a lab letter!'

He threatened to throw me out of the industry. But, since my demand was reasonable, I did not back off.

'Mr Chopra,' I said, 'I have come this far in the industry through my own efforts, and without the backing of any godfather or inherited connections. Moreover, this industry is not your backyard garden.' I filed a lawsuit against him in the Bombay high court as well.

It wasn't about the money, but about my work ethic and dignity. The court instructed Mr Chopra to deposit the dues with the registrar of the court before the release of the film. The news sent shockwaves through the industry. Some people advised me to withdraw my suit; some counselled me not to 'make enemies if I wanted to continue in the industry'. The actor Sanjeev Kumar tried to comfort me by saying, 'A similar treatment was meted out to me at the time of *Pati, Patni aur Woh.*' But I did not relent. Rs 40,000 were the unpaid dues. Thirty years later, after I won the case, I got five times the amount with interest, which I donated to charity. For me the lawsuit was simply an act of unwavering defiance, a refusal to surrender my values.

In hindsight, I regret not speaking out against all the muck thrown at me by film magazines and gossip columns at that time. I did not fall into the trap of appointing an agent or a secretary to promote my public image or lobby for new opportunities. Despite being surrounded by negativity, I managed to find serenity within myself. I won't deny that it disturbed me to see the way others around me landed new roles. This repulsion led me to make poor personal decisions that did not serve me well. I often internalised the anger I felt towards others and directed it inwards.

In 1971, Basu Chatterjee came to meet me at Café Samovar in the Jehangir Art Gallery. He had seen my work in theatre. 'Have you seen the Marathi movie *Mumbaicha Jawai*? I am remaking it in Hindi with the title *Piya Ka Ghar*. Would you like to play the hero in it?' When I responded in the affirmative, Basu-da said, 'Go and meet Tara Chand-ji of Rajshri Pictures and negotiate the deal. He is the producer,' he said.

However, I said no to his suggestion. Basu-da got very upset at this. So, I clarified my position. 'As the director, if I'm the hero you have chosen, then introduce me to him with the dignity I deserve. I will not sit alongside other aspirants gathered in Sheth-ji's office.'

Basu-da stood up, expressing his displeasure at this unexpected reaction from me. In retrospect, as a newcomer in the industry, I shouldn't have hesitated to visit the producer. But I was a man driven by my instincts, a man with a non-mainstream attitude.

My career path, if someone were to trace it, is punctuated by self-sabotaging decisions. I consistently avoided typecasting myself, rejecting similar kinds of roles or roles lacking any challenge, even if the projects offered were lucrative.

One major mistake I made, which I didn't regret then and still don't, was giving up a highly lucrative advertising assignment to promote Ariel washing powder. In hindsight, it was an impractical decision. The Fortune 500 company Procter & Gamble had invited me to create television commercials for Ariel. The brief was to make a realistic advertisement involving interviews with housewives. Procter & Gamble agreed to shoot the ad without any known faces, on actual locations instead of erecting sets. I also did not want the product to be aggressively thrust down the consumers' throats and proposed that the product be shown only in the last frame, without the model exhibiting it in her hands. Initially, the company was reluctant to deviate from the conventional route, but soon my idea grew on them. The first cut was tested through a market survey. They were overwhelmed with the findings. The company signed a three-year contract with me. Every year I would shoot the advertisement in Mumbai, Chennai, Kolkata and Delhi. I was paid handsomely, but I quickly got bored of churning out the same kind of material year on year. When after three years, I refused to renew the contract, the company officials were shocked. Finally, after a long-drawn-out discussion, I agreed to make one pilot advertisement to launch the washing powder in the Bangladesh market. I did that, and then stopped making ad-films. It is a regular and sensible practice in the industry, to chase ad film assignments, to build a corpus of wealth, and then to run one's office without any insecurity. But I did not follow this path for long.

In the industry, I often noticed that, despite dedicating months of hard work, small-time artistes, spot boys and light boys often went unpaid for months after their assignments were over. Producers would make excuses like the film didn't do well or had incurred heavy losses—using these reasons to withhold payments and roll the money instead into their next project. This practice kept these workers tied to the producer. How does a film's commercial success or failure justify withholding their rightful earnings? If they were paid on time, they could have chosen their next project freely, without any financial constraints. Many crew members used to approach me on the sets with an appeal to help them recover their dues. Out of compassion, I would often admonish the producer's representatives.

In those days, it was a common practice to transact in cash. A suitcase full of money used to be handed over as payment. But I insisted on cheques instead. My demand used to be accepted grudgingly. I might be that rare star who bought his own bungalow in Juhu and never got raided by the Income Tax (IT) Department. Of course, being subject to an IT raid was considered a matter of pride in those days!

When I became a producer myself, I deliberately steered clear of the practices that used to annoy me. Even in the 'pre-Sandhya era', as I call it, even though we had paucity of funds, I never failed to settle anyone's dues. Sandhya, with her Left-leaning and lawyerly approach, adopted the discipline of paying all the technicians and equipment providers immediately after the work was over. She persuaded actors to work for lower salaries in case of a financial crunch but never lowered the compensation of the unit members. She took out life insurance policies for all the technicians, entered into formal agreements with the most senior members of the unit, and adhered to the mutually agreed upon payment schedule without fail. After we earned huge profits from the film *Anaahat* in 2001, all my unit members were given a bonus. Jaya Bachchan graciously distributed their cheques to them, honouring my invitation to do so.

On the one hand, I never actively engaged with the mainstream Hindi cinema circle, that is known as Bollywood. On the other, even in the parallel film space, I was considered an outsider, since the National School of Drama or the FTII alumni didn't share the 'alma mater' connection with me. My popularity as a successful commercial hero proved to be a hindrance in gaining acceptance from my peers in the parallel film space. Since, I had received the Filmfare Award for Best Actor for *Gol Maal*—one of the most sought-after awards and a symbol of immense popularity—I was not given the National Award for it. This was something the legendary cinematographer Subroto Mitra, who was on the jury for the National Award, told me. I felt like Abhimanyu, trapped in a labyrinth with no escape. The film industry's tight-knit and often impenetrable social structure is well known. Industry insiders often have their finger on the pulse of things through their networks. From Filmfare and Screen awards to National Awards, every award is subject to intense lobbying.

When I acted as the chair of the jury for the Screen Awards, my jury selected *Udaan* as the best film of that year. I was criticised for not considering a big-budget film like *My Name Is Khan*. A few years later, the then editor-in-chief of the Indian Express Group spilled the beans about how there had been threats that the awards ceremony would be boycotted, how there had been pressure on the jury members to select specific films for some categories at least, and so on. Our collective decision to stand firmly behind a young director like Vikramaditya Motwani was comforting to me.

A similar incident occurred a few years later. I was made chairman of the committee appointed to decide India's official selection for the Oscars. The committee included prominent people from the Hindi and Bengali cinema industries and mainstream supporters of the southern film industry. The two groups were active right from the start. Chaitanya Tamhane's Marathi film *Court* and a Tamil film made it to the committee's shortlist. As both the films had been unanimously chosen, a lobbyist who had been pushing a big Hindi film felt cornered. He tried hard to publicly accuse me of partiality, but the committee finally voted, by majority, that *Court* would be sent to the Oscars.

I used to often wonder why the Marathi theatre and film industry did not capitalise on my widespread popularity as a Hindi film star. Today, I believe that the Marathi film industry turned a blind eye to my success in Hindi cinema because both my films in Marathi, *Bajiravcha Beta* (Bajirao's Son) and *Tuch Majhi Rani* (You are my Queen), failed badly early on in my career. I once said to the great Marathi comedian Rajabhau Gosavi, 'Basu Chatterjee is making nice, feel-good films with me; senior actor-director Rajabhau Paranjape has been making light-hearted films in Marathi with you for so many years. You paved the way for understated comedy and left a lasting impression on my mind, which I drew upon during my acting career.' My words moved Rajabhau Gosavi to tears. He said to the established producer Sharad Pilgaonkar, who was sitting with us, 'Cast us both in a comedy.' After a few non-committal 'cheers', Pilgaonkar promptly forgot about Rajabhau's suggestion.

But one of my favourite music directors, who was also my neighbour, Sudhir Phadke aka Babuji, once invited me as a Hindi movie star. When he was elected the president of the Akhil Bharatiya Chitrapat Mahamandal, he organised events across Maharashtra to raise funds. Along with veteran actors Dada Kondke and Nilu Phule, he invited me as well to the fundraiser. The event was scheduled to conclude with a film festival titled 'Ayodhya's Raja Te Akriet'—this festival covered the journey of Marathi cinema starting from *Ayodhyecha Raja* (Ayodhya's Raja) to the movie *Akriet* (Misbegotten)—in the US. The then information and broadcasting minister, Vasant Sathe, banned the international screening of my directorial debut *Akriet.* The order was conveyed to the Film Corporation as well. Sathe had seen the film during its special screening in Delhi. He objected to its international screening because he thought the country's image would be tarnished if the poverty and cruelty shown in my film was exhibited outside India.

I decided to send a letter urging Prime Minister Indira Gandhi to intervene against his decision. The great scholar Durga Bhagwat, Maharashtra's favourite writer-satirist P.L. Deshpande, prolific playwright Vijay Tendulkar, theatre doyen Sombhu Mitra, theatre scholar Kumudben Mehta and many more celebrity artistes signed that letter in my support. Chief of the National Centre for Performing Arts (NCPA), Dr Narayana Menon personally handed over the same to Indira-ji. After returning from Delhi, Dr Menon narrated the whole story to us: upon reading the letter and the names of the signatories, Indira-ji laughed and said, 'We seemed to have pushed all the right people over to the wrong side.' She picked up the phone and gave Sathe a reality check, ordering him to immediately lift the ban. As Dr Menon was leaving, Indira-ji said, 'Is this Amol Palekar the same actor who acted in the play *Hayavadan*?' When he nodded in the affirmative, she said, 'I still remember that performance. Convey my good wishes to him.' The call to lift the ban came from the ministry even before he had arrived from Delhi with the prime minister's message.

Though all the signatories, including myself, had taken a very strong anti-Emergency stand, Indira-ji demonstrated a commitment to free speech by supporting me. This reflected the unique political fabric of that time. In stark contrast, today's political climate labels those with opposing views as enemies and traitors. The erosion of civil discourse goes to show that our cultural and socio-political fabric has worn thin.

Perhaps due to my innate inclination to stay away from politics, or for some unknown reason, I haven't ever played the role of a politician, nor have I made any films based on politics—the play *Kaala Vajeer, Pandhara Raja* (Black Queen, White King) being the only exception.

The NCPA was established in 1969 by the then prime minister, Indira Gandhi. (Initially, the institution operated from the Bhulabhai Desai Institute, later moving to its current location at Nariman Point.) I had the opportunity to perform my play *Vallabhpurchi Dantkatha* there during a week-long festival in the presence of legends like Pandit Ravi Shankar, Guru Krishnankutty, P.L. Deshpande and Jamshed Bhabha. I have witnessed at close quarters the NCPA's transformations under the leadership of luminaries like Dr Narayana Menon, P.L. Deshpande, Vijaya Mehta, and later Dr Ashok Ranade. In 1992, the NCPA decided to produce the play *Kaala Vajeer, Pandhara Raja,* written by Dr Samir Kulkarni.

In 1989, a prominent Maharashtra politician was arrested for allegedly murdering his opponent in broad daylight. A play inspired by this event came to me, and I was offered the lead role. Although the script's unembellished language was effective, I was alarmed by its thematic structure that reinforced right-wing ideologies. After a detailed discussion, Dr Samir Kulkarni agreed to make some changes to the script, and the project moved forward. However, during rehearsals, due to the lack of clear direction, I had to search for my character's nuances entirely on my own. 'More energy, Palekar!' was the only instruction the director, Vaman Kendre, gave. Relying on my professional discipline, I managed to complete all the shows. Years later, I realised that the invisible forces behind the play's production lost interest in booking further shows because the altered script deviated from the original purpose of promoting rightist ideology and glorifying the political leader.

Then in 1983, Babuji approached me with a proposal to direct a film on the prolific writer, great poet and bold warrior Veer Savarkar. Babuji was my neighbour in Shivaji Park, and his son Sridhar was my childhood friend. 'We want to create a globally acclaimed film, akin to Attenborough's *Gandhi*, that will resonate with audiences worldwide. We are looking for a visionary director who has a command over both the subject matter and the craft of cinema. Not only me, but the trustees of Savarkar Pratishthan, too, are confident in your ability to take up and fulfil this responsibility.' The international accolades received by *Akriet* and my presence as a director at international film festivals likely contributed to their confidence in my abilities. By then I had heard that eminent directors like Hrishikesh Mukherjee, or Hrishi-da, as he was fondly known, Basu Bhattacharya and Ram Gabale had already pulled out of the project after a brief attempt at filming. Babuji had decided to produce this large-canvas film through crowdfunding, that is, by collecting donations from numerous people, ranging from house workers, office clerks to wealthy patrons. This put a colossal weight of responsibility on my shoulders.

I said to Babuji, 'First I will study Savarkar's writings. An accomplished writer Vishram Bedekar has written the screenplay and dialogue for you; I have great respect for him, let me read the script. Then we discuss the scale of the film—'

'Tell me about your monetary expectations, Amol,' Babuji said before I could even complete my sentence.

'Without discussing the script, I cannot grasp your vision as a producer or develop my vision of "Savarkar" as a director. Once we are clear, we will pull in the best technicians of national and international repute. Only after that I can give you an idea of the budget and my remuneration. But I am more interested in discussing the artistic content of the film first.'

After that initial interaction, I spent the next few days reading Savarkar's abundant literature, I read up on his concept of Hinduism, his struggles in the Andaman Islands, and much more. Then I read the screenplay written by Bedekar and requested for a meeting with the trustees.

'He [Vishram Bedekar] has written a screenplay that will appeal solely to a Marathi-speaking audience; that too within the framework of commercial cinema. Bedekar's script fails to capture the magnitude of Savarkar's legacy,' I said.

Though my comments upset the trustees of Savarkar Pratishthan, I continued.

'*The Message*, a film made by director Moustapha Akkad on the life of Prophet Muhammad, starring Anthony Quinn, or *Lion of the Desert*, also starring Quinn, the life story of Omar Mukhtar, a revolutionary leader who fought unsuccessfully against Mussolini in Libya, or *The Battle of Sutjeska* starring Richard Burton, which shines a different light on Marshal Tito's life, are my benchmarks.' I was trying to convince the trustees by giving examples of iconic international films. They did not agree with my opinions, but my sincerity struck a chord with them. After that, Babuji took me to Vishram Bedekar's residence. Upon hearing my response to the screenplay, Bedekar commended my honest, analytical critique with a wry smile. He said, 'I don't have either the enthusiasm or the time to rework the screenplay as per Amol's expectations and vision.'

Then, another meeting took place with the trustees where I shared my directorial vision and artistic approach. I picked out multiple incidents from Savarkar's life and his traits that needed to be highlighted. He had to be portrayed as a revolutionary hero, who had endured a harsh exile in the Cellular Jail of Andaman Islands, also known as 'Kala Pani'. He had to be shown as a sensitive poet, a visionary leader with strong political views, as the originator of the concept of Hindutva, and much more. I proposed that once those details were finalised, the texture of the screenplay and the length of the film could be determined. I also firmly conveyed to the trustees that I wasn't interested in creating a biased, propaganda film presenting a one-sided portrayal of his life.

Multiple meetings were held, but the trustees could not reach a consensus. One of the trustees, the great historian Babasaheb Purandare felt that all the events of Savarkar's life should be covered with equal dramatic intensity, even if the film's length ran up to four or five hours. So I asked him a simple question: 'As a producer, would you be willing to present a balanced portrayal of Savarkar, including his flaws and controversial ideas, even if you disagree with some of them?' His silence spoke volumes.

As a director, I needed clarity from the producers on whether the film's goal was to evoke emotion or to appeal to the intellect. I used a parallel example from Babuji's music world: when composing music, the music director must decide which instruments to use, which ones to put in the foreground, which phrases to accentuate and at what points, and whether to make the tune evoke pathos or joy. Each decision must be made consciously. Had I received an appropriate briefing from the trustees, I would have been able to create a memorable film, without taking any fees for the same.

Later, I watched the film *Veer Savarkar* (Savarkar, the brave), directed by Ved Rahi. The gap between the producers' vision of creating a globally impactful film and the final product was heartbreaking. I felt a sense of relief for having turned down the project and preserved my creative integrity. Subsequently, I directed *Dhyaasparva* (An Era of Yearning), a film about R.D. Karve's lifelong crusade in the field of family planning. I am very proud of that film.

When Sandhya and I made *Thaang*, the film Censor Board gave us a tough time. The film, which tells the story of an urban couple whose lives are plunged into turmoil when the husband's relationship with a man is discovered, was expected to receive an adult-only certificate. Titled *Thaang* in Marathi and *Quest* in English, the film was made in two languages, starring Mrinal Kulkarni, Rishi Deshpande, Shishir Sharma, Sachin Khedekar and Vijaya Mehta. The films were reviewed by separate committees for each language. While *Quest* got an 'A' certificate, the committee reviewing *Thaang* proposed a ban, claiming that 'the subject is very provocative and it is not in the interest of the society to get exposed to such subjects'.

In our defence, we cited many works from Marathi literature that had explored similar themes, some of which were written as far back as three decades earlier. Realising that the board members were firm in their stand, we decided to employ an aggressive approach. We asked them to give their decision in writing so that we could appeal against it in court. To us it was preposterous that the film had been granted a certificate in English, but not in Marathi. Following a heated debate, the board cleared the film with an 'A' certificate. The takeaway was clear: we must stand up against unjust impositions, no matter how arduous the battle may be.

Of course, the story of *Daayra* (The Square Circle) remains to be told. In 1996, my film *Daayra* became a huge success at the international film festivals in Toronto, London and France. But the film did not make it to the prestigious Indian Panorama section of the annual International Film Festival of India (IFFI). Nagpal, a journalist from Delhi who was on the selection committee that year, was strongly opposed to my film. 'How can you consider films that have songs as parallel cinema?' was his biggest dilemma. Gulzar saheb's *Maachis* was also disqualified for the same reason. I took the initiative of organising a parallel festival showcasing four or five such films rejected at IIFI. Our alternative festival, held in Thiruvananthapuram, received overwhelming support from the local audience and national media. *Daayra* went on to win the Special Jury Award at the National Awards in 1997.

A past insult or hurt from several years ago might have contributed to my impatience and snappy behaviour with the media.

The night my film *Akriet* released, my senior journalist friend, Sudhir Nandgaonkar, called me. 'Isaac Mujawar [the editor of an established film magazine called *Rasrang*] has written a rave review of the film. Pay *Rasrang* for a front-page advertisement immediately.'

I didn't like the implied quid pro quo arrangement. 'If a senior journalist like Isaac has made such a demand, I will definitely not obey your advice,' I replied curtly.

Soon another friend, thoroughly immersed in the film industry's protocols, Jayant Dharmadhikari, also called me. 'The readership of *Rasrang* is the target audience of your film. Isaac Mujawar's article will pull in significant patronage from the middle class, educated viewers. Consider this a benefit, and place the advertisement.'

But I did not change my decision. Assuming that what my informants told me was true, Isaac overnight, changed his glowing review to a scathing takedown. Such behind-the-scenes matters often don't come to the surface. The bitter memory of that incident and the unfair review still continue to hurt. Sometimes I ask myself, what did I prove, and to whom? Was it my very impractical attitude, or my ego? Looking at the paid publicity culture and the bribery involved in the conferment of awards, I am relieved that I exited the industry long ago.

My intolerance at being controlled by others would either provoke me to act or lead me to withdraw. The control could come from various sources, whether government authorities, the ruling elite, or industry heavyweights. Once in April 1985, the then information and broadcasting minister, Vitthalrao Gadgil, asked me to meet him. He wanted me to take over as the president of the Children's Film Society of India (CFSI). I was astonished to be offered a position that stalwarts such as V. Shantaram and Ram Gabale had previously held. My immediate response was 'Why me?' Gadgil promptly gave an equally frank answer.

'Balchitra Samiti was formed in 1955 with an aim to produce good films for the younger generation, and to expose them to the medium of cinema at an early age. Unfortunately, that organisation failed to perform as was expected of it. An organisation in disarray needs new and youthful energy to revitalise it. You are adored by common people across the country; the organisation will benefit from your fame and artistic vision. Although traditionally it is a three-year tenure, I have suggested to the prime minister to give you six years.'

I gave my consent to Gadgil on two conditions: I would not take any compensation for this work, and secondly, none of the committee members would make any film using the organisation's funds. I started working with four very capable colleagues, who were senior to me. We organised the first International Children's Film Festival in Bengaluru on a grand scale. Ramakrishna Hegde of the Janata Party, who was in the opposition at the time, strongly championed this festival.

About two-and-a-half years into my tenure, my team and I faced a major roadblock.

'The programmes of the Balchitra Samiti are not a priority for us,' a senior official from the ministry said at an annual general meeting. Naturally, a statement like this sparked a heated debate. If this endeavour wasn't important to the government, why were we brought in to invest our time and energy in it? Even after a huge argument, the officer refused to retract his statement. In protest, I announced my resignation. This happened sometime in September 1987. Immediately afterwards, my colleagues and all other committee members resigned as well.

A few months later, I received a message asking me to meet Prime Minister Rajiv Gandhi at the Mumbai airport. At the time, he had not yet accepted our resignations, and I assumed he wanted to discuss them. The then Maharashtra chief minister, Shankarrao Chavan, and his cabinet ministers, who were there to welcome the prime minister, seemed to have no clue why I was there, standing in a corner.

When Rajiv-ji disembarked, he bypassed protocol and came directly to me. Placing a hand on my shoulder, he said, 'If you face any hurdles in CFSI's work, call me directly.' His affection for me was evident in his behaviour. 'I don't possess the diplomacy to resolve administrative disputes. Also, I am not interested in the non-creative operational issues.'

'If one has to escalate even the smallest issue directly to the prime minister, doesn't that indicate a serious flaw in the system?' I asked him sincerely. I insisted that he accept my resignation. Although my team and I had resigned, we knew the government would struggle to organise the next International Children's Film Festival without our support. So, we conducted it smoothly in Bhubaneswar. In hindsight, I feel that small disputes should be resolved through dialogue and mediation. Retreating is the easy way out. Now, sometimes, I regret having lost the opportunity to do something innovative and beneficial for children.

Surprisingly, even after this, Rajiv Gandhi insisted that I take over the reins of the second Apna Utsav, to be held in Mumbai. The first Apna Utsav was held in Delhi, and it had made headlines for all the wrong reasons, ranging from financial mismanagement to its lack of accessibility to the public, sparking widespread criticism. Apna Utsav had been started in 1986 with the aim of reviving the country's nearly extinct local folk arts and introducing younger generations to the richness of traditional art forms. Since I liked the concept, I agreed to design the artistic programmes without any remuneration. It was decided that my role would be titled 'creative director'. The country was classified into seven cultural divisions, and the heads of these divisions were involved in planning various programmes with the best artistes available.

For the Mumbai festival, it was decided that the inaugural programme would be held at the Andheri Sports Complex and the finale at the Wankhede Stadium. Rather than conducting all the programmes at a standalone venue, it was decided that they would be arranged across Mumbai from the east to the west. The magnificence and talent of the participating artistes—always at the bottom of the totem pole—shone through when they presented their art. To this day, I can feel the lingering pride and satisfaction at how flawlessly the programme was conducted.

Late one night, while I was preparing for the children's film festival in Bhubaneswar, the former finance minister of Maharashtra, Dr V. Subrahmanyam, rang me. 'We have decided to field you against Shiv Sena from Shivaji Park.' The assembly elections of 1985 were imminent. I realised that Congress seniors were trying to draw me into politics after seeing my interaction with Rajiv Gandhi at the airport. 'You are missing a big opportunity,' Dr Subrahmanyam said when I refused.

Immediately after my return to Bombay, I got a call from the one and only Balasaheb Thackeray. 'I heard that you rejected the Congress's offer. If you are willing, we will give you the ticket.' Again, I refused politely, telling him that I wasn't interested in politics. I still remember his parting words, 'think and tell me'. I have always maintained that autonomy and independence from politics are crucial for questioning the system. As for Balasaheb, he always took a thoughtful and discerning approach when interacting with me, sometimes even reconsidering his decisions. I recall two incidents that testify to this.

In 1996, the Maharashtra government decided to honour artistes for their contributions. The first Maharashtra Gaurav Award was conferred upon the writer P.L. Deshpande. While accepting the award, P.L. criticised the then ruling party for 'preferring dictatorship over democracy'. Unable to stomach this criticism, Balasaheb lashed out at P.L. with a scathing denunciation. Due to this, much resentment spread in Maharashtra's intellectual and cultural spaces. I declined an award that Balasaheb was to present to me in protest against his harsh remarks about P.L.

After a few days, I ran into Balasaheb by accident. I was visiting the accomplished singer Suresh Wadkar's studio to attend a song recording for a Marathi film directed by the great theatre director Damu Kenkre. All of a sudden, Balasaheb arrived. Damu was his neighbour and friend. As I stood up to leave, he asked me to sit back down. After the recording was over, he took me to the upper floor of Suresh's house. As he sipped beer, he clarified that what he had said about P.L. had been twisted and misinterpreted. He pointed out that it was hypocritical for P.L. to accept an award from a party that he criticised publicly. Hearing his logic and the thoughtful way he expressed his point, my grudge against Balasaheb melted away.

Then the MAMI incident happened.

In India, international film festivals were usually organised by the government. Dissatisfied with the shortcomings of the ruling government's management of film festivals, prominent figures from the film industry conceived the idea of a grand, annual private international film festival. Hrishi-da, Yash Chopra, Shyam Benegal, Amit Khanna, Manmohan Shetty, Kiran Shantaram and I were selected as the founding trustees. I was tasked with organising the opening ceremony. When naming the festival Mumbai Academy of Moving Images—in short, MAMI—we drew inspiration from renowned international festivals, like those held in Venice, Berlin and Cannes, which are named after their host cities. While planning the flow of events for the inaugural evening, I suggested avoiding speeches, so that we could keep government officers and political leaders off the stage. The trustees honoured my suggestion.

However, one day before the inauguration, we received a message dictating to us that Chief Minister Manohar Joshi and the Minister for Culture Pramod Navalkar must be allowed on the stage, or the event would be cancelled. This spread panic among the executive members. We called an emergency meeting during which Kiran Shantaram received a call. He handed me the phone with trembling hands. On the other side of the call was Balasaheb. He questioned me about our stance to not include government officials in the festival. I replied frankly: 'You will be proud that, for the first time, the film fraternity is coming together to hold this grand international event without any government aid or funding. You being an artiste yourself will appreciate our efforts. We mean no offence to any individual or party. Besides, the first two rows in the auditorium will be exclusively reserved for dignitaries.' Balasaheb was persuaded. 'All right, let's have a beer session soon' were his parting words. The inauguration was a resounding success.

After Sandhya and I moved to Pune in 2000, a group of like-minded residents from our area established a trust called Hirwaee to partner with the Pune Municipal Corporation in an attempt to revitalise the city's central area and promote environmental conservation. However, this initiative quickly escalated into a fierce fight—an interesting story in itself.

On our daily walk through the peaceful Prabhat Road area, we came across a narrow, winding path cutting through a posh residential area. It had been reduced to a squalid dumping site, attracting trash and construction debris from all over the neighbourhood. Besides posing a health hazard, it had created a safety issue, it had become a den for criminal elements. According to Pune's city development plan, designed at the end of the eighteenth century, this stretch of land was originally reserved as 'the left canal' of the watershed. Once upon a time, Pune was nestled within ten to twelve hills, which were the crowning glory of Pune's natural splendour. Small canals were created to divert rainwater flowing down from those hills so that it would be spread throughout the city. But, as the city grew, the hills were eroded, illegal buildings were erected in their place, and the canals were blocked. Cement and concrete roads were built, and beautiful, scenic spots were defaced.

In 2002, on the occasion of Gandhi Jayanti, Sandhya and I embarked on a clean-up drive, engaging the local residents to restore the abandoned canal area to its former glory. The campaign continued over a few Sundays, as a result of which, the 1.1-kilometre stretch became garbage-free. Inspired by international examples of pedestrian corridors, we decided to designate the track as a vehicle-free zone, exclusively for walkers. Then the idea of beautifying the area emerged. A ten-year, public–private partnership agreement was signed in December 2002. Our initiative served as a shining example to citizens to take ownership of civic duties, beyond merely pointing fingers at the government. We dreamt of creating healthy lungs for the city by planting lots of indigenous trees. We planned, among other things, a sitting area for senior citizens, a small outdoor auditorium for young performers, a play area for kids, and an open-air library. Public toilet units were also to be built at both ends of the stretch. A renowned landscape designer was appointed to design and execute the plan. Hirwaee also proposed that it would assume the responsibilities of nurturing the garden, tending to the trees and keeping the track spotless. The trust did not claim ownership of anything. No trustee desired to have their name displayed on the signage announcing their contribution. The project's budget was pegged at Rs 40 lakh, with the trust slated to contribute half of the amount.

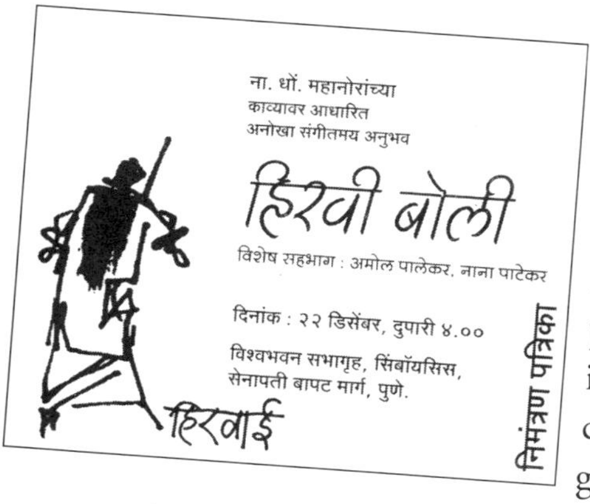

Sandhya conceived of a unique fundraiser which centred around nature-themed poetry recitation. The event, titled 'Hirvee Boli' (Nature's Songs), featured the renowned Marathi poet-lyricist N.D. Mahanor's poems, which were transformed into lyrical songs by the gifted music composer Anand Modak. A talented group of doctor-artistes performed these songs, while the versatile actor and my dear friend Nana (Patekar) and I recited a few of Mahanor's poems. Initially, we had planned to perform only once, but on public demand, two back-to-back programmes of Hirvee Boli were presented that evening. Only half an hour before the first show, I had received the terrible news of the demise of my friend Dilip Kulkarni in Mumbai. Without Nana and Sandhya's support that day, I couldn't have mustered the courage to recite the poems. People loved both the concept and the presentation. The event and the project both received praise from the media and residents. Almost Rs 16 lakh was collected that evening. We deposited the whole amount with the municipal corporation. As it often happens, our success and funds caught the attention of opportunistic politicians and builders; what happened next was the same old tale of manipulation and politicking for nefarious purposes.

The vultures set their sights on this strategic location, and attempts to acquire the land via the local government began in earnest. A fraudulent scheme was devised to unjustly grab the land by building a road on it, while profiting from the sale of transfer rights. Proposals were brought before the standing committee for finalisation; actions were manoeuvred overnight, while citizens remained in complete darkness. Representatives of all political parties stood in support of this deceitful proposal. I received threatening calls from local politicians; some tried to lure me with bags full of cash and a contract to produce three films. Banners were hung up in front of my house saying, 'Has Palekar ever touched a bicycle?', 'Has Palekar ever reached late for office due to being stuck in traffic?' The only way a common man can deal with this kind of bullying is to go to court.

Hemant Naiknavare, a forthright trustee of Hirwaee and a builder himself, and Sandhya managed to save the site after a seven-year-long battle in court. That stretch of land was saved, but during those seven years, the area fell into neglect due to the court having ordered a status quo. A project worth Rs 40 lakh was now estimated to cost Rs 80 lakh. Such a huge amount was not within the reach of Hirwaee; however, we let the Pune Municipal Corporation (PMC) use our funds since we had committed to it. The PMC took over the beautification drive, but the end product was a disappointing departure from our original plan, lacking the elegance we had envisioned. The sole consolation was that we managed to preserve the canal space for the safe use of the pedestrians. Today, thousands of citizens use the canal every day.

In an ironic twist, every political party claims credit for the canal's transformation in their election manifesto. Even though many of our senior trustees are no more, we find solace in believing that they are still connected to us through this serene green oasis.

Every individual, group or organisation has to fight a battle distinct from others. The spark that ignites rebellion varies from person to person. Each revolt or opposition has its own separate strategy and weapons.

The poet Namdeo Dhasal dedicated his book *Golpitha* to

> *all the movements and souls that resist systems that oppress, exploit and marginalise the common man, denying them power, wealth and respect.*

For most people—or my fans—it is often challenging to reconcile the 'real me' with the person they see on the reel. The contrast between the simple, stumbling 'boy next door' seen on the silver screen, and the reserved, quiet Amol Palekar in real life, who stands firm in his opinions, does not seek anyone's validation or praise, stays away from the crowd, does not give much emotional response, is often difficult to comprehend. I feel that people don't like that gap in these double roles. The realisation that 'Ram Prasad/ Lakshman Prasad' is different in reality from their expectations is somewhat disconcerting to people. It's possible they are thrown by the conflicting images of the same man. This is the little catch in my double role. It's a delight for me to introspect and decipher; I am beginning to like it.

Despite all these contradictions, I am humbled by the overwhelming respect and adulation I get from people of all ages, across the globe. Whether it is a bus driver in a northeastern state, or a police officer in Lucknow, whether it is a tamasha performer in Maharashtra, a teacher in Kerala, a shopkeeper in Karnataka, a janitor in Rajasthan, a government official in Delhi, an artiste in Kolkata, a young professor from Hungary, or a student in his thirties from Stanford—I receive love from everyone. And all this love that I have received over the years, this is my greatest treasure.

What else do I need?

In the Labyrinth of Accidents

As I ponder the complexities of life, a haunting visual often surfaces before me: an orange being squeezed by a sharp-edged fruit crusher, and its juice being separated from the pulp. This visual evokes a sense of desolation in me. To me, the pulpless juice is as unappealing and sterile as a dull uninspiring existence. But then why remove the essence from life? With this recurring, unsettling visual, I remain resilient and energised, ready to embrace a life of vitality. Not succumbing to monotony is a choice that I make while crafting and determining my own route. I believe that because I am an atheist, I found the freedom to take ownership of my own decisions and to forge my own path, unencumbered by external expectations or divine interventions. My atheistic perspective towards life has honed my mind, affording me a sharp edge of clarity, critical thinking and, above all, the courage to defy convention and conformity.

Atheism, in its very essence, is a profoundly abstract concept. It exists beyond the realm of tangible, physical manifestation. Once enthralled by that abstraction, the mind is free to face a blank canvas. Painting the unique mosaic of existence then becomes easy. That said, I don't subscribe to the idea that every enigma one encounters in life needs to be decoded. I like to find beauty in the unknown. It's okay simply to exist amidst the unknown. The unresolved pieces of life's puzzle often linger, suspended in air, sometimes manifesting in my dreams, taking on vivid forms and shapes. Upon waking, those forms persist in my mind. It's an absurd dance of blurred images without any articulation. I rush to my studio holding a paintbrush and start to unlock the secrets of the images whispered to my waking mind. Whatever is drawn on the canvas is truly my expression, but the creative odyssey begins in an abstract expanse. It's a deeply personal discovery of oneself. The painting is intimately tied to my being, yet its tendrils continue to remain in the air; though they may be invisible, they form an unseen yet unbroken bond, connecting my inner world to the surreal outer world soaked in ultramarine blue.

It is also not easy to be an atheist.

As far back as I can remember, I have always felt a natural disconnect from the concept of God or divine existence, a sense of doubt that has only deepened with time, shaping my thoughts and beliefs. Refraining from imposing any religious beliefs or practices on my sisters and me, my parents took a refreshingly neutral approach to religion or theism. They remained untethered from the influence of spiritual gurus, unswayed by the trappings of rituals, and uninterested in pilgrimages or temple visits. They did maintain a small shrine in our two-room home though. It housed Shiva, a young Krishna and one or two other deities. Their daily routine did not involve puja or prayers. However, my mother used to follow the tradition of lighting an oil lamp at the shrine every evening, infusing our house with a warm, soft glow. Although I'd had a sacred thread ceremony, I never wore the *janeu*. During Ganeshotsav, we used to bring home a Ganapati idol and enthusiastically decorate our house with flowers. My sisters and I would sing the traditional *aartis* with joy. My mother used to say, 'Ganapati is brought home not as a religious practice but as a symbol of joy and colour.' I knew that my parents were not atheists.

In 1952, when our father's health declined and he had to take an early retirement, my youngest sister, Unnati, was only five years old. Our family faced serious financial challenges. My mother took up a job to support us. In those days, women who stepped out of the house to work were often met with disdain and criticism. This period marked a significant change in our lives, as my sisters and I witnessed the struggles of our parents to sustain our household. I recall that during that period, a man used to come to our home and recite shlokas. This continued, at least for a few days. Due to my maternal aunt's bedridden condition, her family would often visit Haji Malang, to perform rituals and seek blessings. But my parents never participated in those activities.

Most residents of Shivaji Park, where we lived, were Hindus, which created a strong sense of community and entrenched a cultural identity in the area. There were a few Catholic families too, as well as one or two Jewish neighbours. A Parsi colony was situated across Tilak Bridge in Dadar. On one end of Cadell Road, in the direction of Mahim, there was a predominantly Muslim neighbourhood which is still known as Kapad Bazar; on the other end, a unique blend of communal harmony existed, where a Ganesh-Maruti temple, a mosque and a church shared the same corner. Religious inclusivity was evident. Our immediate neighbours included mostly upper-caste Brahmins, and a few Saraswat Brahmins and Somvanshi Kshatriyas; the one Catholic neighbour was an exception.

Every year, on 6 December, Chaityabhoomi, the cremation site of the great Babasaheb Ambedkar, would witness a sizeable gathering of Buddhist followers who would pay homage to his legacy. My school friends, too, were mostly Brahmins. But when I enrolled at the Sir J.J. School of Art, I made friends belonging to diverse religions, castes and ethnic backgrounds. The atmosphere there was truly cosmopolitan. Initially, Menon, Aarya and I formed a tight-knit trio; the group later expanded to include Doss, Patel and Siddiqui, forming a dynamic circle of six friends. During lunch breaks, we used to share each other's food—a scrumptious mutton dish from Patel's tiffin, Doss's Syrian Christian beef recipe, a delicious fish curry from my meal and vegetarian delicacies from Aarya's dabba. Life had a wonderful variety. Later, when I was employed with the Bank of India, my colleagues there came from varied backgrounds too.

In my later life, my in-laws embraced a beautiful tradition of celebrating several festivals, regardless of their religious origins—thus fostering a genuine spirit of inclusivity. But over time, we all observed a disturbing trend where public spaces increasingly started being converted into religious places of worship, which was often driven by political agenda. Thus, suddenly emerged a Udyan Ganesh idol in Shivaji Park in 1994-95. The Siddhivinayak temple ascended to unparalleled heights in front of my own eyes. Eventually, I began to understand the political undercurrents that lay behind the transition of small temples into iconic landmarks, and how they transformed our country's religious fabric.

I have never believed that our daily affairs are controlled by astrological signs and constellations; or that some supernatural force is saving or directing my life; or that certain days are auspicious, while others bring adversities. I firmly believed then, and do so even today, that the events of my life are a direct result of my context, actions, decisions and choices. Embracing that belief, one must always be alert to take full ownership of one's failures and lacunae, and forsake excuses. An ongoing self-reflection has become a habit with me. I keep assessing and reassessing my own actions or decisions, as if peeling off the dead skin in order to keep my core intact. One doesn't get the chance to blame someone else for one's own failures. One cannot experience 'the lightness of being', nor can one yearn for solace. Even so, in my life happiness has often tipped the scales, outweighing difficulties. Not that I have not faced my share of troubles. Several times in life,

With Baba, Aai, Unnati, Akka & Neelon-tai (in the 1950s)

(From left to right) B.S. Patkar & Akka, Arun Mantri & Neelon-tai, (seated) Advait Mantri, Baba, Aai & Unnati (in the 1970s)

With Shalmalee
in Australia

with Christine, Shalmalee, Kaarin,
Sandhya and Samiha

With Sandhya,
Samiha & Shyamang

With schoolmates & teachers
from Bordi School (1959)
—I am with the peacock feather-fan

The trio from
Sir J.J. School of Art (1961)
with Jagdish Arya & U.G. Menon

during critical moments of decision-making, many circumstances arise to challenge our resolve, probing the depth of our conviction and beliefs. I recall many such instances.

The day *Anaahat* was released in 2001 was apparently one of the most inauspicious ones. We had no clue that it was *Sarvapitri Amavasya*; not that it would have mattered in any case. Most slots for shows in movie halls are freely available during *Pitru-paksha* as no producers release their films in those fifteen days. Most Hindus observe rituals during that period to pay homage to their ancestors. Releasing our film during *Pitru-paksha* was a purely practical decision on our part. We never looked for a propitious or holy day. This was sacrilege in the opinion of many of our friends, who advised us to change the date. Ironically, the film became a resounding success; it celebrated a fifty-week run, playing to packed houses, garnering both critical accolades and substantial commercial gains. The same friends who had criticised our decision, on our success said that 'the new moon had blessed us'.

Dr Atul Biniwale, who is a renowned physician in Pune, is Sandhya's close friend. Interestingly, he is also a veteran badminton player, and this shared interest has formed a strong bond between him and me, as I have the same passion for the game. I went to him for an annual check-up in the third week of September 2021. With no pressing health concerns or symptoms, visiting Atul was merely a routine chore. At one point during our chat, I casually mentioned to him that I occasionally experience a sensation where it feels like my heartbeats are coming from my abdominal area. Atul promptly sent me for an abdominal sonography. Once the diagnosis of abdominal aortic aneurysm (AAA) was confirmed, the doctors recommended urgent surgical intervention. Two specialist surgeons with expertise in this type of surgery came in from Mumbai. These experts usually are in such high demand that patients typically need to book appointments several months in advance. But in my case, both were available on any day in that particular week—because it fell during *Pitru-paksha*! Within four days of the diagnosis, that is, on 29 September, the procedure was successfully done. My recovery was so fast that on the twelfth day from the surgery, I chauffeured Sandhya to Solapur for her work commitments. I guess it's safe to say that we indeed are 'blessed by our ancestors'.

Paradoxically, despite my rationalist journey, I have experienced unexplained, unexpected events and mysterious circumstances. Those who believe in the power of fate might attribute it to mere coincidence. I am not a determinist. Rather than delving into complex philosophical debates on determinism or Kant's discourse on free will, I have chosen to trust my intuition and my own experiential insights. I view those four unforeseen incidents as accidental turning points, which have transformed my life, leaving an indelible mark on my existence forever. The first of the four serendipitous accidents led me to discover the field of visual arts; the second one thrust me into the world of theatre and cinema; the third empowered me to take the director's chair; and the fourth brought an unprecedented twenty-five-year streak of peace and happiness.

Sigmund Freud would simply dismiss my views at this point. 'There is no such thing as accidents. They are hidden truths; they are simply manifestations of our subconscious desires,' he would argue. But for a subconscious desire to become a driving force, isn't it necessary to have some latent connection or underlying context? These four accidents, unmoored from any commonality, drifted into my orbit like fragments of a narrative floating in zero gravity and turned my world upside down. As I attempt to discern a thread of coherence among these four accidents, I feel bewildered. This bewilderment is akin to being immersed in the sprawling, unbroken long takes of Jancsó's cinematic masterpieces.

I must write more about my favourite filmmaker. Miklós Jancsó's cinema is a journey through the subconscious, where boundaries between reality and fantasy dissolve. His use of long takes and deliberate pacing creates a meditative state of unconventional storytelling. His world-famous films like *The Round-Up* and *Red Psalm* unfold with a hypnotic rhythm, transporting viewers to a world where time and space blur. His innovative use of camera movements and composition create a dreamlike atmosphere. Whenever I think of the four accidents in my life, I find myself lost in the labyrinthine corridors of Jancsó's cinematic universe. I sense a very strong bond between myself and him.

As the ashes of the Second World War settled, a new wave of cinema emerged in Europe. The new filmmakers sought a more experimental approach. This marked a seismic shift in European cinema, of which Jancsó was a key figure. In 2013, just a year before he passed away, Sandhya and I had the privilege of visiting him at his home in Budapest. We were struck by his warmth and simplicity. Despite his advanced age and frailty, Jancsó's eyes twinkled as I conveyed my deepest admiration for his work and the impact it had had on my aesthetics. Conveying my feelings to him was a cathartic experience. I always felt that despite his greatness, he remained underappreciated outside of Hungary and the cinephile circles. Other than the Best Director award at the Cannes Film Festival in 1972 for *Red Psalm*, he didn't receive any international honour that was due to him. My attempts to lobby for a lifetime achievement award for him at MAMI were unsuccessful. I failed him and myself in not pushing hard enough to make this award a reality.

Jancsó's films were never mere entertainment; they were powerful allegories, laced with political subtext and scathing critique of the ruling regimes. He fearlessly confronted the brutalities of fascism, the repression caused by communism and the violence emanating therefrom. Power, oppression and resistance were his favourite themes. His cinematic style was a radical departure from that of his contemporaries. His use of stark landscapes and minimalist dialogues created a dreamlike atmosphere, both haunting and hypnotic. Imagine the audacity, the innovative spirit and logistical complexity of capturing eight to ten minute long takes on 35 mm reels when there was no digital technology available. His experimentation with extended takes, shot in a single uninterrupted sweep, was a testament to his commitment to cinematic artistry. Each take was a high-wire act, requiring precise planning, meticulous choreography and an almost intuitive connection between the director, his cast and his crew. The resulting footage was the hallmark of his distinctive style. His films were masterclasses in brevity and precision, with a typical length of seventy to ninety minutes, achieved through just ten to twelve shots. Those unfamiliar with the craft of filmmaking too can understand his technical mastery.

'I use long takes to make the viewer understand that he isn't seeing reality; what he's seeing is unreal, it's a fantasy. Only then are they forced to think about the underlying meaning.' His quote convinced me not to spoon-feed audiences, and taught me the power of restraint in filmmaking. By leaving some fragments unconnected, the narrative can become a catalyst for reflection, debate and personal interpretation, lingering in the viewer's mind long after the credits roll. The unpredictability of Jancsó's style kept the audiences on the edge of their seats, as each new shot unfolded like an accident. Each following shot was like a domino falling, triggering a cascade of spontaneous, unscripted reactions.

The long take in my life's journey commenced with a natural inclination towards visual arts. From my family home in Shivaji Park, two different roads led to the Dadar train station. The two routes took one past either the Samarth art studio or the Pam art studio. I had a habit of stopping by the studios where giant size film posters were hand-painted. I never went to the station without stopping on the way to marvel at these grand artworks. It was here that for the first time, I was exposed to the technique of gridding the photos of film stars into squares in order to enlarge and paint them on a massive scale. Hours would fly by without my registering the passage of time as I stood entranced, surrounded by the scent of linseed oil and turpentine.

When I was in the seventh or eighth grade at the Balmohan School, Sinnarkar sir, my art teacher, was once guiding the class to draw and paint a hibiscus flower and its leaf. He did not like the way I had drawn it. 'Have you ever touched a hibiscus leaf? Compare its rough texture to the smooth representation you have drawn on paper,' he said in his poised tone. He then brought the leaf to life with delicate watercolour strokes. That lesson helped me understand the interplay between texture, form and colour. To nurture my interest in painting, my mother used to enrol me in art classes every year during summer vacation. Pradeep Jog was a friend from my school days at Bordi. His father, who was a sculptor, inspired me to opt for a career in visual arts.

I joined the Sir J.J. School of Arts in 1960. Prof. Shirgaonkar was the head of the department of drawing and painting at the time. I acquired the techniques of expressive pencil strokes and of adding depth through shading in my artwork from him and Prof. Solapurkar. Prof. Palshikar, Baburao Sadwelkar, Sukhadwala and Sambhaji Kadam were some of the other teachers who taught me the nuances of portrait painting. Just a week after my admission, our dean, Prof. Dhond, took us on a field trip to the Victoria Terminus train station for a session on sketching. Setting up his folding chair, easel and paper in front of the building, he produced a stunning watercolour painting of the scene in just forty minutes. It was a marvel how he had conveyed the dampness and gloom that lingered there after a drizzle. Years later, when I travelled to Moscow, I was struck by a cityscape uncluttered by advertisement boards, which brought back memories of Prof. Dhond's painting. Mumbai's once-glorious cityscape and historic architecture have been marred by the proliferation of digital banners, advertisement boards and tangled electrical wires. As an artist, Prof. Dhond had excluded those distracting elements from his painting, opting to depict only what he intended to convey. Thus, in my early years at the art school, I discovered the remarkable impact of visual arts and the artist's ability to shape perception and curate reality.

Numerous experiences during that time had a profound impact on my life. I remember one such day: our portrait painting class started around 10 a.m. After a while, Prof. Palshikar entered the classroom. He was observing everyone's work. He approached me and said, 'Why have you ruined your painting? Last night before we left the room, I saw your work. You were doing fine.' I was totally disheartened. He scraped the painting with a knife, removed all the layers. I burst into tears. He asked me to start afresh. I just sat in stunned silence for a while. Then I took a deep breath, composed myself and began anew. I struggled well into the night to finish the portrait. Prof Palshikar visited the classroom to see my progress. 'Do you see the difference in the colour balance and composition now? The subtlety and charm of the grey hues were absent in the previous simplistic black-and-white contrast. Artistry lies in uncovering the complete range of grey shades.' His words etched a lasting impression on my mind. It taught me to face challenges with calm persistence, steady determination and patience. Prof. Palshikar's message remained a guiding force for me throughout my career in theatre and film.

In the third year of art school, I was given the Gladstone Solomon Award. The fact that my name was chosen by luminaries like Gopal Deuskar and Prafulla Dahanukar, meant a great deal to me. By the fifth year, I had the privilege of knowing international celebrities like K.H. Ara, K.K. Hebbar, Vasudeo Gaitonde and M.F. Husain. My association with great art and artists expanded my horizons, boosting my artistic growth.

After completing my graduation from art school, I started exploring different avenues to earn money. The fact that my parents never inquired about my financial plans or future stability weighed heavily on my mind. Although I knew the fine arts would not yield immediate financial returns, unlike the applied arts courses, I had still chosen to pursue it. I had two options now: to accept a teaching position in the art school, or to pursue a career in film art direction, following in the footsteps of the all-time set designer of Raj Kapoor's films and a painter, M.R. Acharekar. I did not like either of these options.

For about a year, I did advertising agency assignments, struggling to find meaning in them. I was thoroughly bored. Then someone advised me to explore opportunities in banking. Wamanrao Varde, who was a prominent figure in the banking and trading industry, referred me for a position at the Saraswat Bank. After a few months, I landed a job at the Bank of India. For several months, my daily routine involved working at the bank during the day and pursuing my passion for painting at night. In the evenings, I would visit art galleries, interact with artists and engage in stimulating discussions about the art world.

One day, I went to the Taj Art Gallery to inquire about potential opportunities to showcase my work in a solo exhibition. The manager asked me to submit my work for review, which would determine the feasibility of hosting a show. I was a bit annoyed. 'Why should you assess my work if I am paying rent for the space?

If you were to sponsor my show, I would understand.' The manager was caught off guard by my directness. In the evening, I went to meet Ara (K.H. Ara), and he sensed my disappointment. I narrated the whole episode. 'Though not to the manager, will you be willing to show me your work?' His question left me speechless. The thought of showing my work to such a master painter was intimidating. He came to my parents' humble abode, where I had arranged my canvases in the small balcony for his viewing. Standing before my paintings, he shared with me a tender memory from his initial days. His father had worked as a car mechanic in Hyderabad. Upon Ara's arrival in Mumbai, he also had taken up a job in a garage to make ends meet. In his free time, he would sketch with charcoal on the garage walls. On seeing this, the foreign owner of the garage, Walter Langhammer, who was a renowned painter himself and the art director of the *Times of India*, bought papers, colours and brushes for Ara. From those modest origins, Ara rose to become a world-renowned painter. By relating this story, he was indirectly asking me not to get discouraged. The next morning, he called the manager of the Taj Art Gallery and requested her to reassign his cancelled exhibition dates to a promising young artist. When she agreed, his face lit up with a warm smile, aimed towards me. Even now, I vividly recall that smile on his face, radiant with his unwavering belief in me. The very next day, I returned to meet the manager of the gallery with Ara's recommendation letter addressed to her.

While I was getting ready for my first solo show, I had no idea how to get leave from my job at the bank. My supervisor refused outright to grant me any time off. Since I was still on probation, he directed me to my departmental head. With a mix of nervousness and determination, I approached my boss, Mr B.N. Atal. I was aware of how the mere sound of his footsteps entering the bank instilled fear in the entire staff. After a few moments of hesitation, I disclosed to him that I wanted a ten-day leave. He was surprised. He asked me to sit down and allowed me to share the details of my activities. 'Technically, you are not eligible for leave, but I will allow your absence for ten days provided you sign the attendance register daily.' His graciousness offered a turning point in my life. I was able to retain my job and still hold my exhibition. I have never forgotten the kindness he showed me.

Many eminent artists, most of my art school professors, colleagues from the bank, friends and relatives attended my exhibition. Shortly after, I received a new commission to create two wall murals for the Bombay Port Trust's newly constructed hospital. Once again, Ara graciously provided a recommendation letter that significantly strengthened my application. The second recommendation was given by my teacher Prof. Palshikar. He was delighted to discover that my rough sketches for the proposed murals had departed from the realistic approach. 'Amol is a deserving, talented candidate who merits a chance to express his artistic abilities.' His words proved to be the deciding factor, confirming my selection for the assignment. The chairman of the Port Trust sealed the deal. For the next two months, I worked tirelessly to complete both the murals.

Soon after, I received a time-bound assignment, to draw a portrait of the chairman of Johnson & Johnson. He was to return to his home country. Having attended my exhibition, he had liked my work. He sat for me for two hours each day, and I was able to complete his oil portrait in just one week. Despite not being a strictly realistic representation, he enjoyed my expressive portrayal. My work was very well rewarded and I earned a substantial amount for my efforts. Receiving one lakh rupees in 1967-68 was beyond my wildest dreams. This early experience in my career gave me the confidence and reassurance that I could succeed while staying true to my artistic vision and style.

In 1966, when I was working with the Bank of India, my sister Unnati, who was three years younger than me, was studying at St. Xavier's College in Mumbai. As a part of her college's annual festival, she was performing in a play. She invited me to attend one of her rehearsals. There I met her friend Chitra Murdeshwar, who was also performing in the play. I admired her independent and energetic spirit. It drew us closer, paving the way for a lasting relationship. Around that time, a parallel movement in Bombay known as the 'Film Forum' enabled M.S. Sathyu, Basu Bhattacharya, Basu Chatterjee and Shyam Benegal to showcase alternative foreign cinema, distinct from the mainstream Hollywood films, at a movie theatre called Tarabai Hall on Marine Drive. Chitra and I started attending those evening shows regularly.

One day, Satyadev Dubey visited St. Xavier's to meet Chitra. He offered her Chitralekha's role in his play *Yayati*. The well-known actress Sulabha Deshpande had recommended Chitra for that role. Dubey used to hold rehearsals at the Indian National Theatre's (INT) warehouse near Mahalaxmi Temple on Peddar Road. The first time I accompanied her to the rehearsal, rain was pouring down hard. I saw a short person, dressed in half pants and a T-shirt, with curly hair similar to Sathya Sai Baba's, pacing back and forth. Chitra murmured in my ear, 'That's Dubey.' Glancing at his wristwatch, he remarked, 'Glad you arrived five minutes ahead of time.' Then Chitra introduced me to him as a 'friend'. As he turned around, I noticed a big stick in his hand. 'Our rehearsal will finish in two hours,' he announced to me, implying that I should now leave. In the future, as I got to know him better, I saw him in various moods and avatars, with the stick emerging as a key prop.

A few days later, after the end of a rehearsal, Chitra came out, and Dubey followed her. After a short but intense inquiry about me, he unexpectedly asked if I'd like to act in his play. He immediately added, 'Don't think that I have seen some great talent in you. You seem to have a lot of time, hence I'm asking you.' And this is how I came to be cast as Ponkshe in his production of *Chup! Court Chalu Hai*.

This marked my life's 'second accident', thanks to which I became an actor without seeking or expecting the title of an 'actor'. Accidentally, at the age of twenty-three, 'painter Amol Palekar' became 'actor Amol Palekar'. Once my debut show at the Tejpal Auditorium in Bombay ended, I went to the Walchand Terrace hall, and sat there, savouring the moment. Dubey handed me a copy of the *Times of India*, and asked me to read out aloud the critical review of the play written by the seasoned theatre critic Dnyaneshwar Nadkarni. My performance had been called 'suave' in Nadkarni's piece. I found it difficult to comprehend his words. Dubey said, 'You are now ready to learn acting, but first, learn the basics. Work on your stage presence. Why are you standing so stiffly? Relax your shoulders. Release the tension.' As he finished his initial instructions, he threw in an additional command, 'Try standing on just one foot.' That was his way of praising my work. The image of a young Dubey standing beside a pillar in the Walchand Terrace hall remains etched in my memory.

Our performance of *Chup! Court Chalu Hai* in the Hindi State Theatre competition at Nagpur was very well received. Immediately thereafter, Dubey started rehearsals for the play *Suno, Janmejay* (Listen Janmejaya). He paired me with another newcomer, Nila Bhagwat. She was asked to practise in one corner of the room, and I was assigned to another corner. Dubey began by teaching us the fundamentals, instructing us on posture, movement, vocal projection, the difference between pitch and octave, and on how to use these to add depth and emotion to our performance. We were also taught physical exercises to enhance our agility and overall stage presence. Even though Dubey was engaged in rehearsals with veteran actors Amrish Puri and Kanti Madia, he closely monitored our rehearsals, keeping a watchful eye on our progress. We rehearsed with a sense of apprehension, aware of the stories we had heard about Dubey's volatile nature and of the stick that was said to be his tool for discipline.

The second performance of our play saw a dismal turnout, with a mere thirteen spectators occupying the vast seven-hundred-seater Tejpal Auditorium. Kanti Madia proposed cancelling the performance. With fierce determination, Dubey retorted that we would perform regardless of the size of the audience. Those thirteen people were the genuine audience, who had braved the heavy rain and purchased tickets. Their dedication to theatre was evident in their presence. Turning towards me, Dubey ordered me to perform with the utmost energy and zeal. That moment held a crucial lesson for me, one that I didn't recognise at the time.

In a short span, Dubey's Theatre Unit ventured into producing Marathi plays alongside its Hindi productions. Walchand Terrace witnessed the staging of a variety of important plays like *Still Frame, Aadhe Adhure, Pagla Ghoda, Gidhade, Vallabhpurchi Dantkatha, Hayavadan* (Horse Face)*, Anushthan, Achcha Ek Baar Aur, Punashsha Hari Om, Sambhog se Sanyas Tak,* to name a few. That venue served as the epicentre of the parallel theatre movement, attracting talent and ideas. As dusk fell, the venue became a pilgrimage site of sorts, with theatre enthusiasts and artistes flocking to it. Walchand Terrace was sanctified by the presence of iconic personalities such as playwrights Girish Karnad and Vijay Tendulkar, great poets like Chintamani Tryambak Khanolkar, Bhawani Prasad Mishra, Dharamvir Bharati, art lovers and patrons like Kumudben and Arvind Mehta, theatre practitioners like Dr Lagoo, Arvind and Sulabha Deshpande, Dina Pathak, Tarla Mehta, Pearl Padamsee, Badal Sircar and Shyamanand Jalan, theatre conservator Pratibha Agrawal, eminent singers like Jitendra Abhisheki, great painters like Vasudeo Gaitonde, Tyeb Mehta, Akbar Padamsee, and established directors like Rajindarnath and Sai Paranjpye, to name a few. The walls and pillars of the Terrace were electrified by creative energy and artistic pursuits such as music and poetry recitations, heated discussions, critical appreciation of art, script and play readings, etc. The Terrace became the hub for contemporary cultural narratives. Being a part of that dynamic environment was a privilege, and I felt grateful for these vibrant experiences.

Many years later, after Sandhya and I had bought a house in Bandra's Sahitya Sahavas, Dubey became our neighbour and started visiting us frequently. By then, he had mellowed down significantly. He would come over with a sense of entitlement and affection, as if there had never been any conflicts between us in the past. He would often ask Sandhya, 'Why didn't I meet you earlier?' He once suggested translating a one-act play she had written into English and offered to direct it. However, his health gradually declined. When I held his hand in the hospital for the last time, I expressed my heartfelt gratitude to him, 'I will never be able to repay your debt, Dubey.' His legacy will live on in me until my last breath.

On 21 January 2012, I was invited as the chief guest to the All India Marathi Theatre Festival. This happened a month after Dubey's passing, which I found rather cruel. I attended though, representing experimental theatre artistes who were systematically ignored by the mainstream theatre community. And I used this opportunity to pay tribute to Dubey, who was never acknowledged by the mainstream theatre community.

'Even before the famous court case against the Censor Board for *Sakharam Binder*, Satyadev Dubey, as a producer, had fearlessly and successfully fought for *Gidhade*. The debt that Indian theatre owes to Satyadev Dubey can never be repaid. Dubey never surrendered before the hypocrisy of fighting censorship on one hand, while accepting another form of backdoor censorship at the hands of political parties, the ruling goverment, the underworld or theatre practitioners themselves. It must be noted that Dubey, whose mother tongue wasn't Marathi, loved Marathi plays immensely and enriched Marathi and Hindi theatre with his work for nearly five decades. It is deeply unfortunate that my mentor, a torchbearer of experimental theatre, was never honoured on any platform.

Thanks to Dubey's efforts, eminent playwrights like Badal Sircar, Mohan Rakesh and Girish Karnad, who were writing in other Indian languages, found synergies with Marathi theatre. Dubey also introduced Marathi playwrights—from Vijay Tendulkar and C.T. Khanolkar to Chetan Datar—to the theatre world outside Maharashtra. From seasoned artistes like Amrish Puri and Alaknanda Samarth to today's generation of actors, like Kishore Kadam and Amruta Subhash, Dubey nurtured and polished many talents. It might be hard to believe, but it was Dubey who fought for national recognition of the contributions of successful commercial playwrights like V.V. Shirwadkar and Vasant Kanetkar. Dubey took his final exit on 25 December 2011. Until his last breath, Dubey lived and breathed theatre. If not during his lifetime, then let us—in the presence of all theatre artistes and enthusiasts here today—at least pay homage to Dubey posthumously. This would justify my presence here today. Let us stand and observe two moments of silence in his memory.'

The third life-altering accident happened to me around 1978-79. After the consecutive silver jubilee hits of *Rajnigandha*, *Chhoti Si Baat* and *Chitchor*, I became established as a successful star in Hindi cinema. The subsequent box office successes of *Damaad* and *Gharaonda* brought a steady stream of new film offers. Despite this, I continued to dabble in experimental theatre. I maintained a strict rule of not stepping onto the stage or facing the camera without meticulous rehearsals, without honing my skills to perfection. The great actor Sombhu Mitra instilled in me the awareness of keeping my performance fresh even after multiple shows and despite knowing by heart an audience's response to various scenes. I applied this skill not only to theatre, but also to my roles in films. Over time, I developed the ability to maintain the integrity of my performance despite multiple retakes in a film, a discipline I acquired through Sombhu-da's training.

My flourishing career in films coincided with a period of technological advancements and transformation in the film industry. The heavy Mitchell camera used to shoot *Shantata! Court Chalu Aahe* (Quiet! The Court is on) and *Bajiravcha Beta* had become obsolete, and was replaced by the more portable Arriflex, with a zoom lens, enabling easy close-ups without moving the camera closer to the subject. Filming on actual locations instead of confined studios became routine. The director of *Bicycle Thieves*, Vittorio De Sica, once asked Raj Kapoor why, with such beautiful sunlight in India, he resorted to Hollywood's practice of using intense artificial lighting on sets inside dark studios. This question, asked during the first international film festival held in Bombay in February 1952, spurred significant changes in Indian cinema, prompting luminaries like Satyajit Ray, Raj Kapoor and Bimal Roy to film on actual locations.

Another major change that occurred during this period was in sound recording. The Arriflex camera was a noisy machine, and it was impossible to shoot with a synchronised sound while using it. This led to all films being dubbed. This meant that every actor's dialogue had to be re-recorded after the film had been shot, either by themselves or through dubbing artistes. Exposure to numerous excellent global films at the Film Forum expanded my understanding of the stylistic, thematic and technical advancements in cinema. Influenced by directors like Ingmar Bergman, Akira Kurosawa, Jean-Luc Godard, François Truffaut and Sergei Eisenstein, I became increasingly eager to create films finding my own expression.

In 1978, a group of four Kannada producers approached me with a proposal to direct and star in a bilingual film based on a Kannada short story *Agantuk*. Its storyline was quite different from the kind of stories being made into movies at the time: a Western photographer visits India to capture wildlife. He takes a mute village youth as his guide. Attracted by the promise of decent pay, the village boy readily accompanies the photographer. However, while wandering in the forest, a tiger attacks the boy, and instead of saving him, the photographer keeps clicking photos. Finding the plot intriguing, I agreed to make the film. With Tom Alter as the photographer, myself as the mute youth, and Chitra as a village girl, we began shooting in the Bandipur forest. After two sessions of seven or eight days each, the producers withdrew from the project, as distributors and financiers had rejected it, fearing it was not commensurate with my popular image of a romantic hero. The film was shelved.

Just before my directorial journey ended prematurely, around 1979, a well-established Mumbai producer had offered me his new film, *Footpath*, to direct and star in. I loved the script, which had been created by the renowned writer Rahi Masoom Raza. It told the story of a young man making a living by selling tea on the footpath, a girl selling flower garlands and a neighbourhood goon. The script, which avoided villains and melodramatic scenes, bordered on the genre of parallel cinema. I recall a beautiful scene in which the goon takes the tea seller and the flower girl to a fancy hotel to celebrate a big earning. The girl feels like she has entered a massive palace with shiny floors, a moment wonderfully captured by the lyricist Naqsh Lyallpuri in a song. I was cast alongside Rameshwari and Amjad Khan. As the film's form gradually came to life during the meetings at Rahi saab's home, the producer began to insist on changes. He wanted a different lead actress after Rameshwari suffered an eye injury. I suggested deferring the shooting of her scenes. Then he suggested we replace our music director, Jaidev, who was deemed ill-omened at the time. Firmly refusing to go along with this, I withdrew from the film, saying, 'Choose another director you prefer.' Amjad Khan also backed out, as he had joined the project only to support my sincere directorial effort to make cinema that veered off the beaten track.

The industry had set certain unwritten rules, placing utmost importance on commercial returns. It was understood that filmmaking should therefore adhere to this set framework of success without any deviations. In this environment, the emotional support I received from someone like the *Sholay* star Amjad gave me immense strength. A few years later, around 1981, we worked together in the film *Plot No. 5*. During that time, I expressed my gratitude to him. In the course of our conversations, I also congratulated him on his outstanding performance in *Shatranj Ke Khilari*, particularly praising his sensitive portrayal of a gentle character, one that went completely against his rugged and masculine image. With slightly misty eyes and a voice full of emotion, he said, 'Yaar, the industry gave me nothing but criticism for *Shatranj*. Today, for the first time, I've heard a few kind words, and that too from a fellow artiste like you, who values experimentation!' Saying so, this hefty man gave me a tight hug. With a smile, he added, 'I don't usually drink, but let's indulge a little tonight to celebrate this moment.'

After these episodes, I realised that if I wanted to make unconventional films, I needed to become my own producer. I started working on a film based on Arvind Gokhale's story 'Navri'. Gokhale turned down the offer of writing the script due to prior commitments; however, he praised my career choices and suggested the names of a few potential screenplay writers. His approach was entirely professional, and I appreciated it. Following his advice, I approached Vijay Tendulkar, who agreed to write the script after understanding my perspective as a director. After visiting Phaltan to observe wealthy families from the Mali community, Tendulkar started writing at my bungalow, Chirebandi. He often used to read out the scenes and discuss them with me. Despite our on-going discussions, I found the final script inadequate and dry, which eventually put a courteous end to our collaboration.

A few days later, Tendulkar unexpectedly brought me a thick file, a prize-winning NFDC script, offering it as a substitute. I insisted on paying a separate fee for this new script. Initially he hesitated,

Handwritten screenplay by Vijay Tendulkar, based on Arvind Gokhale's story titled 'Navri'.

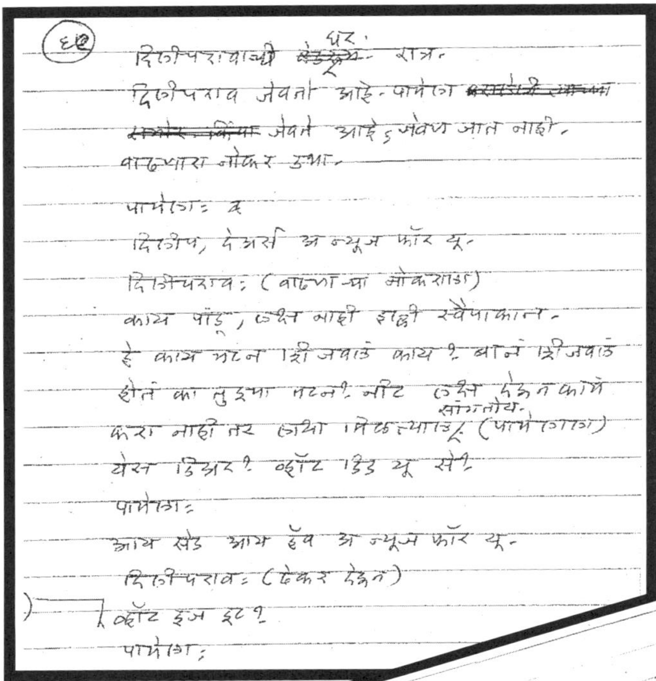

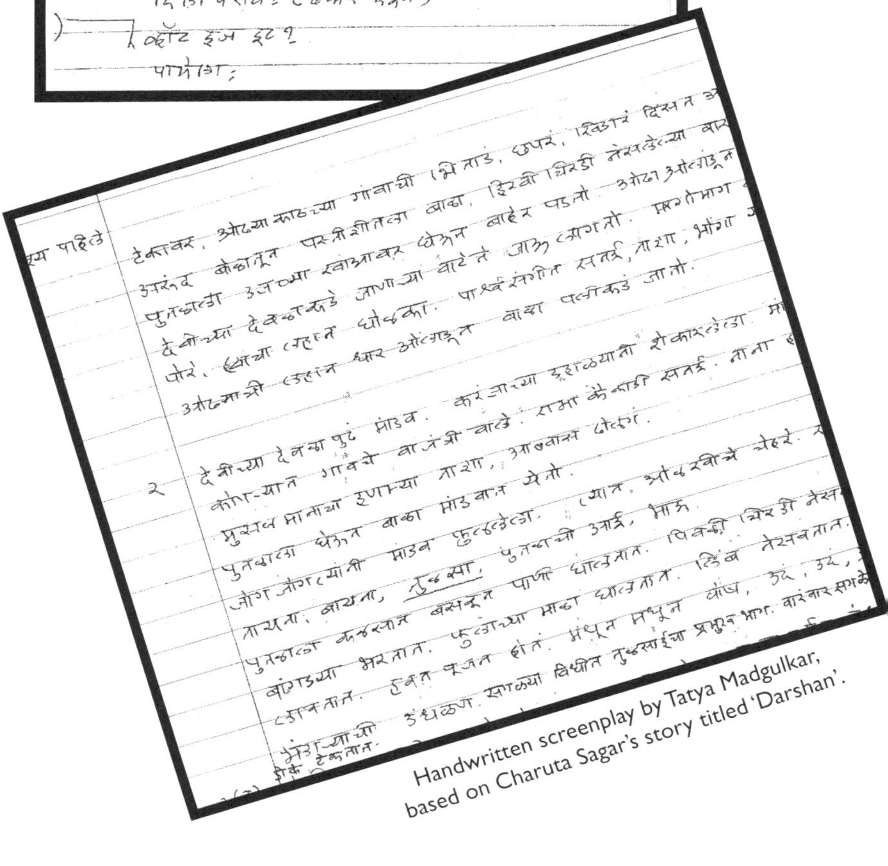

Handwritten screenplay by Tatya Madgulkar, based on Charuta Sagar's story titled 'Darshan'.

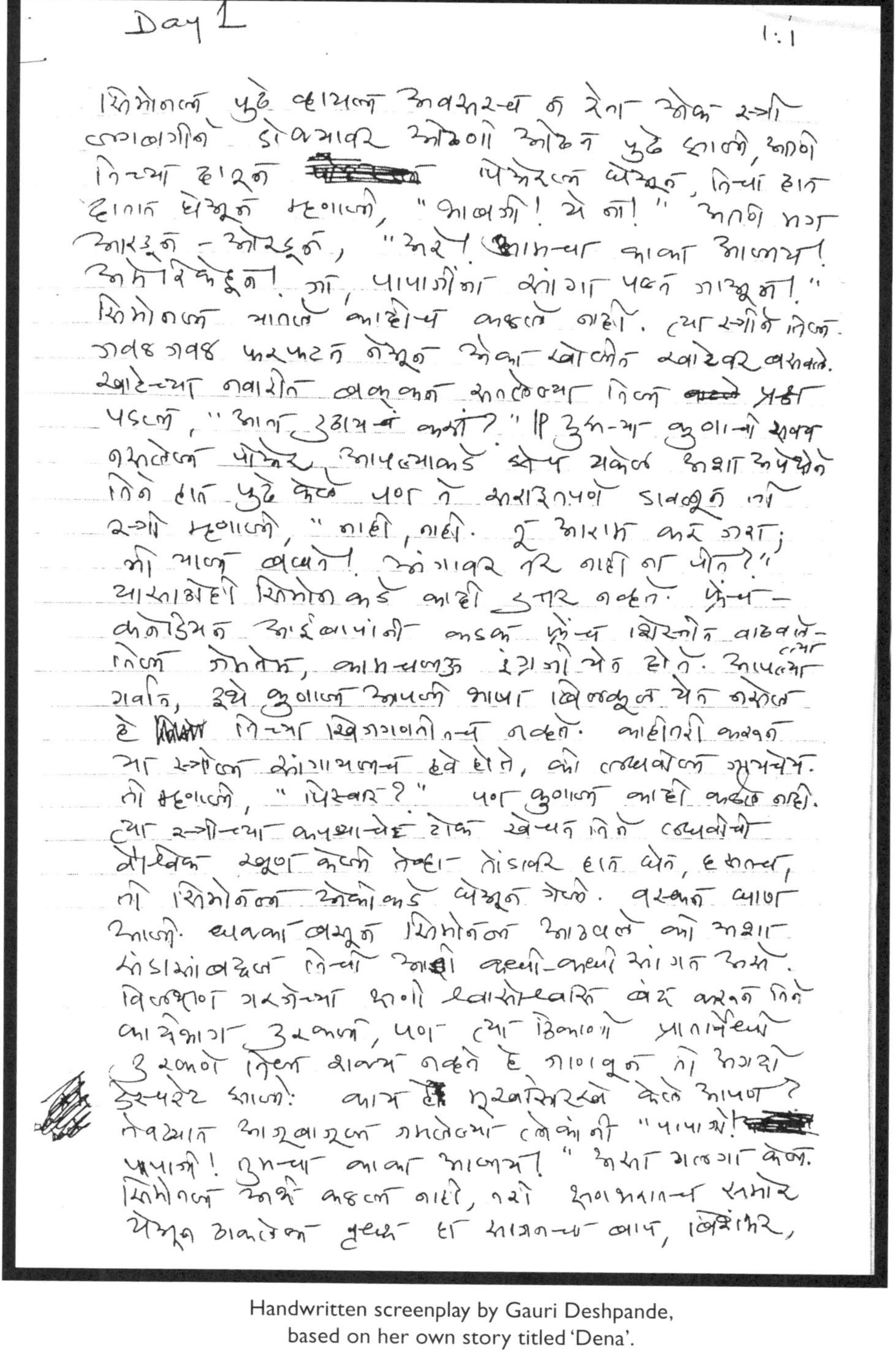

Handwritten screenplay by Gauri Deshpande,
based on her own story titled 'Dena'.

but later he agreed to accept. This led to me directing my first film. Originally titled *Bali* (Victim), I renamed it *Akriet*, and it became the first Marathi film after the film *Sant Tukaram* to win international awards. It marked a turning point in my career, leading me to direct about fifteen films over the next several years.

Akriet was based on the Manwath village murder case. A shocking case for all of India, it involved the abduction and mutilation of women and girls for occult rituals in the Parbhani district of Maharashtra between November 1972 and January 1974. The girls would go missing and their mutilated genitalia would be discovered later. A total of twelve females lost their lives at the hands of perpetrators who offered human sacrifice to be able to produce an heir as well as unearth a hidden treasure. It was clear that black magic, human sacrifice, witchcraft and sorcery had been used in these murders. The village head, Uttamrao Barhate, and some nomadic people of the Pardhi tribe were arrested by the police and the trial began to punish them with hanging and life imprisonment. In 1976, the Bombay High Court acquitted Barhate and his Pardhi concubine Rukhmini due to lack of evidence. However, four Pardhi people were sentenced to death.

After the first reading itself, I decided not to portray the cruelty of the entire incident in a sensational or cheap manner. What fascinated me about the case was that a man who enjoyed being with many women could be in love with a woman from a lower caste and could go to any lengths for her. At that time—and, in fact, even today—making films with love triangles or love stories as the central theme was a surefire formula for commercial viability. But I decided to focus on the human relationship from a different angle. As a director, I felt the need to go beyond the point at which Tendulkar's script ended, and show the harsh social reality of caste hierarchy. Uttamrao's character, who arrogantly says, 'If I didn't have money, I too would have been hanged. I had to spend four and a half lakh rupees to prove my innocence', represented people who were able to be above the law because they wielded power. The need to comment on social inequality through the final frames of the film grew more intense during the filming. And after watching the film, Tendulkar did not object to it.

I liked the core and the elaboration of that script for two different reasons. Playing the lead role of Mukutrao (the village head) was a fantastic challenge for me as an actor. I had the opportunity to create a formidable villain. Before that, I had played a character with shades of grey in *Bhumika*. But with Mukutrao, I got the chance to portray an unapologetically wicked man. I changed my look, getting a military haircut and joint eyebrows. Moreover, since there were many shirtless scenes, gaining ten to twelve kilos of weight was necessary, and I did it.

The second reason I liked the script of *Akriet* was that Chitra played the role of Mukutrao's mistress, Ruhi. She was an incredibly talented and seasoned actor. Despite this, she wasn't considered for roles in either Marathi or Hindi cinema. Much of the blame for this was put on me. Since I was a star of Hindi cinema, she felt that the parallel theatre and film industry treated her unjustly. This issue had started creating a lot of tension in our relationship. Since *Akriet* was my own production, giving her an important role temporarily quelled the tension. I also registered the film production company 'Dnya' in her name. This company later produced television series like *Kachchi Dhup* and *Naqab*. Her ownership rights in all the content created under that banner were kept intact.

I decided to produce *Akriet* without taking a loan, reinvesting in it what I had earned as an actor in films and saved. Due to our limited budget, it was necessary to complete the shooting in the shortest possible time. And with meticulous planning, we completed the entire shoot in approximately twenty-eight days.

After visiting multiple locations, we decided on a small village by a river called Jambulpada. This village was later washed away in a flood on 24 July 1989. With a young and inexperienced team including Debu Deodhar, Baba Majgaokar, Shashank Shankar, Vijay Shirke and Haider Ali, I started my career as a director. Bhaskar Chandavarkar composed the film's music. However, despite initially agreeing to do the background score, he backed out at the last moment. An accomplished music director, Ashok Patki filled in for him.

On the very first day of shooting, a major problem arose. The house where we were to shoot for the next week was being readied for the scene. Just a few hours prior, the owner of the house had passed away in Bombay. Yet his wife, neighbours and all of us in the village were completely unaware of it. An Ambassador car arrived on the location bearing the sombre news of the houseowner's demise. 'Do not inform his wife about this just yet,' one of the houseowner's relatives requested us. In telling the wife about the death, there were two concerns on our minds: firstly, that she might lock up the house and depart for Bombay, and secondly, that the villagers might perceive our arrival as a bad omen and ask us to leave the village and cancel our shoot. However, contrary to our apprehensions, the lady of the house said, 'Continue your shoot,' and, handing over the house keys to me with complete faith, she got into the Ambassador and left. Still, this unexpected situation caused a significant delay on the very first day of shooting.

Later, a similar problem arose which had to be handled deftly. The scenes of a police station were to be shot inside a temple premises, though outside the sanctum. Before we began, the local villagers insisted that the actors remove their footwear outside the premises. Immediately, a gram panchayat meeting was called and we pleaded for the actors to be allowed to keep their shoes on. It would look unreal and strange if we were to show on screen people entering a police station without shoes. Besides, we were not even entering the temple's sanctum. After a long deliberation, the villagers finally accepted our request. To reciprocate their gracious gesture, we decided to change one detail in our scene. Instead of using a chicken leg, Haider Ali, who played the character of the sub-inspector, crudely chewed on a drumstick.

Mangesh Desai, a veteran in the industry, agreed to do sound mixing and re-recording after watching the trial run of *Akriet*. Not only that, he postponed a big film like *Silsila* from a major banner for me. Despite being known for his hot temper, Mangesh Desai did not let his disposition get in the way of our working relationship. He explained many technical aspects of filmmaking to me with great affection. Thanks to him, we were able to explore myriad new dimensions of sound.

The Special Jury Award at the Three Continents Festival in Nantes, France, recognised the film's technical aspects as being of high international standards. I remember feeling very accomplished at the time. Despite the film's meagre budget, every technician and artiste involved in *Akriet* had delivered their finest work.

In those days, there was no independent distribution system for Marathi films like there was for Hindi films. All major producer–directors used to distribute their Marathi films themselves. But I sought the help of renowned producer–director Vishwas Sarpotdar as a special distributor for *Akriet*. I wanted to release the film at the Plaza Cinema in Dadar, where it would have appealed to and garnered the patronage of the educated middle-class audience who were my loyal fans. However, Plaza wasn't available. So the idea of releasing the film in Dadar's Kohinoor Cinema came up. But we were uncertain whether the story would appeal to the labour class and mill workers who were Kohinoor's regular patrons. Finally, we were constrained to agree to Kohinoor Cinema. As expected, the film ended up being commercially unsuccessful due to lack of pre-publicity. However, the film per se and my performance were widely appreciated. A renowned film critic like Khalid Mohamed lavished praise on *Akriet* in the *Times of India*. My directorial debut received nationwide coverage in almost all the English newspapers. This overwhelming response and critical acclaim offset my financial loss.

Just as unexpectedly as these three accidents altered my life for the better, Sandhya Gokhale came into my life and filled it with sunshine. Actually, she entered my life not once, but twice. The first time she arrived, she flashed like a comet and vanished without leaving a trace. The second time she came, all the tracks trodden until then changed. The speed at which the last twenty-five years have passed, the number of things we have done together—be it jointly producing eight films, organising my art exhibitions or theatre festivals, raising our younger daughter Samiha, attending various international exhibitions, concerts and festivals, hosting countless feasts of exquisite cuisine, reading literature, listening to various types of music, watching innumerable films and plays together, taking long walks, the worldwide travels with long car drives and plane journeys, the endless discussions and debates on various issues, our two cats, my non-trivial illnesses, our cars and houses, our owl collection and numerous small things acquired over the years with an abundance of joy … we have lived and experienced a lifetime of love, happiness and peace, and all of it continues to enrich our shared existence.

If I had to capture it in today's visual language, it would be a shot captured by a drone of a vast, sprawling blue ocean … and of a human figure slowly appearing—floating on the surface of water, on his back, with arms and legs spread out. As the drone moves towards the water, that figure slowly starts becoming recognisable as me. The sea is as calm as I am. As the drone moves a little to the side, Sandhya's hands supporting my back become visible. Despite her efforts to stay unseen and hidden, the drone's camera doesn't miss her hands. However, the drone cannot capture her tireless efforts to shield me from the ocean's turmoil. This shot encapsulates the essence of our relationship.

Around the year 1990, one afternoon, a lively young woman came to see me on the recommendation of Ramdas Bhatkal, a veteran publisher, who was producing a television serial in Marathi titled *Paulkhuna* (Footprints).

> She: I've heard that you are directing a series on female characters in Marathi literature. Could I be considered for the role of the protagonist in Gauri Deshpande's story? I identify with the female protagonist's traits and qualities, which makes me confident that I can bring a nuanced portrayal to the role. But to be honest, I have no prior acting experience.
>
> I: That particular series is in the planning stages, it will take a few months.
>
> She: All right then, I'll leave. I'm going to be in India only for six months. If the series is ready to be filmed within that time, maybe you could consider me.
>
> I: Six months? So, you don't live in India?
>
> She: No, I practice law in the States. I'm here for six months for a professional assignment.
>
> I: I'm about to start shooting a Hindi series for Doordarshan. It's based on Vrindavan Lal Verma's Hindi novel *Mrignayani*. It is about a tribal girl whose fighting spirit captivates King Man Singh during a hunt, leading him to fall in love and eventually, marry her. I could offer you a role in that.
>
> She (refusing outright): I'm not that proficient in Hindi. Besides, to portray that period, I would be required to dress in traditional costumes, which I'm not too comfortable in.
>
> I (trying to control my annoyance at this): All I hear from you is 'no' this and 'no' that. Why did you show up here in the first place?

She: I came with just one role in mind. I think I could play it well because it aligns with my personality.

I: You've never acted before, so why are you so confident? You'd need to take lessons in acting and Hindi.

She: True, but I don't have that much time.

I (expressing as much displeasure and irritation as possible): All right. Before leaving, leave your photos at the producer's office.

She: Sorry, I don't have any photos to share. And since I'm not looking to pursue any other roles or opportunities, it's pointless to leave anything.

After this short yet fiery exchange, the woman who had come riding on her high horse left. Just as swiftly, I crossed her name off my list. But somehow, I couldn't shake her from my thoughts.

Seven or eight years of complete silence, and then, out of the blue, I received a call from her.

'I am Sandhya Gokhale. I've heard you're making a film based on G.A. Kulkarni's story 'Kairee' (Raw Mango). I love that story. I've also tried writing something based on it. May I send it to you?'

Even today, I marvel at how I immediately recognised her voice. In reality, the first time she had come to see me, she was Sandhya Dabholkar (Dabholkar being her surname before her divorce). So there was no question of recognising her by name. Besides, there had been no contact in the intervening years.

I said, 'The script of *Kairee* is ready. Have you come back to India for work again?'

She said, 'I have been practising law in Mumbai.'

Following our reconnection, I noticed her name popping up in newspapers about her involvement in two or three legal matters dealing with social issues. Occasionally, I noticed her at music concerts at the Dadar Matunga Cultural Centre, or at the Yashwantrao Chavan Centre Auditorium where she would come to watch movies. A few times, we exchanged some pleasantries.

At the time, I was considering challenging some provisions in the law relating to censorship. To get her opinion on that, I went to her office. We started working on the petition. Despite spending ten years in America, her familiarity with Marathi literature, classical music and the intellectual–cultural activities overall in India was astonishing. Her confident grasp of issues, unwavering opinions, passion for social causes, infectious enthusiasm and unassuming nature … all of it was irresistibly magnetic. Progressive values coupled with strong patriotism, a strict demeanour but a tender heart, reticent yet always willing to go the extra mile to assist others—the paradoxical blend in her personality fascinated me. I was quickly drawn to her warmth, her independent spirit and keen intellect.

One more incident contributed to my growing fascination with her. The Ministry of Women and Child Development approved a grant for my then proposed film *Kairee*. I was given a lengthy contract to sign. Wanting Sandhya's opinion as a lawyer, I handed it to her. After reading it, she said, 'If you are asking for my advice, I would say, don't sign it. It's unjust on their part to impose such one-sided terms on you.'

I said, 'In my experience, artistes are often the ones in need, and those in need are rarely allowed to challenge government authority or contracts.'

To this, she said, 'One has to take the leap at least once.'

I accepted her advice. After much back and forth, the ministry accepted eight of her twelve objections. Others who had already signed their contracts approached the government for redrafting their terms as well. I was struck by Sandhya's advocacy for parity among the parties, a perspective I hadn't considered before. With equal promptness and effectiveness, she secured a grant from the MacArthur Foundation in America for *Dhyaasparva*, enabling me to complete the half-finished film.

While I was emotionally getting involved with her, Sandhya remained engrossed in her professional work, always going to court in her black robes. Her daughter, Samiha, was her breath of life outside work. Sandhya's respect for me as an artiste and as a person was evident, but it took me many months to figure out how to go beyond that.

I decided to directly enter her world and meet her parents. 'Our daughter is simple and won't fit into your film world. She stays away from parties and crowds' was their main concern. Sandhya though set three conditions for me to consider. I immediately accepted two of those conditions. She didn't want me to bring any part of my wealth, bungalow or material assets from my past life into our new life together. Having created her own career from scratch, she refused to accept handouts or favours from a new partner. I relinquished everything I had, freeing myself from the burdens of my past. According to her second condition, raising her daughter would always be her top priority; accepting that was easy. Her third condition, demanding absolute transparency and trust in the relationship, was the most difficult one for me to grapple with. She laid out her entire past before me, but my past wasn't as linear. My life was more complex than hers, with a multitude of people, relationships and incidents. I was apprehensive that if she came to know everything about my past, she might reject me. It's not easy to strip yourself bare! But I realised the immense value of my 'confession' at that time. Once I crossed that threshold, I felt as light as a feather. Sandhya accepted me with all my flaws. Not only me, but she also embraced my sisters, Shalmalee, her companion Christine and son Kaarin with all her heart. Sandhya brought me closer to my two sisters, bridging the distance between us.

What I admire most is her remarkable maturity in navigating the challenging time following my separation from Chitra. Society tends to accept even toxic or dysfunctional relationships, but frowns upon couples who choose to part ways. Forced to decide where their loyalties lay, many of Chitra and my mutual friends had to choose either her or me. Many of them drifted away from me. Sandhya and I settled down in Pune and the chances of meeting these friends decreased. Over time, many tried to mend fences, admitting their lapse of judgement, but by then, I had distanced myself from them. Throughout all this, Sandhya stood firmly by my side. She also took on the responsibility of film production even though it wasn't her true calling. I had no idea her shoulders were so capable. Without her exceptional abilities, we wouldn't have achieved what we did in life. Without her, my ultramarine blue expanse would have never achieved its ideal saturation.

She was the driving force behind my writing this memoir. Her encouragement ignited the spark and I penned four hundred pages in my own handwriting. When she inquired about my emotions on completing the manuscript, I recalled a tale about a Zen master and his young disciple. They had to cross a stream, and the water level was rising. A beautiful young woman, stranded in the middle, asked them for help. The disciple was puzzled: how could they help her without falling prey to temptation? Just then, his master picked her up, swiftly crossed the stream, set her down on the bank, and walked on. The disciple was stunned. After days of confusion, the disciple asked the master, 'You broke the principle of avoiding the touch of women. How could you just lift that drenched woman?' The Zen master smiled and calmly said, 'I left her behind the moment we crossed the steam. You are still carrying her.'

That's how I felt. I underwent a complete catharsis. Everything has been drained out. I need no baggage now … no colours either. The 2024 elections are round the corner—by the time this book is published, the sky will be overcast again. The sooner I exit from this deepfake world, the better. That exit too should be an accident—unexpected, yet permanent.

Even though I am entangled in the labyrinth of these four accidents, I am still free. I am tranquil, nestled in the warmth of a womb's embrace. When I attempt to make sense of these accidents, I remember Arun Kolatkar's poem *Takta* (*The Alphabet* as translated from Marathi by Prof. Vinay Dharwadker), a favourite of mine, which masterfully obscures clarity in a rich brocade of absurdity.

THE ALPHABET

anvil arrow bow box and brahmin
cart chariot cloud and compost heap
are all sitting in their separate squares

corn cup deer duck and frock
ganesh garlic hexagon and house
all have places of their own

inkpot jackfruit kite lemon and lotus
mango medicine mother old man and ostrich
are all holding their proper positions

pajamas pineapple rabbit and ram
sacrifice seal spoon and sugarcane
won't interfere with each other

sword tap tombstone and umbrella
warrior watermelon weight and yacht
have all found the eternal resting place

The mother won't put her baby on the compost heap
The brahmin won't season the duck with garlic
The yacht won't hit the watermelon and sink

Unless the ostrich eats the baby's frock
The warrior won't shoot an arrow into ganesh's belly
And if the ram doesn't knock down the old man
Why would he need to smash the cup on the tombstone?

Echoes from Within ...

The question 'Who am I?' has been a riddle for the ages, mused upon by psychologists, literary titans and philosophers alike—Aristotle, Freud, Descartes and the modern proponents of the '4E perspective'. It is a query not confined to intellectual giants; it is pondered by every introspective soul, including me. As we transition from self-awareness to the 4Es (embodied, embedded, enacted and extended cognition), the external environment permeates our subconscious, merging and surfacing to form the intricate identity we call 'me'. The eighty years of my life have allowed me to watch the subtle ballet between conscious insights and subconscious influences, deeply intertwined with my relationships, surroundings and the physical world. Through the lens of Marxist/Leninist objective reality or Sartre's existentialist human contingency, I have come to understand myself and the world. All have etched their marks on me, shaping the contours of my being.

Thus, I've been on a quest to discover myself. Sometimes I lie awake at night staring into the darkness. In those sleepless moments, I look at myself—there I am, lying on the bed, eyes fixed on the ceiling; it's as if I'm inverted and floating parallel, gazing down at my own body. I cherish this moment. It evokes the surreal self-portrait of M.C. Escher, my favourite graphic artiste. I vividly recall the tears that blurred my vision as I gazed at that 1935 print in the Museum Escher in The Palace in The Hague. The distorted reflection of himself in an elliptical ball held in his hand, with the backdrop of books from his Roman home, his suit and hat denoting affluence but in a surreal form—was that a direct or a subtle revelation of his inner self, or a metaphorical representation of his identity? In that suspended state, 'I', an outside observer staring down at 'me', possessed a deeper understanding of myself than the real 'me' ever did. The outsider probably possesses the objectivity to fully comprehend the nuances and complexities of my personality.

I feel envious of him as 'he' must be observing the transformations of my inner self, as I evolve alongside the changing landscape of my surroundings. Envious, because I couldn't grasp those changes in real time; only in hindsight, years later, did I notice them.

In a way, it's liberating not to be vigilant 24/7. I believe that having to be constantly alert can be exhausting, and can internalise restlessness and fear. This same restlessness stirs at night. A lingering sense of restlessness has been a permanent fixture of my consciousness for the past decade, showing no signs of release. I feel fossilised. Everything around me has transformed so drastically—roads, bridges, flyovers, buildings, tunnels and known-unknown-close-distant people; all have changed. Fellows indoctrinated in toxic ideologies, their minds infected with poisonous thinking, they are busy spreading their venom like a virus that causes an epidemic. But I have encased myself in a protective shell. My icy exterior remains unbreakable. Though the external attacks cannot shake me, my inner suffocation is so intense that I feel I might shatter the ice with the carbon dioxide I exhale. How did everything change so drastically? How did I overlook the saffron tendrils unfurling on the ocean? The once-vibrant landscape has turned monochromatic. If the five elements are also going to turn orange, I'd rather disintegrate into pieces. Let those fragments of my being turn black, a colour that embodies the spirit of resistance. Whether history remembers me or not, I will be grateful to that outsider 'I' for observing my defiance and resistance till the last breath.

Today, all this is stirring in my mind because the Supreme Court has decided to send the eleven convicts in the Bilkis Bano case—the merciless, inhuman rapists who were released despite being proven guilty—back to jail within two weeks. Technically, I ought to view it as 'justice' being served in her case. The state was condemned for conspiring with the convicts, and the verdict in her favour was accompanied by scathing criticism of the ruling authorities. Bilkis was twenty-one years old and five months pregnant when she was gang-raped and seven of her family members, including her three-month-old daughter, were slaughtered. Given the relentless suffering she has been subjected to from 2002 to the present, I believe the scars inflicted upon her by the system will never heal. The absence of true justice renders us helpless and powerless. The sting of incompetence continues to throb. Bilkis's persecution is not an isolated incident; countless individuals exploited by those driven by power, greed and prejudice are denied justice, whether it is the victims of the atrocities in Una district of Gir Somnath, or the victims of the Khairlanji murders, or the Dalits targeted in Shabbirpur, Saharanpur, Bhagalpur, or those who were massacred or brutalised in the Manipur riots. Projected justice is often an illusion. In the virtual space, social media or other platforms on the internet, one has to decipher the truth for oneself, something in which we always fall short. Therefore, I refuse to accept the illusions presented to me and instead choose to live mindfully in the present, with my conscience guiding me.

I have always preferred to stay away from this virtual world. Somehow I have mastered the art of being informed without being invested in the world that drives these advancements. Of course, throughout my life I've had to pay the price of maintaining my distance from that world, a price I have willingly paid. In spite of that, I had the privilege of having many people converge with my life—some entering like a fleeting glimpse for a short while, leaving a lasting impression on my mind.

I travelled miles to specifically watch Vithabai Bhau Mang Narayangaonkar's tamasha. While dancing, she suddenly stopped and scolded a group of hecklers by asking, 'Don't you have mothers and sisters at home?' She berated them so harshly that the hooligans had to leave with their faces covered. Once they bolted, as if nothing had happened, she proudly performed a Lavani to the tune of '*Mere Naina Sawan Bhaado*' and the beats of a dholak. She possessed a remarkable talent for captivating her audience while maintaining a sense of decorum. I admired her initiative to breathe new life into the traditional folk art of tamasha by reinterpreting it in a modern context, rather than confining it to static gallery displays. When I met her after the programme and saw her humility, I wondered if this was the same fierce Vithabai that I had seen a little while ago. She excitedly expressed her admiration for me and asked for a photograph of me to be taken with her daughter, a request I couldn't resist fulfilling despite my usual reluctance.

Similarly, during the Apna Utsav, I met Gulabo. The ease with which she performed the Kalbelia, a Rajasthani folk dance form, capturing the audience's heart with her graceful footwork, is still fresh in my memory. Though the photograph might have been lost, the feeling of her loving arms around me stayed with me. There were many more people like Vithabai and Gulabo whom I never met again after those brief encounters. Yet, like whispers in the wind, our fleeting interactions have left an eternal echo in my heart. Though many of the kindred spirits with whom I shared a deep and abiding connection have passed into eternity … the bonds though remain unbroken in my heart.

My love for Marathi literature was innate. In our household, books were a staple gift for birthdays, festivals and celebrations, fostering a love for reading and learning. When I was in the school at Bordi, Dugal sir taught us Marathi. He would often commend me on my essay-writing skills, boosting my confidence. Once, he asked me to read *Ritu Chakra* by Durga Bhagwat, an erudite writer. I went to the library and immediately read it. That day, I experienced a new level of awareness that changed my perspective. Besides the prescribed textbooks, I developed a liking for extracurricular reading. What began as a habit of casual reading has developed into a profound love affair with literature. Even today, I consistently read different genres, new writer-poets, and even pieces of literary criticism. I categorise the books I read into distinct groups, such as 'worth reading', 'forgettable', 'timeless classic', 'mediocre', etc. As my reputation grew, authors began presenting me with signed copies of their latest works, which I have lovingly preserved, keeping them dust-free and cherished. I even shared a deep and lasting bond with some writers, especially G.A. Kulkarni and C.T. Khanolkar aka 'Aarti Prabhu'! Their creative brilliance, nuanced style and expansive imagination unlocked new realms of consciousness for me.

Poetry is the genre that moves me the most. My elder sister Neelon-tai had bought Mangesh Padgaonkar's collection of poems *Gypsy* especially to read out to her siblings. As I grew older, my focus shifted from unravelling literal meanings and chasing interpretations to the interplay of rhythms, tones, imagery, etc. To introduce Shalmalee to the world of Marathi literature, despite her English medium background, I would recite literary pieces by Vinda Karandikar, G.A. Kulkarni and Khanolkar to her. Like a masterful engraver, Aarti Prabhu's poems instantly etched a firm place in my heart. But my preconceived notion of Khanolkar, shaped by his poetic voice, was starkly contrasted by the reality of his persona.

In 1963, during my third year at J.J., Professor Sambhaji Kadam and I often discussed classical music and literature, beyond visual arts. As we engaged in such art-related conversations, the reserved facade often presented by Kadam sir would crumble, revealing his sensitive, kinder side. Once he proposed that we perform a Marathi one-act play at that year's annual gathering. He chose *Jevha Arsa Bolto* (When the Mirror Spoke), a play by a budding writer named Khanolkar. He also declared that I would play the lead role. His decision to choose me, a novice with no acting experience, remains an inexplicable mystery to this day.

One evening, Kadam sir introduced me to a person on the college premises. 'Meet Shri Khanolkar,' he said, pointing to a man wearing thick round glasses, a light blue kurta and pajama, standing around shyly. I greeted him formally. 'And he is "Aarti Prabhu" as well.' This revelation left me momentarily speechless. Could tender lines

Cover done by Amol Palekar

Cover done by Sambhaji Kadam

Cover done by Dinanath Dalal

such as *'Phule mazi alumaalu, vaara baghe churagalu'* (The delicate blooms I adorn are often tousled by the wind) emerge from someone so unassuming? I wondered if the same hands had written the two collections of poetry, *Jogwa* and *Divelaagaan*. Although I felt embarrassed about my doubts, my reservations about him persisted even after several interactions. I expected his behaviour to match his creative genius, but he often acted differently. He never hid his need for money, which bothered me. As I've mentioned earlier in the first chapter, he made certain compromises related to his compensation for *Avadhya*. He initially sold the film rights to his novel *Chaani* to Govind Nihalani (who had begun making plans for a movie adaptation starring Bhakti Barve), but later transferred them to V. Shantaram. I never detected a flicker of shame or guilt in his eyes while he reflected on these experiences. When I decided to make the film *Ankahee*, I entrusted the commercial negotiation with Khanolkar to my co-producer, Jayant Dharmadhikari. I managed to avoid another embarrassing situation and financial entanglement with him.

Despite these uncomfortable traits, I continued to love Khanolkar's poetry deeply and enjoyed his extensive body of work, including novels, one-act plays and dramas. Each of his plays contained a spark of brilliance, though for some plays, plot progression remained incomplete. An exception was his one-act play *Aapule Maran Pahile Mya Dola* (I Witnessed My Own Death), which I vaguely remember as being complete in every sense. Directed by Madhav Watve, its first (and possibly last) performance remains etched in my memory. Citizens besieging the royal palace, forcing the king to stand in place of his statue to save his life. For an hour and a half, the brilliant actor portraying the king, Datta Bhat, stood motionless without uttering a word; this portrayal set a new standard in subtle yet powerful acting. Playing the king, Bhat masterfully portrayed the changes that take place in the king's personality while he listens to the criticism from his subjects besieging his palace. Despite the various activities on stage, the audience's focus remained, unwavering, on the silent and still Datta Bhatt.

My production of Khanolkar's play *Avadhya* pleased him greatly. He wrote in the preface, 'The intention behind giving the play to Amol Palekar was that he would look at its experimental possibilities from a different perspective. I am proud to acknowledge that he has brought *Avadhya* to vivid life, demonstrating his capabilities.' Khanolkar also liked the cover illustration I created for the play, finding it more fitting for the essence of the play than those done by Dinanath Dalal for *Jogwa* and Sambhaji Kadam for *Divelaagaan*.

In 1972, there was a buzz in the theatre circles that Khanolkar would direct his play *Chawhata* (Public Square) himself. The anticipation was high, and the inaugural performance at Ravindra Natya Mandir became 'house full'. Esteemed personalities from both the parallel and the commercial theatre were present. The third bell rang, the auditorium's lights dimmed, and Khanolkar stood in the spotlight in front of the curtain. He began speaking, but his words were barely audible even to the front row. Yet, no one from the balcony shouted for him to speak louder; everyone strained to hear their beloved poet and playwright. As the curtain began to rise, Khanolkar nearly lost his balance but recovered. The play started. For the next one and a half to two hours, various characters appeared and interacted on stage. Gradually, it became apparent that the actors were fumbling with dialogues and were uncertain about their movements. Events happening in the town square were not yielding a cohesive narrative and dialogues. The second act ended, with most of the audience silently leaving during the interval. A few loyal fans like me stayed until the end. After the play was over, I went backstage to meet him. In the make-up room, the cast stood with guilty expressions on their faces. Khanolkar sat alone, huddled near a water cooler in the wings, crying softly. I stood silently for a while before leaving. On the way back, I recalled his lines *'Ek phataka kavi, tyala wahawa havi'*

(A torn poet seeking applause) from his collection *Nakshatranche Dene*. Why did a poet, so honest in his expression, make such a futile attempt? Writing a play and staging it are two different processes. Spontaneous expression isn't sufficient for all art forms; mastery over technique and craftsmanship is necessary. Didn't he realise this? Unable to muster the courage to discuss *Chawhata* with him, I sought solace in his poetry.

Amidst all these slightly sour memories, there is one deeply touching memory that I cherish. Over five decades have passed, but the joy of witnessing a sublime, creative moment remains fresh. In 1970, during the rehearsals for the Marathi version of *Pagla Ghoda*, I struggled with translating a Bengali nursery rhyme. One evening, Khanolkar visited Walchand Terrace. I opened up to him about my inability to translate Badal-da's nonsensical Bengali rhyme into Marathi. After watching the rehearsal for a while, he wrote a few lines on a piece of paper in one go, and handed it to me.

His translation perfectly captured the essence, rhythm and melody of the original Bengali song. I still visualise him reciting those lines in Marathi to me, clad in his crumpled white kurta and round glasses.

(Marathi translation)

आंब्याची ग आंब्याची, पाने पाने जोडीची
फुटला चाबूक सुटला घोडा
राणी राणी बाजू दे, पगला घोडा दौडत ये।।
पिसाळला ग पिसाळला,
झाला घोडा वेडापीर बंदूक रोखू नको उशीर
ऑल राईट व्हेरी गुड, दाल रोटी बिस्कुट-फूड।।

(Original Bengali)

आम पाता जोडा जोडा, मारबे चाबुक छुटबे घोडा।
ओरे बीबी शोरे दाडा, आशछे आमार पागला घोड़ा।।
पागला घोड़ा खेपे छे, बोंदूक धोरे मेरेछे
ऑल राईट व्हेरी गुड, दाल रोटी बिस्कुट-फूड।।

Together spread the mango leaves …
the mango leaves,
Strikes the hunter, gallops the horse
Rani, Rani, make way,
Galloping comes the mad horse.

In 1976, after the untimely death of Khanolkar, Bhaskar Chandavarkar, along with some members of the Pune Theatre Academy, planned a tribute for him. This unique attempt involved presenting Khanolkar's poems in various ways—by singing, by using recorded songs and by reciting some of them. Bhaskar had already announced that he had decided to do only five performances of that programme and to give all the earnings to the Khanolkar family. Accordingly, we performed in Mumbai and Pune. Despite not being formally invited, Chitra and I joined the effort out of our gratitude for a great writer. We travelled between Mumbai and Pune for the rehearsals.

The first performance at Pune's Balgandharva Theatre ran to a full house, with many literary figures present in the audience. The applause I received for reciting the long poem *'Bakarichi Don Pore'* (Two Baby Goats) still resonates in my ears, giving me a sense of fulfilment. I went to the wings and lit a cigarette. The praise I received from my co-actors in the wings made me even more relaxed. Suddenly, someone said, 'Hey, your next poem …' and almost pushed me onto the stage. Which poem, what words …? I was completely blank. I kept trying to remember desperately. Even after a long pause, I couldn't remember anything, so I turned back towards the wings. In the corner, Meena Chandavarkar quickly flipped through the pages of the script and stopped at the required page, then looked at me. In an instant, everything came back to me vividly. I went to the designated spot and started, '*Aatalya aatach halti band shyamal megh*' (Inside it stirs, closed dark clouds). That day, I learnt a valuable lesson: an actor must sustain the required intensity and focus, and remain in control until the very end, whether in a play or a film.

A few years later, P.L. Deshpande and Sunita-bai, his multifaceted 'better half', publicly recited Arati Prabhu's poems. I was specially invited. During the programme Sunita-bai singled out my rendition of the poem '*Bakarichi Don Pore*' for praise, saying, 'it's intimidating to recite poetry in front of such a talented artiste', which was a moment of immense pride for me. Khanolkar was one of the links between Sunita-bai and me; the other link was G.A. Kulkarni. It took fourteen long years to bring to life my film *Kairee*, from conception to completion, a journey marked by perseverance and determination. During the initial phase, P.L. and Sunita-bai read its screenplay and dialogue. Sunita-bai noticed the subtle nuances and also figured out that scenes from two of his other stories. I was delighted to share with her my fond memories of stimulating conversations with G.A.

G.A. was often perceived in the Marathi literary world as a quiet, reserved and aloof individual, but my personal experience with him revealed a more nuanced personality. G.A., who I would see playing cards with his non-literary friends at the Dharwad Club in the evenings, was very different. I was amazed by his ability to become completely absorbed in an activity as seemingly frivolous as playing rummy. Above all, I was overwhelmed by his warmth and affection. Following my initial visit to Dharwad to obtain permission to adapt his short story 'Kairee' into a film, I had the privilege of spending numerous hours with him over the next few years. Often, I would make changes to the screenplay and discuss alternative possibilities with him. His responses would spark new ideas. Once, hearing about the difficulties in arranging funds for the movie, he said, 'You dared to go against the current and created your film *Akriet*. Instead of continuing the journey of a successful hero, you made the antagonist the main character. You will keep forging ahead ... don't worry.' For some reason, such unexpected encouragement had a profoundly uplifting impact on me.

He always exercised the right to keep his life private; even so, he not only allowed me into his home, but also gave me the opportunity to sit beside him and eat traditional meals cooked by his sister, Prabhavati, while discussing fundamental questions about art in depth. On one such morning, while Chitra, Shalmalee and I were staying at the forest guesthouse in Dharwad, he arrived. He had with him a cassette of *Mugdachi Goshta* (The Story of Mugdha) recorded in his own voice and some stories from *Bakhar Bim Chi* (Bim's Chronicles), which he gave to Shalmalee as a special gift. The air became heavy with unspoken gratitude and love, feeling like a gentle hug from a revered family patriarch, leaving me at a loss for words. After a while, when he got up to leave, Shalmalee quickly touched his feet, and he lovingly patted her head. When I bent down to do the same, he seemed a bit embarrassed and mumbled something indistinct; then he turned away, and quickly disappeared. This image of a stalwart, who zealously guarded the sanctity of his personal space, walking away has never faded from my mind.

He continues to inspire me in more ways than one. One particular conversation about spontaneity has stayed with me, and I can still vividly recall his words: 'Every morning, without fail, I sit at my desk for two hours. Most of my initial drafts fall short of my standards, and I don't hesitate to crumple them up or tear them to shreds. But when a few lines show promise, I become obsessed with refining them. What may appear to be a single page of decent writing is actually the culmination of countless rejected drafts, torn papers and relentless editing. This process of iteration and improvement is essential to my craft.'

There is a widespread misconception that the technical aspects of art such as technique and practice have less value than the creative process, with some viewing the former as unglamorous and uncreative. Art is not necessarily always intuitive. We tend to look upon a director who can narrate a story spontaneously, without a ready screenplay, as a great artiste, but are inclined to think of the discipline of reading a well thought-out script as something inferior. I have always insisted that an artiste ought to seek the discipline needed to nurture artistic talent; they ought to make the effort required to build physical agility, they must inculcate patience to practise the same piece repeatedly in rehearsals, and they should have control over technical aspects. This is required of an artist(e) in any creative field. The fact that G.A. shared my conviction amounted to a vital validation of my thought process.

When G.A. passed away, it felt like I lost an essential support in my creative journey. I missed the chance to share the final version of the script of *Kairee* with him and to get his feedback. I feel sorry that I didn't get to express my gratitude and share the triumph of completing the movie with him. The dream of watching the first trial of the film with him also remained unfulfilled. However, the thought that G.A. would have liked *Kairee*, crafted out of many crossed-out lines and discarded drafts, somewhat reassures me. After his passing, many people suggested that I publish our correspondence or write a book about our relationship. Some others did capitalise on their association with him; however, I found it inappropriate. What we shared was personal and private. Since he was protective of his privacy in life, publishing anything without his consent didn't align with my ethics. But now, before I take my exit from this world, I will hand over our correspondence to his sister.

What label can I assign to these relationships? How can I fit them into any mould? Such bonds have left an enduring legacy in my heart, becoming a treasured part of my life … seeped into my existence … elusive yet cherished in my palm!

Similarly, the bond I shared with Basu Chatterjee, whom I always called Basu-da, cannot be confined to conventional labels. Between 1973 and 1980, parallel to our professional relationship, our bond as guru and disciple flourished, nurtured by mutual love, admiration and respect. While Basu-da was making the Hindi adaptation of the famous Marathi film *Mumbaicha Jawai* (The Son-in-law of Mumbai). I missed out on this opportunity of working under a major Hindi film banner alongside Jaya Bhaduri, who had become a star after the film *Guddi*. I have mentioned this incident in an earlier chapter. Still, in 1973, Basu-da came to meet me again, this time with producer Suresh Jindal at Samovar in the Jehangir Art Gallery. Basu-da started narrating the story: 'There's a boy, let's say you, and a girl—a new girl, Vidya Sinha ...' After a few sentences, he paused and said, '*Yaar*, why don't you read this story instead?' He handed me a one-and-a-half-page short story, titled '*Yahi Sach Hai*' (This is the Truth), written by the renowned Hindi writer Mannu Bhandari. After reading it, I bombarded him with questions, 'How will you make a two-hour film out of a story so short? There is no love triangle nor a big plot; besides you're making it with new faces! How will you manage a narrative that unfolds without any dramatic plot twist or a clear antagonist?' Basu-da, with his characteristic smile, asked, 'Would you like to work in a different kind of film such as this one?' My enthusiastic 'Yes' propelled him to hand over the script and dialogue of the film *Rajnigandha*.

During the preparatory phase, Basu-da requested me and Dinesh Thakur to rehearse with Vidya Sinha, using our experience from the theatre, to calm her novice nerves. We met at Basu-da's small apartment in Adarsh Nagar, Worli. By the time the actual shooting began, the three of us had great camaraderie. Our friendship lasted for many years until Dinesh's death ten years ago and Vidya's five years ago.

Dinesh, raised in Delhi, and I, having grown up in Bombay, landed up having scenes with Vidya in opposite settings—my scenes were located in Delhi and Dinesh's in Bombay. The talkative nature of the 'Sanjay' character was the complete opposite of my real-life quiet nature. Immersed in his office, its politics and his colleagues, Sanjay would keep losing track of time. Crafting Sanjay—a loquacious character who never explicitly expresses love but conveys it through his eyes—without making him seem selfish, was a challenge. I drew inspiration from Ramesh Chacha, the elder brother of producer Suresh Jindal, using his North Indian warmth and simple-heartedness to shape Sanjay.

Basu-da never narrated stories or explained the characters or did demonstrations for actors. It wasn't his style. However, if something felt off, he usually immediately corrected it, saying, 'No, no, what's happening here?' I portrayed Sanjay without any corrections from him. I felt energised by the delight visible on his face when he declared 'Cut!'.

After the Delhi shoot of *Rajnigandha* was over, there was a small party at Ramesh Chacha's house. The writer Mannu Bhandari and her husband Rajendra Yadav, both significant contributors to contemporary Hindi literature, were present there. They were keen to know about the new experiments and progressive journeys taking place in Marathi literature, while I was eager to learn about the diverse streams prevalent in Hindi literature. To my surprise, the otherwise reserved Basu-da spoke at length about my role in Mohan Rakesh's play *Aadhe Adhure,* making that evening unforgettable.

After the completion of the Delhi-Bombay shoots, and the editing, dubbing, re-recording and other post-production work of *Rajnigandha,* Basu-da and Suresh started approaching distributors, but to no avail. They faced rejections everywhere. While this was happening, I was engrossed in the triple entanglement of banking, theatre and family life. Nearly a year and a half passed. With no distributor willing to buy the film, Basu-da offered it to Rajshri Pictures, who released it nationwide on a commission basis. Basu-da called me in a cheerful tone, 'Our film is being released, Amol.' Banners and posters started appearing all over Bombay. My face was splashed on huge posters and banners suspended in mid-air, and I started getting recognised by people who would approach me on the streets.

In September 1974, *Rajnigandha* premiered at the Akashwani Theatre opposite Mantralaya. Suresh, Basu-da, cinematographer

K.K. Mahajan, Dinesh and I stood in the foyer for the first 11 a.m. show. Vidya was absent. Having seen only snatches of the movie during post-production, I was now eager to see the entire film on the silver screen. However, Basu-da insisted on me waiting outside. Though, there was no fear of failure or any insecurity. Basu-da peeked inside after a while and, with a satisfied smile, said, 'They are laughing, yaar. Everyone is enjoying themselves.' Then K.K. entered the hall, took a round and, lighting a cigarette, gave us a thumbs-up. The audience's positive reactions during the intermission reassured us. A very anxious Suresh approached me then and asked, 'What do you think, Amol? Will the film work?' Taking a puff of my cigarette, I replied, 'Why should you worry? Even if it doesn't work, we can carve two ad-films out of it—using any part of Dinesh's scenes for a cigarette advertisement, and any part of mine for a toothpaste commercial.' My response angered Suresh so much that he walked away. Even in our subsequent meetings, his displeasure didn't seem to subside. My sarcastic humour didn't sit well with him. Self-deprecation and objective evaluation of one's own work

Rajnigandha (1974), with Mannu Bhandari, Vidya Sinha, Basu-da, Dinesh Thakur, Suresh Jindal (at the press meet in Delhi)

are uncommon traits in the film industry. But I have always admired Suresh's dauntless spirit to do something different. His production of *Shatranj ke Khilari* was an outstanding achievement, worthy of tremendous praise and pride.

I was confident that the songs of *Rajnigandha*, composed by the master music director Salil Chowdhury, would become immortal. However, I was a bit uncertain about his decision to use Mukesh's voice in the song '*Kai baar yun dekha hai*'; but since I didn't have to lip-sync to it, I ignored that concern. Mukesh even won the National Award for 'Best Male Playback Singer' that year for this song. My belief was that presenting a simple story in a simple manner would forge a strong connection with the audience, and that belief got validated by the success of *Rajnigandha*. After the inaugural 11 a.m. show ended, the audience surrounded Dinesh and me. When the Marathi viewers especially came up to me to shake my hand, I saw a different shade of affection and pride in their eyes. Showered by praise, I felt fulfilled.

Rajnigandha became a hit. Rajshri Pictures released it in all major cities across the country in their characteristic 'restrained' distribution style. It celebrated silver jubilees in Bombay and Delhi. Of course, it wasn't given any grand publicity, advertisements or pomp. The commercial success of the film was discussed with tight lips. Nonetheless, I started receiving numerous offers. The meeting with the producer I.M. Kunnu, that took place thereafter, was amusing. He supported directors like B.R. Ishara, known for making bold films like *Chetna* while maintaining the mainstream tag. He came with an offer for a film and started asking me questions like, 'How many films have you accepted recently? What is your expected remuneration?' In response, I asked him counter-questions like, 'What is the subject of the film? Details of the protagonist's character? Can I read the entire script?' He probably didn't like that and gave up on me during the meeting itself. Around the same time, actors from FTII (Film and Television Institute of India), like Anil Dhawan, Shatrughan Sinha, Satish Kaul and Romesh Sharma, were making the rounds of producers' offices. That was something I could never do.

Once again, I got a call from Basu-da. Over coffee at Samovar, he started talking about a new film. 'You must have seen the Hollywood movie *School for Scoundrels*, but perhaps you don't know the old film *The Secret Life of Walter Mitty*.' I knew that P.L. Deshpande had made the film *Gulacha Ganapati* (A Simpleton) basing it on *Walter Mitty*. Basu-da spoke of blending the two stories into an entertaining fusion, and then handed me the complete script of *Chhoti Si Baat*. Although the film was being made under the big banner of B.R. Chopra Films, there was no change in Basu-da's simple, minimalistic style. The shooting started at 9 a.m. at the Kodak office in Fort. Around 10:30 a.m., Ashok Kumar made his entry. After formal introductions, Basu-da began shooting my scene with him. Most of the scene involved my silent reactions to his extensive dialogues, and the shooting got over in no time. While the arrangements for the next scene were underway, Ashok Kumar went to Basu-da and asked in Bengali, 'Where did you find this young man? You said he came from theatre, but I couldn't find even a hint of theatricality in his acting.' Since they didn't know that I understood Bengali, they spoke openly about me within earshot. I tried to maintain as neutral a face as possible. By the end of the day though, I was chatting easily with Ashok Kumar, addressing him as 'Dadamoni'. Not only that, but when he found out that I had studied painting at the Sir J.J. School of Art, he warmly invited me to his penthouse opposite the Jehangir Art Gallery. He even invited me to his bungalow in Chembur a couple of times. In later years, Dadamoni was the only artiste from the Hindi film industry who consistently attended each of my painting exhibitions.

Working with the comedian Asrani gave me a glimpse into the industry's mannerisms. Probably because of his success on account of *Guddi*, *Sholay* and *Abhimaan* doing well, he got into the habit of arriving late for shoots. A few days into the shooting of *Chhoti Si Baat*, while getting ready, he asked me, 'I hear you come early?' 'No, I come on time,' I replied. With a slight smile, he said, 'Yes, yes, you're doing just one or two films now, later …' The conversation was interrupted by someone telling us that the shot was ready. During lunch, I explained to him my definition of professionalism. The number of films I did, how many shifts I worked, or what remuneration I got—those things became irrelevant once I committed to a film. My professional code dictated that I deliver my utmost effort in the time frame committed to the producer. Keeping my word and not causing inconvenience to others was a part of my discipline. Just like me, legendary artistes like Dev Anand and my contemporary Amitabh Bachchan would arrive at the studio punctually at 9 a.m. I wish Asrani had been present to witness their punctuality. Years later, while working together on a film, he made a slightly awkward request. 'Yaar, you're finishing scenes in a single take. You're the hero … stretch out the shooting a bit. I'm working on a "per day" basis …' The adage that the film industry only remembers an artiste's most recent success was constantly reinforced by such incidents.

While the shooting of *Chhoti Si Baat* was going on, I received an invitation to attend the Filmfare Awards ceremony. Basu-da insisted that I attend the event at Shanmukhananda Hall in Matunga, Bombay. Moreover, he kindly offered me a suit that had been tailored for use in the film, saying, 'Wear this.'

That evening, I gazed in amazement at the glitz, the big stars from previous generations and my favourite music directors. I wondered, 'Am I really amidst this illustrious crowd?' Suddenly, an announcement was made for me to present an award. Thunderous applause erupted from the topmost, third balcony. Before I knew it, the entire auditorium had picked up the applause. My heart pounded so loudly that I feared others might hear it as I walked up to the stage. I was also worried about tripping over the cameras and their thick cables lying along the way, and making a fool of myself. But with a deep breath and a confident smile, I completed the task assigned to me. As soon as the ceremony ended, I saw a man in a pristine white suit and hat approaching me. When he got closer, I realised it was the great O.P. Nayyar! Grasping my hand firmly, he said, 'Welcome to the clan.' I stood there in a daze for quite some time. Then David (Abraham Cheulkar) saab came close, lovingly embraced me, and said, 'This is just the beginning, young man.'

One evening, while having drinks at Basu-da's place, I asked him, 'Didn't you get angry when I refused *Piya ka Ghar*?' With a slight smile, he said, 'Yes, I did. However, upon reflection, I realised your point. I really appreciate your honesty. Besides, I have always enjoyed watching your theatre performances.'

Portraying Arun in *Chhoti Si Baat* was an entirely different kind of fun. While crafting a character totally opposite to Sanjay from *Rajnigandha*, I incorporated some of Basu-da's mannerisms. Additionally, P.L. Deshpande's acting in *Gulacha Ganapati* nudged me in the right direction. Dadamoni's constant praise on the sets boosted my confidence. Since this was my second film with Vidya, there was no awkwardness between us, rather a lovely friendship. 'It's unfair, Basu-da, we are the hero-heroine, but you haven't given us a single romantic scene,' she would tease him. While the song *Janeman Janeman* played in the background, he interspersed scenes showing Dharmendra romancing Hema Malini in a garden, with scenes of Vidya and me shown sitting across each other inside the Express Tower office. I loved the contrasting scenes Basu-da came up with. Salil-da's music was indeed a great asset and a decisive factor in the success of the film. He chose Yesudas, a Tamil singer, to record the song '*Janeman Janeman*'. Through this song, Yesudas garnered countless fans in the Hindi film industry.

On 9 January 1976, *Chhoti Si Baat* hit the theatres and became a 'super hit'. It received six Filmfare nominations and Basu-da won an award for the Best Screenplay. That year, both *Chhoti Si Baat* and *Chitchor* were nominated for the Best Film category, and I was nominated for the Best Actor award. The film *Kabhi Kabhie* had thirteen nominations, and *Mausam* had eight. Basu-da never told us that the producer, B.R. Chopra, didn't like *Chhoti Si Baat* at all. Moreover, he kept it a secret from us that he had distributed the film through his own company, Cine-Eye. The press show and premiere were held not in Bombay, but in Madras. Praise from the non-Hindi speaking audience there was heartening. I cherish to this day the long chats with Kamal Haasan and his then wife Vani Ganapathy, as well as senior director K. Balachander's detailed analysis of how well I had handled the nuances of both my personas in *Chhoti Si Baat*.

At the press conference following the Madras premiere, the first question posed to Basu-da was, 'Is this film based on a Western movie?' Even before the questioner could finish, Basu-da replied, 'This film is not inspired by just one movie, but rather combines elements from two separate storylines.' His transparent, candid admission drew a big laugh. Both Vidya and I received ample publicity. The film enjoyed immense success in Bombay as well. Afterwards, many producers and directors insisted that I take on a name that would obscure my Marathi identity. They tried to persuade me by citing examples of V. Shantaram, C. Ramchandra and Master Bhagwan. However, Basu-da never suggested I change my name. And as I ascended to greater heights of success, such suggestions became increasingly rare.

As *Chhoti Si Baat* was being wrapped up, preparations for *Chitchor* were underway. I was introduced to Zarina Wahab, who had just graduated from FTII. I received a warm welcome at the Rajshri

Pictures office. I was called to attend the recording sessions of the songs beautifully composed by Ravindra Jain, and sung by Yesudas and Hemlata. I was also invited to participate in the four to five days' session to discuss Basu-da's script and dialogues, and arrangements were made for a special car to drive me to the out-of-town shooting and back. All these privileges signalled my ascension to stardom.

Most of the shooting took place at locations in Panchgani and Mahabaleshwar. Just as Basu-da had requested my assistance to guide Vidya during *Rajnigandha*, he now sought my help to support Vijayendra Ghatge, a debonair actor, in honing his craft. Vijayendra was also accommodated in my room at the guest house. One morning, I woke up to see this young man practising different expressions in front of the mirror. I watched him with curiosity. Shortly after, he confidently explained to me the acting training he had received at FTII. I told Basu-da later, 'He is confident that he already knows everything about acting, so please don't involve me.' Basu-da laughed and arranged for Vijayendra to have a separate room. During the shoot, Basu-da, quite unlike his usual self, frequently questioned Vijayendra: 'What's going on? Are you acting? Why are you doing this?' Zarina, also from FTII, was a natural and spontaneous actor. She had no inclination towards method acting. During our rehearsals, whenever I would compliment her on her performance, she would feign innocence and ask, 'What did I do that was so great?' The spark of her lively nature ignited a natural chemistry between us, and our friendship has endured long after the cameras stopped rolling for both of us.

For the first time, in *Chitchor*, Basu-da decided to film songs with the actors lip-syncing. After a quick assessment of my singing, he declared, 'Amol, you sing well and have a good understanding of music. My tension has eased.' The close-ups he took of me singing the song *'Jab Deep Jale Aana'*, based on Raga Yaman, were his way of endorsing me. I was elated. The legendary tunes I got to perform were a treasure. And even after five decades, people, including the young generation, still love to listen to them, which gives me a special joy. In Indian films, playback singers significantly enhance a hero's image. Just like the Raj Kapoor–Mukesh, Rajesh Khanna–Kishore Kumar and Shammi Kapoor–Rafi pairings became iconic, the Amol Palekar–Yesudas duo also achieved an immortal status in Hindi film music.

Basu-da planned to shoot the entire sequence of the song *'Aaj Se Pehle'* in a moving car. Vijayendra was to drive in the happy part, and I in the second sombre part of the song, K.K. Mahajan carried the camera on his shoulder and sat on the Jeep's bonnet with an assistant. In those days, we didn't have the various grips available now to shoot such scenes. We secured K.K. with ropes. As monitors showing what the camera were capturing didn't exist then, Basu-da had to sit next to K.K. on the bonnet, to ensure the desired framing of the shot. To help me lip-sync correctly, our sound assistant sat crouched in the back seat, playing the song loudly. The three of us—Zarina, Vijayendra and I—sat in the front. Each shot required such meticulous preparation. As an actor, I encountered challenges like performing in a confined space without revealing its limitations, precisely angling the sun-gun's light to illuminate my face, lip-syncing convincingly to the playback singer's voice and persuading the audience that the voice was actually mine.

Around 1971, seasoned editor and director Raja Thakur, after watching my stage performance, asked me to play the lead role in his Marathi film *Bajiravcha Beta*. His previous Marathi films, *Mee Tulas Tuzhya Angani* (I'm the Holy Basil in your Yard), *Ranglya Ratri Ashya* (Such Colourful Nights) and *Mumbaicha Jawai* (Mumbai's Son-in-law), had been major hits. Following my consent, he honoured me by setting up a meeting with the renowned writer S.N. Navare to discuss the script's finer points. Later, on the first day of the shoot, when I arrived at Bhagwan Dada's Asha Studio, Rajabhau played a devotional song sung by the veteran composer-singer Sudhir Phadake. Then, he said, 'Today we are filming a song with you.' Following my debut film with Dubey (*Shantata! Court Chalu Aahe*), this was only my second occasion to be in front of the camera. I was a bit scared. Following a few rehearsals, I managed to grasp the technique of lip-syncing, singing with gusto and not just miming the words. But singing while playing the ektara with one hand and manjira (small cymbals) with the other proved impossible. I finally told Rajabhau in frustration, 'I don't think I can do this; please get another actor.' Rajabhau smiled, patted my back and reassured me, 'Don't worry, we'll make this song look so beautiful that it will leave you amazed.' Using different lenses and clever framing, Rajabhau masked my flaws and brought the devotional song to life. The valuable lessons I learnt from Rajabhau became a guiding force in my career. I believe his mentorship was crucial in my being able to make the voices of Bhupinder in *Gharaonda*, Yesudas in *Chitchor* and Kishore Kumar in *Gol Maal* sound like my own. Instead of retreating with an 'I can't do it' attitude, this incident taught me the determination to find innovative solutions, navigate difficulties and stay committed to my aspirations.

Basu-da filmed all the songs in *Chitchor* without the help of a choreographer, using his natural narrative style. At the time, even though it was customary for choreographers to handle song picturisations, they mostly remained unacknowledged, unlike these days, where the choreographers are stars in their own right and are duly acknowledged. The songs in Bimal Roy's *Do Bigha Zamin* (Two Bighas of Land) were choreographed by the great dancer Sachin Shankar, and the song '*Khaike Paan Banaras Wala*' in *Don* was choreographed by P.L. Raj. Gopi Krishna's younger brother Madho Krishna was also a renowned choreographer. Taking this practice into consideration, the producer of *Chitchor*, Raj babu (Raj Kumar Barjatya) tried to provide Basu-da with all the help he needed for the picturisation of the songs.

One evening, when the picturisation of the song '*Gori tera gaon*' began, Basu-da said with a chuckle, 'The production assistants have been pestering me since morning, asking me when they should bring out the peacocks?' For the line '*Ji karta hai, mor ke paon mein payaliya pehna doon*' (I wish to gift anklets to a peacock), Raj babu had made extensive preparations to showcase a peacock. Basu-da firmly refused, causing some unrest for a while in the production team. For the line '*Chandni raaton mein, haath liye haathon mein*' (Holding hands on a starry night) from the same song, a set had been created in the studio with a moon hanging in the sky and a small bridge path going below, which was entirely against Basu-da's style. When I asked him about this, he didn't respond. However, by then, I knew that he had the talent to adapt to the producer's demands while still maintaining his artistic integrity, that he would find a middle ground in this instance too by subtly adjusting his approach.

During the making of *Chitchor*, producer Raj babu personally ensured that justice was done to every scene in the script. I had a special admiration for Rajshri Pictures and Raj babu. Compared to the expensively made mainstream films like *Kabhi Kabhie*, *Dus Numbri* and *Laila Majnu*, Raj babu and his brother Kamal babu (Kamal Kumar Barjatya) were committed to creating wholesome entertainment on modest budgets. They consistently produced and distributed films that were morally uplifting and suitable for family viewing. This was their hallmark. Of course, their extensive experience as distributors and their ownership of a chain of theatres were also significant assets that bolstered their work as producers.

After the film was completed, only the cast and crew were invited to the trial screening. Everyone loved the movie, and Basu-da was pleased too. However, we both became uneasy upon hearing that it would be released in only one theatre in Bombay. Basu-da took me to the Barjatyas' office. The explanation given by Raj babu and Kamal babu, with respect to Basu-da's concerns, left me perplexed.

'This film is going to be a huge hit, a super hit. But we don't want to release it in the usual way. People should have to make an effort and go long distances to watch this film instead of easily getting tickets at every corner. Once this atmosphere of exclusivity is created, we will release it everywhere.' Their strategy proved successful. *Chitchor* premiered at a theatre in Andheri on 10 January 1976, without any pomp and show, and ran 'house full' for a hundred days. Following this success, it was gradually released all across India, making 'Amol Palekar' a household name. This earned me the reputation of a trailblazing hero—whose career launched with a remarkable trio of silver jubilee successes—resulting in a flurry of producers clamouring to work with me.

I soon took the bold decision of resigning from my banking career and devoting myself entirely to the world of arts.

For my first three films with Basu-da, I did not discuss fees or any other practical matters with him. Following Satyadev Dubey's advice to trust Basu-da's sense of fairness, I accepted whatever amount he decided to pay me without any complaints or negotiation. For all of the six films we worked on together, I adhered to this principle. Later, Basu-da's key technicians and long-term associates like K.K. Mahajan and Narendra Singh left him on account of the conservative remuneration, but I happily continued working with him until the end.

Discussing fees with mainstream producers, outside the parallel cinema circle, made me uncomfortable. The contrast between my humble middle-class roots and my suddenly inflated market worth caused a jarring sense of incongruity, which I found difficult to reconcile with. Accepting a six-figure amount made me uneasy. When I declined the then prevalent practice of giving a portion of the remuneration in cash, alternatives like cars, foreign trips or other gifts became ubiquitous offers. A producer named A.V. Mohan insisted on signing me on simultaneously for three films. Another new producer, Mohan Rao, offered me a one-lakh-rupee cheque, saying, 'We'll make a film on any subject you want, just say yes without thinking twice.' That's when I decided to move from my small apartment in Gamdevi to a bungalow in Juhu.

'Chirebandi', my source of happiness for many years, was located inside a quiet bungalow society in Juhu. Some people viewed my bungalow as a symbol of my impractical and unconventional thinking, suggesting that I should have allotted those funds towards a more practical investment such as getting an office. Veteran film producer Sharad Pilgaonkar advised me, 'Instead of acquiring a bungalow, if you set up an office in the Naaz Building and invest in production or distribution, you'll blend in with the industry folks and go far.' Interestingly, his first film was titled *Ha Maaza Marg Ekla* (This is My Lonely Path). However, ironically, in real life, he advised me not to take such a solitary path.

A middle-class Marathi man like me constructing a bungalow like Chirebandi in a film-centric neighbourhood, with music director Laxmikant on one side, Shatrughan Sinha and Jeetendra nearby, Dharmendra across, Amitabh Bachchan on the other side, and immediate neighbours like Biswajit and Khayyam Saheb, raised eyebrows in the industry. Taunts like 'someone who wears slippers has bought a bungalow here' were heard. The distinctive name of the bungalow was also a subject of much conversation, with many seeing it as a reflection of my individuality. I named my bungalow 'Chirebandi' to shield myself from the film industry's culture of deceit and superficiality, though the irony and sarcasm eluded most people. The charming house nestled amidst a lush garden and had three generously sized bedrooms on the first floor, while the ground floor had my office and a spacious meeting room for discussions on literature, music and visual arts. The house was always bustling with the energy of artistes, theatre enthusiasts and friends, who would often congregate there.

I threw an open house every year on New Year's Eve for theatre folks. The debates, discussions and laughter that resounded in Chirebandi are now impossible to track. Many litres of alcohol must have been consumed by various people there. Vijaya Mehta held a meeting there with Smita Patil and me for the adaptation of the hugely successful play *Mahasagar* into a film. The walls of my home witnessed countless script readings, discussions and Jaidev-ji's rehearsals with Bhimsen Joshi. Parts of *Naqab* and *Ankahee* were shot in Chirebandi. Many enduring memories were made on its permises. After the first private screening of *Ankahee,* Shabana Azmi and Javed Akhtar brought a Mughlai dinner feast, and we spent the night deliberating over and appraising the nuances of the film. Whenever artistes like Badal Sircar, Anil Chatterjee and Devika Mukherjee visited Bombay, Chirebandi would be their home. Young painters and sculptors like Navjot Altaf, Deepak Shinde and the Balbir-Latika Katt duo used Chirebandi freely as if it was their own residence. After Sai Paranjpye and Arun Joglekar separated, Arun and their son Gautam stayed at Chirebandi for nearly two years.

The only film-related gathering that took place at Chirebandi was to celebrate my winning the Filmfare Best Actor award for *Gol Maal.* Gulzar saab and Utpal Dutt had also received awards for the film, and so, they, along with Sharmila Tagore and Tiger Pataudi, made it a point to join in the celebrations. Such joyous gatherings usually lasted until dawn, with an elaborate spread of food and drinks fuelling the merriment.

Our close-knit family comprising Chitra, Shalmalee and me shared our beautiful home with friends and relatives for almost two decades. A loft with a ladder to climb up and a rope to come down added a touch of adventure to Shalmalee's room. She and her friends would make a ruckus by jumping up and down in this loft. The swing in our garden and a big jungle gym made for a wonderful play area for

Shalmalee, her friends and the three daughters of the neighbouring Patwardhans.

After finishing a film shoot, playing for at least an hour with our handsome black Labrador, Napoleon, was a surefire remedy for relieving my fatigue. In striking contrast to Napoleon's compliant personality, his son, Junior, turned out to be quite independent. Those two furry members of my family had a blast at Chirebandi since there they could run around, play and soak up sunshine to their heart's content. Junior's life was unexpectedly cut short after he accidentally consumed some toxic substance. His loss took a toll on Napoleon, who stopped eating. Despite the doctor's best efforts, his condition continued to deteriorate, until one fateful morning, when he gently rested his head in my lap and slipped away. His frozen eyes are still etched in my memory. Their bodies were buried in our garden. The presence of both Napoleon and Junior remained eternal to the essence of Chirebandi.

Initially, Chitra genuinely loved the house. The path from starting with nothing to acquiring a magnificent bungalow had been a long and challenging one, but the sense of pride and fulfilment we felt was overwhelming. The property, once a symbol of our shared dreams, lost its lustre as our bond began to fray, becoming a burden she no longer cherished. It was a large house, and the responsibility of its upkeep and staff management became an increasingly daunting task, weighing heavily on her mind. She began insisting that we sell the bungalow and get a small apartment. Despite her desire to get rid of the house back then, ironically, she accepted it without hesitation when I willingly relinquished it to her after we parted ways. Chirebandi's crucible revealed the true nature of those I thought I knew intimately, exposing the true nature of my relationships with them and the hidden facets of their personalities. I derive immense pride in having preserved my beloved home's integrity, refusing to let it become a pawn in any negotiations or a resource to be exploited for personal gains.

During the making of *Do Ladke Dono Kadke* (1979), instead of giving us the script and dialogues to read, Basu-da showed us the Bengali film, which was to be remade in Hindi by Hemant Kumar's son Jayant Mukherjee, with his wife Moushumi Chatterjee, Asrani and me. The story of two petty thieves getting unwittingly involved in a major kidnapping case, and the ensuing chaos, was perfect for Basu-da's gentle, humorous style. Asrani and I formed an unstoppable duo; our performances were completely in sync. Seasoned actors like Keshto Mukherjee, Dina Pathak and Nilu Phule were our co-actors. And yet, the film sank both artistically and commercially. This failure was a sobering reminder that even the most carefully crafted recipes could go awry.

Later, during a conversation about it with Hemant-da in Calcutta, he said to me, 'The films I produced (*Bees Saal Baad* and *Kohraa*) fell in an unusual sub-genre of thrillers. Besides, I was unsure if the Hindi movie-going audiences would accept Biswajit as the lead actor. But both those films were wildly successful at the box office. *Khamoshi*, on the other hand, had all the winning elements. A talented director like Asit Sen, a superstar like Rajesh Khanna, a mature actress like Waheeda Rehman, Dharmendra in a sensitive role to elevate the emotional triangle, and my popular songs … yet the film flopped completely. Youngsters like you should analyse these dynamics.' Saying this, Hemant-da affectionately patted my back and walked away. Later, Basu-da told me something. Jayant was insisting on using Yesudas' voice instead of Hemant-da's for my role, which was causing disagreements between the father and son. When I asked, 'Didn't you explain it to Jayant?' Basu-da replied, 'When discord creeps beyond the office and spills over to the dinner table, it is wiser to stay silent.'

Somehow, I felt that Moushumi never properly engaged with that film, even though it was a home production. Having worked before with big banners, it might have been difficult for her to adapt to Basu-da's restrained style. Surprisingly, the film's failure not withstanding, Jayant and I formed a close friendship. The sound recording of many of the films I directed was done at the Geetanjali Studio, owned by him. I often visited his and Moushumi's home too. Moushumi, who was called 'Indu' at home, always welcomed me with great warmth.

In 1979, while the filming of *Do Ladke* was on, Basu-da gave me the script of *Baton Baton Mein* to read. It was a story about a Catholic family. He also asked me to suggest some unusual faces for the supporting characters. For the role of the heroine's mother, I suggested the name of Pearl Padamsee, who was active in the English theatre circuit; for the part of the younger brother, I thought of Ranjit Chowdhury; and for the character of my father, I recommended the senior Marathi actor Arvind Deshpande. Basu-da got all of them on board for the respective roles. I asked him, 'Should I keep a Bulganin beard for the character of Tony Braganza?', quickly sketching it out on paper. Basu-da immediately approved. My sketching that beard ignited a creative spark, inspiring him to add a novel twist to my character by depicting Tony sketching the heroine on a local train. As the seasons passed, I don't exactly remember when, but the former premier of Soviet Union Nikolai Bulganin's style of beard seamlessly merged with my real-life persona.

Right at the beginning of that shooting, I instantly bonded with Tina Munim. This simple young woman from a middle-class Gujarati family was very open and talkative. Around the time the first leg of the shooting ended, Tina's debut film *Des Pardes* released. Due to her heartfelt insistence, I attended the premiere. I used to tease her about her anglicised Hindi. 'Actually, Basu-da chose a Christian background for the film to cover up your awkwardness in

Hindi.' To this, Pearl, who was a Parsi, said, 'That opened up a nice opportunity for me too.' Arvind mischievously added, 'My Hindi in a Marathi accent gave Basu-da's dialogues the multilingual flavour of Bombayi.'

For a peek into the Bombay of the 1970s, Basu-da's films are the perfect time capsule. Due to his realistic filming style, various locations, bus stops, bridges, roads, buildings, trees, which the people of Bombay have close associations with, can be seen in every frame. The entire shooting of *Baton Baton Mein* took place in the Christian locality of Bandra and on local trains. The shoot was a joy ride for everyone; its playfulness permeated every scene in the film. *Baton Baton Mein* and *Gol Maal*—these two films demonstrated that when the director and the cast collaboratively explore the various facets of the script without overpowering each other, the comedic elements shine through.

Even while the film was being made, it was evident that the four or five songs written by Amit Khanna and the brilliant music given by Rajesh Roshan would make the film immensely successful. By the time the film released, on 13 April 1979, all the songs had already become super hits.

Back then, a film's soundtrack would be made available for sale in the market a month or two prior to the film's release. The songs would be broadcast on the radio. If the producer was very good at publicity, the songs would also be played at the local Ganesh or Janmashtami festivals. Cassette tapes had not yet become common. The images of the film's actors on the outer covers of music records used to be hand-drawn. These covers revealed the actors' appearance in the about-to-be released film. Visual advertisements for the films would also go up before the release. Show-cards and photo sets of 'upcoming attractions' were put up in cinema halls. These too were hand-drawn by artists. There was a special excitement in going half an hour early before the show began to soak in the glitzy atmosphere, devour the publicity material in the lounge and watch the trailers. Once the release date was set, giant hand-painted hoardings would go up on the roads. As an actor, I always wondered if the hand-drawn portraits would be detailed enough to make me identifiable. Many times, the drawings were so amateurish that they made me feel queasy. Still, the artist in me always had a special affection for those painters. The rise of the digital era has led to the decline and eventual disappearance of these traditional art forms.

Despite so many years of consistent success, Basu-da didn't change. Only his hair turned completely grey, and his habit of chewing the corner of a handkerchief after calling 'action' disappeared as the years went by—that's all! In his small apartment in Adarsh Nagar, Worli, his routine of getting up early in the morning and sitting down on the floor to work on a script remained unchanged. Between 1978–79, even with a hectic life of shooting for two films in different shifts and editing the scenes shot in the third, he never skipped his morning routine. Unfazed by success, he persisted with his deliberately chosen unconventional choices, which influenced me greatly.

For the films *Safed Jhooth* (1977) and *Jeena Yahan* (1979), Basu-da requested that I join both the movies as a guest artiste. Saying no wasn't an option. The filming of *Safed Jhooth*, starring Vinod Mehra and Mithu Mukherjee, was done near Mysore. Basu-da was keen on including my family in the outing, as he was planning a family vacation after the shoot, with his wife (whom I addressed as 'Boudi', the Bengali word for bhabhi or sister-in-law) and daughter Rupali, and cinematographer K.K. Mahajan and his wife and daughter. It turned into a family outing for everyone. When asked to shoot for *Jeena Yahan*, I was directing my play *Julus* (Procession) in Bombay and was immersed in its rehearsals. I managed to take out some time and quickly finished my shoot for the film in two days. It was during this time that intense conversations about the Emergency took place between Basu-da and me. When I mentioned to him that my mail was being intercepted and my phone conversations were being listened to, Basu-da said slightly resignedly, 'I am also disturbed. What's happening is not good.' After some time, he took my hand and said, 'I'm not as Left as you or the other Basu (Bhattacharya) are. But you be careful, Amol.' In fact, before getting into film direction, Basu-da had worked at *Blitz* as a cartoonist commenting on political events. But he never commented on politics through his films; nor did he discuss political topics even in private conversations.

Around 1980, Basu-da adapted Sharat Chandra Chattopadhyay's famous novel *Nishkriti* (Deliverance) into the film *Apne Paraye*. The producer duo of the film, Mushir-Riaz, was known for making grand mainstream films like *Mehbooba* and *Bairaag* . Their decision to venture into parallel cinema sparked a lot of talk. Since the story explored intricate relationships and conflicts within a joint family set-up, against the rich backdrop of Bengali culture, I was chosen to play one of the lead roles alongside Girish Karnad as one of the two brothers. To play the role of Siddheshwari, who lovingly holds the entire family together, I suggested the name of the veteran Marathi actress Ashalata Wabgaonkar. Shabana Azmi and Bharti Achrekar were also in the cast.

Bappi Lahiri was the music director. Instead of his popular disco-style songs, he used tunes from the Bengali bhajan, Baul and boatman song traditions, which were apt given the theme of the film. It was also a significant leap in his professional journey. After reading the script, I realised that there wasn't any new challenge in it for me as an actor. I didn't need to make much effort to portray the character of Chander, who loses himself in his music and has no understanding of worldly affairs. As preparation for the movie, I just practised playing the dholak a bit with the help of an assistant, to ensure that I didn't appear clumsy while playing it in my scenes.

The producers had built a large set in the Mehboob Studio at Bandra. Getting to film an entire movie on a set was an exceptional event in Basu-da's career. Most of my scenes were with Shabana. Since we were co-actors from the same acting tradition, the shooting went wonderfully well. Besides, it was an absolute pleasure to film two melodious songs in Yesudas' voice. After the shooting of the song *'Shyam Rang Ranga Re'* was over, Basu-da seemed especially pleased. That evening, Girish and I received an invitation to visit his home. Lyricist Yogesh also joined us. While discussing Shyam Benegal and Girish's multi-dimensional careers, Basu-da's usual reticence fell away; the film society movement pioneer within him must have surfaced. Unlike many others in the industry, he never engaged in the practice of praising someone publicly and then criticising them privately. I cultivated this quality in myself as the years went by.

After that, our meetings became rare. We continued our journeys on our respective paths. On the occasion of my seventieth birthday, I met most of my former heroines at a lunch gathering. In the course of the conversation, we all talked about Basu-da's contribution to our lives. I knew that his health wasn't very good. I called and asked Boudi if we could visit him. She told me Basu-da's response, 'Since when does Amol need permission to meet me?' Vidya (Sinha), Zarina (Wahab), Bindiya (Goswami) and Deepti (Naval), my reel-life heroines, and my real-life partner Sandhya, accompanied me to Basu-da's place. Seeing all of us, his tired face lit up. After a long and nostalgic conversation, we bade him farewell, unaware that this would be our final meeting. He left us a few months later. His beaming smile and serene demeanour from that day remain within me as an indelible last memory.

The mere mention of Basu-da's name unlocks a treasure trove of recollections in me, as of result of which the early phase of my journey in cinema and a pivotal era in my professional life come alive. Another legendary figure I had the privilege of sharing a strong professional relationship and an emotional connection with was Hrishi-da. He considered me his protégé. Hrishi-da came into my life in 1979. Like Basu-da, Hrishi-da too never spoke about political issues, nor did his films comment on the political climate of the time. And yet, their personalities were quite different. Basu-da was reserved, while Hrishi-da was loquacious. Basu-da's scripts and dialogues were always fully prepared for the cast and crew to see before the film went on the floor, but he didn't have a knack for oral storytelling. Hrishi-da, on the other hand, would have the entire film ready in his mind, but would seldom put it all down on paper, preferring to narrate the story himself. He would only give the scenes that were to be shot to the actors. A commonality among the five leading Bengali directors of India cinema—Basu-da, Hrishi-da, Tapan Sinha, Satyajit Ray and Biplab Roy Chowdhury—was that they never demonstrated how they wanted the actors to perform; they never acted out scenes themselves. However, the expressive and graphic narration of the scripts by Tapan-da and Hrishi-da, emphasising the pivotal scenes and characters, enabled me to seamlessly translate the characters from page to screen.

Hrishi-da himself played the sitar. Music was deeply ingrained in him. He was also very fond of all kinds of sports, especially chess. I sometimes teased him, saying, 'You direct films between games of chess.' His command over the medium of cinema, his understanding of all of its aspects was better than Basu-da's. He preferred moving the camera to shoot from different angles rather than keeping it stationary. Hrishi-da loved discussing the beautiful cinematic language he had learnt under the great director Bimal Roy. He also spoke a lot about classical music. Collaborating with both Basu-da and Hrishi-da, I frequently found myself drawing comparisons between their distinct styles, which only deepened my fascination with the technical nuances of filmmaking.

On the set of of *Gol Maal* (1979), with Bindiya Goswami, Hrishi-da

Last meeting with Basu-da, with (From left) Zareena Wahab, Basu-da, Bindiya Goswami, Vidya Sinha

In 1978, Hrishi-da suddenly called me one day. 'I wish to cast you in my film. When can I come to meet you?' I declined his offer to visit me and went to meet him instead. On the way, many thoughts swirled in my mind. He used to attend many of my plays and would praise them generously. Yet, from what I had heard about his working style, I was a bit apprehensive. I had heard that he didn't share the script with the cast, instead told them to trust and follow his instructions. Big stars like Rajesh Khanna, Dharmendra, Amitabh and Shatrughan had to work under his strict direction. So, when I arrived at his bungalow on Carter Road, I had almost decided to say 'no'. I had even rehearsed a polite refusal in my mind to avoid hurting his feelings.

Hrishi-da welcomed me warmly. His elderly mother insisted on feeding me coconut laddus that she had made herself. He then asked me about Shalmalee's recent badminton tournaments. And after this, he began narrating the storyline of *Gol Maal* in great detail. This was the first time, I was hearing such an engaging narration that was bringing the entire film's framework to life before my eyes.

When he started talking about the possible schedule for shooting, I laughed out loud. I told him about the rumours I had heard about him and the refusal I had planned in my mind. We both laughed heartily. Then he recounted how he'd had to change the climax of *Chupke Chupke* at the last moment with just a single shot of Dharmendra entering, since he had arrived to the shoot late.

After much laughter, Hrishi-da said he wanted to make five films with me, and narrated the remaining four stories just as effectively. As I was leaving, his mother insisted that I have another laddu. Despite his difficulty in walking, Hrishi-da walked me up to the gate. True to his word, he made four films with me between 1979 and 1985: *Gol Maal, Naram Garam, Rang Birangi* and *Jhoothi*. Due to scheduling conflicts with Utpal Dutt and me, the shooting of *Jhoot Bole Kauwa Kaate* had to be postponed. And since I got busy with directing my own films after that, I missed out on acting in Hrishi-da's last film, which he later made with Anil Kapoor and Amrish Puri.

Half of *Gol Maal* was shot at Hrishi-da's bungalow and the rest at co-producer N.C. Sippy's bungalow. Perhaps Hrishi-da adopted this style of filming due to his worsening arthritis. In any case, he preferred straightforward storytelling in simple settings over elaborate set designs. I realised this while working in *Gol Maal*. Hrishi-da's meticulous direction enabled me to effortlessly juggle the three roles in *Gol Maal*, making a potentially challenging experience surprisingly smooth. Most people think it was a double role. Watching Ram Prasad and Lakshman Prasad, the audience forgets that the main character is 'Ram', the one striving to find a job. To impress his eccentric boss during the interview, he presents himself as Ram Prasad, and later, when in a bind, he creates another persona, Lakshman Prasad. His lie about the twin brother eventually catches up with him. Watching 'Ram' juggle these personas, the audience forgets the original 'Ram'. I had a history of playing multiple roles. In the play *Hayavadan*, I had played three different roles on stage. So I wasn't overly stressed about essaying the three roles in *Gol Maal*. The distinctions between the characters were already embedded in Hrishi-da's script. However, I added my own flourishes—like buttoning up my shirt tightly, pulling down the kurta intermittently, or twirling a key around my finger—to effectively highlight the differences between the characters.

Working with Utpal-da (Utpal Dutt) and Dina-ben was a true delight. We gave each other useful suggestions during scene rehearsals. Once Hrishi-da had explained the choreography of the scene, he left us to explore myriad possibilities to generate the desired reaction from the audience. After three or four rehearsals, he would decide what to keep and what to discard, and then we'd proceed to the final rehearsal and/or the 'take'. Even for the scenes I wasn't in, Utpal-da and Dina-ben would insist I stay on set and suggest improvements. During the filming of the scene where they end up meeting at a party, I suggested a minor adjustment that opened it up nicely. Utpal-da's attempts to sit on a moving swing a couple of times injected a delightful chaos into the otherwise tense scene. He also gave me some fantastic tips. For instance, during Lakshman Prasad's entry, he advised me to use the comb like a knife—a brilliant idea that added a touch of heroic flamboyance to my character. This improvisational style of rehearsal soon caught on, and Deven Verma and Shubha Khote joined in. Manju Singh, the TV presenter playing my sister, the veteran David saab and the rest of the cast transformed from mere cast members into a cohesive team. This sense of familial bonding during the making of a film is something I've consistently tried to foster throughout my directorial career.

The first shot of *Gol Maal* stands out in my memory for a peculiar reason. After thorough rehearsals, we were ready for the take. Just as Hrishi-da called 'Action!' and I was about to start speaking my lines, I noticed that Hrishi-da and the great writer of the film Raahi Masoom Raza were engrossed in a game of chess. I promptly called 'Cut!' Hrishi-da asked, 'What happened, son?' I expressed my concern about him not watching what I was doing. He reassured me, 'I am watching. Let's start again … Action!' We began the second take, but the same thing happened, and I called 'Cut!' again. After the third time, I told him that I wasn't used to working without the director's attention on the ongoing scene. Somewhat reluctantly, he paused the chess game, and we resumed shooting. Once the first scene was completed and preparations for the next scene began, he resumed his game. He humorously told Raahi saab, loud enough for me to hear, 'Sorry, I couldn't concentrate on the game.' Then, turning to me with a mischievous smile, he said, 'I don't want to earn the reputation of being a director who doesn't pay attention to his actors!'

Deven observed the decline in the number of Hrishi-da's chess matches with Raahi saab and inquired about the reason. Hrishi-da laughed and said, 'Amol has no interest in sedentary games like chess. He likes field games.' In a sense, he was right. My passion for cricket and interest in games like badminton and table tennis often led to frequent discussions and analyses of various matches on the set.

The legendary music director Rahul Dev Burman's enchanting music for *Gol Maal*, especially the song *'Aanewala Pal'*, became immortal. Gulzar saab's lyrics perfectly matched Raahi saab's dialogues, making *Gol Maal* a cult classic. *Gol Maal*'s impact extended far beyond urban elitist circles, catapulting me to unprecedented nationwide recognition, making me a beloved figure in every nook and corner of the country. Recently, the director Rohit Shetty created a series of films with the same title with Ajay Devgn, which also garnered immense popularity. I missed watching the adaptations of *Gol Maal* with stars like Rajinikanth in Tamil, Shiva Rajkumar in Kannada and Madhu in Malayalam. I've also heard that it was remade in Sinhala and released in Sri Lanka.

'What remuneration did you receive for *Gol Maal*?' Someone asked me this question in an interview. In the first meeting itself, Hrishi-da had said he would pay me three lakhs for the first two of the five movies. I never discussed it any further. Apart from that remuneration, when *Gol Maal* became a huge success, he generously offered me a bonus, although the exact amount escapes my memory. The film's influence was immeasurable, exceeding the boundaries of what could be measured by the conventional standards of success. I received the Filmfare Award for 'Best Actor' in 1980. Along with me, Amitabh had been nominated for two movies, *Mr. Natwarlal* and *Kala Patthar*, Rishi Kapoor for *Sargam* and Rajesh Khanna for *Amar Deep*.

The success of *Gol Maal* was so overwhelming that a major crossroads in life appeared before me—a point at which to pause and think about the future. One path that was beckoning was the one Sanjeev Kumar had chosen. He successfully created an image as a capable actor and a star by following the industry norms, using publicists and PR representatives to keep small news about him circulating in the entertainment world, maintaining a small entourage of yes-men, among other things. Sanjeev had used such conventional methods very effectively. Before him, from the previous generation of actors, Raaj Kumar had also created an image of an eccentric yet capable actor-star using the same approach. The advice Shashi Kapoor had given me was also momentous. I don't recall how many offers of situational comedies like *Gol Maal* I rejected after the success of the film. Just the signing fees, if accepted then, would have been enough to sustain my family for five generations. However, my own mental barrier against stardom was so significant that I resisted taking the easy road to success. I was trying my utmost to say 'I am not a star' by evading the crowds that gathered around me in public places or in the offices of my friends, avoiding people asking for my autograph after plays, preferring to stand in line rather than seeking priority or extra attention at other places. Truly, while everyone strives to reach the pinnacle of popularity and maintain that position, often using both overt and covert means to do so, I had reached the apex despite avoiding all of this and seeking something beyond the established framework. I was proud of that. But there was no reason for me to feel guilty about the stardom that had unexpectedly come my way. By then film producers and the industry as a whole had come to accept my ways, recognising and accommodating the rules I had set for my own work.

At a time when all the big stars were routinely working two shifts a day—Dharmendra even working three shifts in twenty-four hours, and Shashi Kapoor starting a new trend of working two hours a day on one film—I had decided to do only one eight-hour shift for a film, preferably from nine to five. And if the shooting had to happen at night, then I would do a shift from two to ten, but only if I had been given prior notice. Besides this, I also decided to work on only one film at a time, dedicating an uninterrupted thirty-day period to its completion. Big producers, who were used to aligning dates of big star casts for shooting, found this very restrictive.

In this complex situation, I once had an honest conversation with Hrishi-da about my doubts. He told me very reassuringly, 'Ammu, what do you want to do? Do only that.'

'I want to direct a film.'

'Then do it. Whatever you need, camera, lights, anything, take it from me. If you want, I will even edit your first film. But I will charge one rupee for it.' On hearing this, I was overwhelmed. I, who had always stood tall, unexpectedly found myself kneeling at his feet. With great affection, Hrishi-da embraced me, softly ran his fingers through my hair, and hurried off to his bedroom. When he returned, he had a 'director's viewfinder' in his hand. 'Keep it with you,' he said, and, not wanting me to see his brimming eyes, quickly retreated inside. How can I ever repay that debt? That moment, the weight of his bequest, is still vividly etched in my memory.

Before Hrishi-da began work on his first film, *Musafir*, Bimal-da had given him this viewfinder—like an iconic vocalist, nearing the twilight of his life, entrusts the hallowed melodies of his heritage to a loyal protégé. That act of handing over something precious illustrates the depth of the giver's love and trust, the recipient's worthiness and the legacy's immeasurable value, symbolising a sacred bond between the one who bequeaths and the one who receives.

In our time, when directors and cinematographers did not have monitors to preview a shot, the viewfinder was used to determine the crucial dimensions of the frame and to decide things like the lens required for the camera and the angle from which to shoot, et cetera. How many great technicians, starting with Bimal-da, must have used this priceless gift that I had received from Hrishi-da. How many frames must have been visualised through this device …

I felt Hrishi-da's presence by my side through the making of every one of my films. I always saw the scenes through the lens of that viewfinder. Later, when monitors became prevalent in film-shooting, I handed over that viewfinder to Bimal-da's daughter, Rinki Bhattacharya.

When Hrishi-da was admitted in the ICU at Leelavati Hospital, Sandhya and I went to visit him. Seeing him lie beyond the glass partition broke my heart. Seeing people in a diminished, helpless state is deeply unsettling for me. I went near him. His daughter-in-law whispered in his ear, 'Dadu, look who's here? Amol has come.' A faint smile appeared on his serene face. The doctor signalled for me to come closer. I held Hrishi-da's wrinkled hand. His weak hands tried to grip mine tightly. As I gazed at his contented smile, I could hardly hold back my tears. Without responding to the barrage of questions from the news channels gathered on the hospital premises, I simply greeted the reporters and got into my car. I felt numb until I returned to Pune. The next day, Hrishi-da left this world. Another void settled in my life.

In 1982, as he had promised, Hrishi-da started working on another film. He narrated its story very elaborately this time. The name of the film was *Naram Garam*. His assistants were to handle the production. Since he had clearly stated the compensation for the first two films with me right at the beginning, our subsequent conversations never touched upon financial matters. Hrishi-da seamlessly fitted the pairing of Utpal-da and me into a backdrop completely different from that of *Gol Maal*. For Utpal-da, this time he wrote up a mildly flirtatious character. Introducing the character of his younger brother brought in a unique element of fun; Shatrughan Sinha had agreed to play that role. For the female lead's role, Hrishi-da was considering Swaroop Sampat, a newcomer who had recently been crowned Miss India. Her father, Bachubhai Sampat, was an acquaintance of mine. That familiarity helped her to quickly overcome her shyness and adapt to the unit.

The outdoor shooting was happening at a bungalow in Juhu. Shatrughan arrived around half-past ten for the nine o'clock shift. Welcoming him, Hrishi-da said, 'Now you have become a big star, haven't you?' Shatrughan grabbed his ears and touched Hrishi-da's feet. He hurriedly started doing his own make-up and getting ready. An assistant came to read out the dialogues for the scene. After reading the lengthy dialogues twice, Shatrughan went and stood in front of Hrishi-da, saying, 'I am ready.' After a brief rehearsal, Shatrughan delivered those long dialogues effortlessly, without missing a beat, earning applause from all of us. Later, while lighting a cigarette with him, I saluted him and gazed at him in awe. Laughing heartily, Shatrughan said, 'If I hadn't done even this much after arriving late, Dada would have stripped me down in front of everyone!' I had previously heard rumours of Hrishi-da's strict discipline, but that day, I saw a glimpse of its impact first-hand. As for my experience working with Shatrughan, it was a sheer delight to get to know someone as open-hearted and gregarious as him.

Naram Garam celebrated a silver jubilee. It won the 'Best Film' award and Utpal-da received the 'Best Actor in a Comic Role' award at the 1982 Filmfare Awards. In Hrishi-da's own words, 'Amol and Utpal are currently the most successful romantic pair.' Which was very well acknowledged by the industry!

What I treasure more than all the success Hrishi-da brought his crew and cast is what I learnt about film production from him. Hrishi-da surprised everyone by deciding to go to the Karnala Bird Sanctuary for shooting some scenes and a song for *Naram Garam.* In the evenings, after work, we—Hrishi-da, Hangal saab (A.K. Hangal) and I—used to have wonderful conversations. Both of them would share memories, good and bad, from their long careers in the industry. Hangal saab described interesting events from his time with the Indian People's Theatre Association (IPTA). Hrishi-da once shared how he had diligently, with proper homework and discipline, worked during the shooting of *Anari* (1959). Every morning, sharp at nine, Nutan would be ready on set with make-up and costume on. However, Raj Kapoor, another legend and her co-actor, would arrive at four in the afternoon as per his pre-agreed schedule. So, Hrishi-da and his unit would finish all of Nutan's scenes before lunchtime. Then, until Raj Kapoor came, they would take her close-ups and preference shots. By the time their joint scenes were ready to be shot, it would be six in the evening. Nutan would pack up and leave. After that, Raj Kapoor's preference shots were taken, and other work would continue until ten in the night. Raj Kapoor, when signing a contract, always gave a warning himself that he was an unaffordable actor. But once he had arrived on set at four in the evening, he would enthusiastically stay on without complaining until his work was done. Shooting such long hours daily, however, was a financial burden for the producer. Within the bounds of conventional filmmaking and aware of the pros and cons of casting superstars, Hrishi-da consciously avoided making grandiose mainstream films.

Hrishi-da always showered me with boundless love. I experienced this during the shooting of *Rang Birangi* as well. In 1983, I received a call from Hrishi-da. 'We need these specific dates for the first leg of shooting for four to five days.' When I said that I wouldn't be available on those dates, he pushed harder. He mentioned that Parveen Babi had taken back those dates from another producer and given them to him. He added, 'Whoever has your dates, I will personally request them to release you.' I felt uneasy with this, and to wriggle out of that awkward situation, I went directly to his house. Hrishi-da asked, 'Ammu, what's the problem?' I told him the truth without any hesitation. 'I'm going to watch a cricket match during those dates.' (This was a West Indies vs India match.) Hearing this, he laughed out loud and said, 'Is that all? We can watch it together on set. I'll arrange for a TV.' Indeed, we completed the shooting while watching the match on the set at Film City. In that atmosphere of bonhomie, gradually, even Parveen became comfortable around us.

In the middle of that shoot, Hrishi-da's gout became significantly more painful. Eventually, despite his reluctance, he had to undergo surgery. When I visited him in the orthopaedic hospital near Haji Ali, he was more worried about the upcoming shoot than his own health. Additionally, he had taken on the responsibility of pulling Parveen out of her depression. He confided in me that he was having doubts about continuing to work in such a stressful condition at his age.

Rang Birangi, based on a short story by Hindi writer Kamleshwar, seemed to be coming together well during its shooting, thanks to the stellar cast that included Farooq Shaikh, Deepti Naval, Deven

Rang Birangi (1983), with Parveen Babi

Verma, Utpal-da and Parveen Babi. However, when we watched the finished film, it didn't seem worthy of Hrishi-da's reputation. The shooting had doubtlessly been enjoyable. I liked Deepti from the beginning, both as an artiste and as a person. I loved her poems and paintings, especially her self-portraits. When she said, 'I'd like to work with you,' I brought her on board *Ankahee*, which I was planning to direct at the time. Due to Hrishi-da's worsening arthritis, much of *Rang Birangi* was shot with him seated, within the space he could manage to navigate. He insisted, 'Work as my assistant, Amol,' and I fulfilled that responsibility.

I knew Parveen from before *Rang Birangi* was made. Satyadev Dubey had taken me to her house once. Later, I took Badal-da to Film City to show him some shooting, and Parveen was also there waiting for the shooting of *The Burning Train*. Seeing Badal-da, she greeted him with folded hands. I knew that before her film career had taken off, she had worked in theatre. I learnt from Badal-da that she had played the lead role of Mansi in his play *Evam Indrajit*. For nearly two hours, she talked to him about his work. I listened in awe. That day, I saw her in a new light, as a sensitive and artistic person who loved the written word, but also couldn't help but notice her vulnerability too. During the outdoor shoot of *Rang Birangi*, she would retreat to a corner after her shot was done. I refrained from intentionally trying to coax her out of her shell. When she was in high spirits, the conversation would flow freely. Seeing her was like gazing upon Gustav Klimt's *The Kiss*, in which a gorgeous young woman, wrapped in shimmering gold, stands with her head bowed in a gesture of quiet reverence. Despite my best efforts to avoid feeling melancholic, the mere thought of Parveen causes a lump to rise in my throat.

Once, in 1984–85, Hrishi-da invited me home and inquired about the progress of my film *Ankahee*, the shooting of which was underway. Then, he mentioned wanting to start a film with Rekha, who was an absolute star. She had been disheartened by the rift between Amitabh and Hrishi-da after the failure of *Alaap*, and was now insisting on immediately starting work on *Jhoothi*, whose story Hrishi-da had chosen for her. Hrishi-da suggested I play her brother's role instead of the hero's. Although the role was small, my relationship with Hrishi-da was such that I could not say no to him. Moreover, the first chance to don a police officer's uniform and take on goons was enticing. Before the shoot commenced, I went to Mohan Studio to give measurements for the costumes. Bhutkar dada, who managed the wardrobe, told me a funny story. Once, when he had given Hangal saab his clothes, the latter had said, 'Oh bhai, I've worn these before in two or three films!' Bhutkar dada had replied, 'Don't you know Hrishi-da's habit? He casts only those actors who fit the clothes already in our wardrobe.' Back in the day, most heroes got their clothes tailored at the famous tailoring shop Kachins. Hrishi-da refused to follow that custom by giving all the costumes to his own tailor Madhav, who skilfully created costumes with fake Kachins labels!

Rekha, Raj Babbar, Deven Verma, Supriya Pathak and I formed the cast of *Jhoothi*. I had previously worked with Rekha and Raj Babbar in *Jeevan Dhaara* in 1982. Since I had very few scenes with them in both *Jhoothi* and *Jeevan Dhaara*, I didn't have the chance to get to know them. Before the shooting of *Jhoothi* began, Hrishi-da introduced me to Supriya with great affection, 'This is Dina-ben's younger daughter.' And to Supriya, he said, 'This is Ammu, my son.' Supriya knew I had worked with her mother in *Hayavadan* and with her aunt in *Pagla Ghoda*. I immediately noticed that she was a very capable actress. One day, after Hrishi-da had okayed a shot, Supriya requested Hrishi-da, 'Could you please do one more take?' I took this opportunity to explain to her a special method of Hrishi-da's. 'He will let you shoot a second take; then he will clap and say "Brilliant", but in the next instance, he will loudly say, "Print the first one."' Hrishi-da laughed heartily on hearing this and shot a retake for Supriya. During the making of *Jhoothi*, I was so preoccupied with my own directorial journey that my connection with the film was limited only to the extent of its actual shooting. The film was released in September 1985 and became a hit.

In 1996–97, when the Mumbai Academy of Moving Images (MAMI) was established, Hrishi-da was appointed as its chairman. Considering his stature in the industry and his experience in running organisations like NFDC and CBFC, MAMI was lucky to have got a very capable mentor. He played a major role in defining the festival's framework and rules. He issued firm instructions that sponsors from cigarette, tobacco and alcohol industries were not to be selected. However, due to his poor health, he couldn't attend the inaugural day. Throughout his career, Hrishi-da played a pivotal role as a guide and advisor on numerous governmental film-related committees.

He even offered extensive support to foster the growth of parallel cinema. Of the forty-two films he directed, only a few were unsuccessful. A few characteristics from his career stand out. In the first few films he made like *Musafir* (1957), *Anari* (1959), *Asli-Naqli* (1962), he worked with the reigning superstars of the time, Dilip Kumar, Raj Kapoor, Dev Anand, and in his later films, he worked with superstars like Amitabh Bachchan, Rajesh Khanna and Dharmendra. And yet, he never made a purely commercial film. Giving importance to small emotional moments in the lives of small characters, he made films that were 'middle of the road', landing somewhere between commercial Bollywood cinema and parallel cinema. He catapulted many new, small and big actors and technicians into the limelight. When he received the Dadasaheb Phalke Award in 1999 and the Padma Vibhushan in 2001, his triumph felt like my own personal triumph. In his eyes, I always saw paternal love reflected, something I had longed for all my life. It granted me a sense of belonging that had eluded me for years.

Jhoothi (1985), with Rekha

A fascinating pattern emerges when I think back to all the titans who have most profoundly influenced my artistic horizons and kindled my intellectual curiosity—all of them shared a common Bengali lineage. Badal Sircar, Basu-da, Hrishi-da, Utpal Dutt, Tapan Sinha, Sombhu Mitra, Biplab Roy Chowdhury—the entry and participation of such eminent artistes in my life shaped it and made it what it is today. Among them, I must also include veteran theatre persons such as Shyamanand Jalan and Pratibha Agarwal from Calcutta.

Basu-da and Hrishi-da never spoke about politics or said anything against the system. But Utpal-da had the spirit of a rebel; I identified with him on that count. He was associated with over forty plays, including *Angar*, *Kallol* and *Mahavidrohi*, in various capacities—writer, actor, director, producer. Utpal-da used the money he earned from mainstream cinema to support theatre; this aligned with my ideology. I, too, spent the money I earned from film acting on theatre. Many of Utpal-da's plays were banned by the West Bengal government, and in 1965, he was imprisoned on charges of sedition. The film-going audience might know him only as a comedian, but it is a very limited and one-sided view of him. It's a pity that the profound scope of Utpal-da's scholarliness became accessible to me very late, only during my stay in Calcutta while filming Biplab Roy Chowdhury's film *Spandan* (1982). After the shoot, I regularly attended the rehearsals of Utpal-da's plays.The rehearsals were inevitably followed by endless conversation, debates and much drinking.

But let me briefly go back to how I came to act in *Spandan*. In 1981, Biplab's *Shodh* won the Golden Lotus National Award. The film, featuring Om Puri and Sushma Tendulkar, was remarkable. Thereafter, Vijay Tendulkar introduced me to Biplab. My role in *Spandan* is one of my favourites. I played a man who had to face many challenges. Due to his financial struggles, my character had been forced to do the difficult job of selling aborted foetuses to laboratories. At home, he was caught up in an emotional tussle with his wife and daughter. Biplab handled this complex narrative in an extraordinarily sensitive manner. The screenplay had been written by Tendulkar, and the dialogues by Surendra Verma. Aparna Sen played my wife, Utpal Dutt played the lab owner buying the foetuses, and Anita Kanwar was the daughter—all three of them outstanding co-actors. Filming in the narrow lanes and slums of Calcutta introduced me to a new, unseen Bengali landscape—its poverty. The Bengali language is typically celebrated for its lyrical and poetic nature; however, while working on *Spandan*, I was exposed to its raw and unvarnished reality, the different tonalities it has outside of the sphere of storytelling. I witnessed a generation that could recite nearly every poem of Tagore's word for word and sing his songs collectively with passion. *Spandan*, made on a very tight budget, broadened and enriched my artistic consciousness. Despite other ongoing films, I gave priority to *Spandan*, completing it without charging a fee. In 1983, *Spandan* won the Silver Lotus

Ashray (1983), with Om Puri

National Award for 'Best Film'. My performance received a lot of praise internationally, but went largely unnoticed in India.

Afterwards, Biplab offered me the lead role in *Ashray* (1983). By then, we had developed a strong friendship, which remained intact until his passing. It was deeply painful to see the end of this man, who, unlike Utpal-da and me, initially did not drink, but ultimately succumbed to alcoholism. While discussing the script of *Ashray*, I noticed his occasional distraction, but ignored it and continued the conversation. During the shoot in Bhubaneswar, I realised that Biplab would start drinking secretly from morning itself. We somehow managed to complete *Ashray*. Whether it was ever released, I don't recall clearly.

In 2007, while making the series *Krishnakali* for Doordarshan, which was shot entirely in Kolkata, I insisted on roping in Biplab, hoping his involvement in the project would take his attention away from drinking. Unfortunately, I failed.

At the very beginning of my career in theatre, the actor who influenced me the most was none other than Sombhu Mitra. In the late 1960s, Sombhu-da announced his retirement from the stage. To mark this occasion, the Indian National Theatre (INT) organised a festival of his plays at the Ravindra Natya Mandir in Bombay. The festival featured some of his most celebrated plays, *Putul Khela* (Doll's House), *Raktakarabi* (Red Oleanders), *Oedipus* (Oedipus Rex) and *Pagla Ghoda*. Watching these productions, performed by Sombhu-da and his wife Tripti Mitra, was a feast for the senses. During the live performance of *Oedipus*, Sombhu-da's effortless movements, especially his agility in navigating the eight or ten steps up and down on the stage, seemed incredible for someone in his mid-sixties. He had just undergone a cataract surgery, yet his energy on stage was remarkable. The thunderous standing ovation he received from the enraptured audience included my own enthusiastic applause.

As I headed home after watching *Oedipus*, my mind was abuzz with thoughts. Sombhu-da's wrinkled face and impaired vision were nowhere to be found in the character he portrayed on stage. His performance had convinced the audience that he was a young, vibrant prince. But what if the same performance had been filmed? The camera would have captured every wrinkle, and his ageing body would have been apparent. It was at that moment that I realised the unique magic of theatre. As a captivated audience member, I was willing to deceive myself while watching theatre. Sombhu-da, in his sixties, appeared to me as though he were in his thirties. This delightful deception, this enchanting exchange, was possible only in the live moments of theatre. Over time, I continued to experience this magic again and again. Yamunabai Waikar, with her ordinary appearance and stout body, would transform into a seductive diva while she performed Lavani on stage. Kelucharan Mahapatra, with his frail physique, would become an irresistible enchantress, seducing a man with his dance. A great Kathakali dancer like Raghavan Nair could depict scenes from *Putana Vadh* (The Killing of Putana) without make-up, costumes or elaborate lighting, making it feel like a lived experience. Such is the spellbinding nature of theatre—a living dialogue between two living, breathing beings.

This awareness came to me because of Sombhu-da. Once, while discussing his performance at his home in Calcutta, I asked him, 'Why did you walk on stage by lifting your heels and giving a slight push? It created a noticeable springy action.' His face lit up as he replied, 'It's wonderful that you noticed. The prince had his feet bound with thorns during his childhood, which left him with a lingering weakness. I adapted my walk to depict that.' I was stunned. He made me realise the importance of putting thought into essaying a role. Moreover, he taught me that a great actor makes the audience believe that what happens on stage is happening for the first time, even though it has been rehearsed and scripted.

Years later, Fritz Bennewitz expressed a desire to stage *Galileo* with Sombhu-da, bringing him back to the stage. The evening before the ticket sales began, people started queuing up on the pavement outside the venue of Ravindra Sadan. The crowd was so huge that the tickets sold out within an hour, necessitating the announcement of additional shows. I met Sombhu-da before that performance.

In 1970, he was awarded with the Padma Bhushan and in 1976 with the Ramon Magsaysay Award.

When this unparalleled artiste passed away, he left behind a humble request: that his body not be put on public display, draped in flowers or paraded in a procession, and that only his close family members attend the funeral. The Bengali community honoured his final wish. Inspired by his modesty, I too have outlined my own final wishes in a similar manner.

As I look back on the love and respect I received from extraordinary individuals like Sombhu-da, I am filled with a profound sense of gratitude and fulfilment.

Another majestic personality similar to Sombhu-da was Tapan Sinha. His direction of *Aadmi Aur Aurat* (1984) remains a golden chapter in my life. I deeply cherish my role in the film. I had watched Tapan-da's earlier Bengali films like *Atithi* and *Shiulibari*. On Dilip Kumar's insistence, he had directed the Bengali film *Sagina* in Hindi as well. When he offered me a role, I immediately accepted. Given that it was a Doordarshan production, I assumed that there would be no significant remuneration. This beautifully crafted film did not reach as wide an audience as it deserved. Even today, it pains me that my performance in *Aadmi Aur Aurat* remains largely unseen, stowed away in some government archive.

In the film, I played a rogue from a small village, a man with a penchant for preying on helpless women. When he discovers that one of the women he targeted is pregnant, his initial rage turns into a desperate effort to take her to the hospital. After ensuring her safe delivery, he bids her farewell with a simple *'Ae Aurat!'* (Hey, woman). This unique love story was shot in the forested regions along the Bengal–Bihar border. One sequence required shooting in the rain. As we couldn't afford a rain machine, we would prepare everything and wait each day for real rain showers. At sunset, we would return to the guest house.

Most of the shooting was completed in the first schedule itself; the editing was also done. In the second schedule, we also finished dubbing. While filming the final scene at the hospital, where I bid farewell to the 'woman', I couldn't bring myself to shed tears, not even with glycerine. After five or six retakes, Tapan-da finally settled on an 'OK' shot. I wasn't satisfied, though. Despite my persistent requests for more takes, Tapan-da announced 'pack up' for the day. That night, I couldn't sleep at all. The next day, I arrived, prepared for the new scenes to be shot with doctors and hospital staff, only to be surprised by Tapan-da who suggested, 'Let's redo yesterday's scene.' I was taken aback. With a wink, he said, 'I can't wrap up the shooting with my protagonist dissatisfied!' I was so moved by his kindness that, for the retake, I didn't need anything else to bring tears to my eyes. In 1984, *Aadmi Aur Aurat* won the National Award for Best Film.

Tapan-da's mastery over cinematic language and his skill at delving right into the essence of the script and creating a film without any frills were exceptional. He reaffirmed the idea that a director's gentle handling is crucial for getting good performances out of actors.

During the shooting of *Aadmi Aur Aurat*, my co-star Mahua Roy Choudhury, who played the 'woman', and I developed an emotional bond, something Tapan-da probably sensed. After the dubbing was done, on the last day of the shoot, Mahua prepared a special Bengali meal and insisted that Tapan-da and I join her. Just before I finally left, she hugged me tightly, standing silently for a long time. Just days later, Tapan-da called with the shocking news of her suicide. What had happened in her life to drive her to such an end? The most painful part was that she never spoke to me about her inner turmoil. Was life so unbearable that she couldn't bear to live it anymore? Looking back, I realise that if she had lived, I might have become closer to her.

Later, Tapan-da invited me to act in *Ek Doctor Ki Maut*, but I was neck-deep in the shooting of my film *Thodasa Roomani Ho Jaayen* and couldn't match his dates. Nonetheless, his love for me never diminished. In his final days, when I visited him, he held my hand tightly with his wrinkled, trembling hands and, in his British accent, said, 'Thank you, Amol, for everything.' I'm still humbled by that gesture and also puzzled as to why someone who gave me so much would express gratitude towards me, when I'm the one who's forever in his debt.

Even today, when I visit Kolkata, my steps naturally turn towards the Tollygunge Club. I linger in Tapan-da's favourite courtyard, reminiscing about our conversations and shared memories there, especially the one time I narrated the screenplay of *Kairee* to him. With a heart full of these golden moments, I eventually leave.

Basu-da, Hrishi-da, Tapan-da, Sombhu-da, Utpal-da and Biplab are not around anymore, but the impact they had on my life will remain with me forever. Tomorrow, I will also depart, but the films we created together will remain, a lasting testament to our friendship and a comforting reminder that a part of all of us will endure.

Badal Sircar was very different from the people in the film industry. He was a highly sensitive playwright and a fiercely committed theatre activist. The rebellious undertones in his plays stemmed from his immense love and concern for the oppressed classes. In 1966, the Maharashtra state government had established a committee for infrastructure and urban development. Badal-da had been appointed to the post of an urban engineer by the union government, which frequently brought him to Bombay. After work, he would naturally gravitate towards theatre folks. One day, Dubey introduced me to him as the translator of his play *Vallabhpurchi Dantkatha.* The Pune-based theatre activist Rajabhau Natu invited Badal-da to Pune to familiarise the local theatre artistes with him. I drove him to Pune, and during that journey, we smoked countless cigarettes, and the conversations that began on that trip continued for the next thirty-five years, even after I had quit smoking!

I owe the opportunity of working on Badal-da's plays to Dubey. This creative journey has been chronicled in various parts of this book. Badal-da's writing was so rich with possibilities that one layer opened up countless others. Compared to writers who wouldn't allow even a dot to be changed, Badal-da's openness was monumental.

In the 1970s, moving away from urban settings, he started taking theatre to villages. During the Emergency, plays like *Julus* and *Teesri Shatabdi* (Third Century) sparked a unique movement. Through plays like *Basi Khaabar* (Stale Food) and *Bhoma* (Bomb), he ignited a rebellion against the government. Witnessing his performance with his comrades early in the morning at Curzon Park during the initial days of the Emergency was awe-inspiring. There was no stage, no set, no lights, yet the surrounding noise faded away, and the growing circle of police officers on horseback around the audience didn't distract anyone. Eventually, the police left. Badal-da's writing, challenging urban middle class stagnation through allegories, still resonates deeply with many. He firmly believed that 'surviving enables everything'. He established the 'Third Theatre' by taking art to rural and oppressed communities, distancing himself from commercial or mainstream theatre and theatre artistes. He was cast into an isolated, different world.

In 2004, I received a call from Kolkata with the shocking news that Badal-da had been hit by a truck and was seriously injured. My local friends in Kolkata had no additional information. I was deeply disturbed and flew directly to his home the next day. He had just returned from the nursing home. Seeing his dire condition, I worried about who would care for him at home and realised he couldn't afford to stay at the nursing home. I had witnessed first-hand how society treated those who refused to conform and instead chose to forge their own path. Feeling distressed, I called Sandhya, who immediately said, 'Give me his bank account details; I'll send money right away.' But I knew Badal-da's self-respect and pride would prevent him from accepting help that might be perceived as charity or debt. I sat beside him, feeling deeply unsettled. I had never seen him so defeated. Then, I thought of an idea: 'We want to organise a festival of your plays. Would you accept a tribute from Marathi theatre artistes and astute Marathi audiences? And you must accept the proceeds from ticket sales too.' He happily agreed.

'If you need to come to Pune for this, you must get well soon. A male nurse will stay here with you for a month to take care of you.' He accepted my plea. I hired a good nurse, instructing him to care for Badal-da as his own father.

After that, Badal-da's spirits lifted considerably. In August 2004, he came to Pune with great excitement and stayed for a while. Luminaries like Amrish Puri, Naseer–Ratna, Vijay Tendulkar, Dubey, Nana Patekar, Shyamanand Jalan, Kulbhushan Kharbanda, Pratibha Agarwal, Jaydev–Rohini Hattangadi, Mahesh Elkunchwar and many others joined this extraordinary event. Sandhya organised a packed three-day festival. On the last day, I staged *Julus* with young men and women from Pune's Jagar group. Badal-da's eightieth birthday was grandly celebrated during this festival of his plays, and he was handed a generous purse of money. With a tinge of sadness and a sense of gratitude, he remarked, 'Though Bengal's audience didn't recognise my contributions, I've been fortunate to receive appreciation from Marathi viewers.'

To invite Puri saab for a reading of *Evam Indrajit* at the Badal-da festival, I had called him. About three decades ago, under Dubey's direction, he had played the role of the 'Writer' most impressively in *Evam Indrajit*. Dubey himself had played Indrajit with intense emotion, yet Puri saab, with his understated acting, had stolen the show every time as the 'Writer' when standing before Dubey. Puri saab did lead roles such as Sukhatme in *Chup! Court Chalu Hai,* the narrator in *Suno Janmejay* and the four men in *Aadhe Adhure*. I acted in those plays alongside Puri saab. However, when Dubey asked me to play Devdutt opposite Puri saab's Kapil in *Hayavadan*, I felt utterly demoralised. At the time, my voice was thin and high-pitched. Every time Puri saab spoke, I would become so enthralled by his voice and delivery that my own energy would diminish. I would hesitate to open my mouth on stage before him. When I shared this with Dubey, he pointed out a quality within me: I had an intuitive sense of which words in a sentence to emphasise on and how to modulate my voice accordingly. 'Use that well. And fight,' Dubey instructed, and my deflated spirit got reinvigorated.

'Hello, Amol, kaise ho?' I heard over the phone when I called Puri saab. After listening to the concept and outline of the Badal Sircar festival, he agreed without a second's hesitation, but on the condition that the rehearsals be held at his Juhu home. Accordingly, Rohini Hattangadi, Mohan Bhandari and I conducted two or three reading rehearsals at his place. On the day of the event, this formidable man arrived as promised, wearing his hat. Instead of reading the last poem of the play, Puri saab put aside the papers, rose from his chair, and stepped forward onto the stage.

इसीलिए तो इस पथ का मैं अंत नही पाता
नहीं कोई आश्वास कि यात्रा के पूरी होने पर कोई देवलोक सम्मुख होगा
या स्नेहस्पर्श से पथश्रम कोई दूर करेगा...
...इसी पथ पर है चलना, इष्ट यही, गंतव्य यही।

Though I don't see the end of this road,
Though heaven is not assured at that end,
Nor a promise offered
To make me forget these aching feet,
I have to follow the same path,
As it is meant to be the goal.

As he breathed life into this grand poem, his powerful voice reverberated inside the hall. The audience was deeply moved, rising to their feet in a spontaneous standing ovation. This outburst of applause occurred even before the curtains had closed. A moment later, behind the closed curtains, this towering man crumbled to the floor as if all his strength had left him. When I rushed to his side, he embraced me tightly, sobbing like a child. Two days later, we learnt that he had been admitted to the Cooper Hospital in Mumbai for cancer treatment. Sandhya and I immediately went to see him. Seeing Puri saab so weak and fragile filled me with a deep sense of sadness. His son later told me that during the rehearsals at his house and just before the last performance, he had strictly instructed the family not to tell anyone about his condition. That same week, Puri saab passed away.

For days, I remained lost in thought. I remembered the first time I had seen that emperor of the stage, whose commanding presence did not require the crutches of any frills or elaborate costumes. With the confident stride of a seasoned dancer, he commanded the stage, his presence illuminating the dark backdrop. As his rich, powerful voice boomed through the open theatre, the audience erupted into instant applause, captivated by his charisma. This was in 1967, when I was fortunate enough to witness the first performance of the play *Yayati* at Rang Bhavan in Bombay's Dhobi Talao area. This was young playwright Girish Karnad's first play, directed by the budding director Satyadev Dubey for the Indian National Theatre (INT). It was vastly different from the typical Marathi plays I had seen until then, which were narratives written to suit the box sets (sets with a proscenium arch stage and three walls) and leaned towards over-the-top performances replete with theatrical exaggeration. That day, I was simply mesmerised by Puri saab's commanding presence.

From then on, I met him regularly for rehearsals. In the evenings, he would bring hot samosas and jalebis for everyone from the Kailash

Parbat restaurant near his office in Colaba. He had taken it upon himself to spoil us all. When we toured for shows, he planned every detail with great attention and care. Initially, Puri saab used to arrive on his Royal Enfield. One day, Dubey lost his balance and fell off his brand new Vespa scooter and got injured. Dubey promptly attached a sidecar to his scooter and gifted it to me. Dubey insisted that Puri saab also get a sidecar for his Royal Enfield, which he did, and used regularly.

The countless memories we created together over three decades run deep, shaping the person I have become. I am aware that my sense of self is inextricably linked to these shared experiences, and I am utterly grateful for the impact they've had on my life.

It's impossible to measure how great Puri saab was as a co-actor. Despite my being much younger and less experienced than him, Puri saab never once undermined my authority as the director when I was directing *Pagla Ghoda* in 1970, simultaneously in both Hindi and Marathi. At the beginning of the rehearsals, I told him, 'Kartik the compounder's personality is that of a poor man who blends in with the crowd. Will you …' He interrupted me, saying, 'Believe me, Amol, I will give you exactly the Kartik you want, one who will easily disappear into the crowd.' And true to his word, by merely changing his body language, he transformed into a humble compounder. At a particularly delicate juncture in the play, I had envisioned a long pause, just after the other male characters confessed to their past sins. I asked Puri saab to hum a tune during the pause. Having heard him sing K.L. Saigal's songs before, I suggested he hum '*Babul Mora*' in every performance of *Pagla Ghoda*. Each time, not only the audience but also the fellow actors on stage would get emotional listening to his powerful voice. I later heard that Dubey, in his own way, had praised me behind my back for this idea; though to my face he had simply said, 'Find a good singer for Kartik's role in the Marathi version as well!'

Today's generation may know Amrish Puri only as the actor with menacing eyes, who roared *'Mogambo khush hua!'* or shouted *'Ja, Simran, Ja!'*. Thanks to Google, some might be aware of his exquisite performances in movies of parallel cinema like *Kalyug, Nishant, Bhumika, Suraj Ka Satvan Ghoda*—but have they taken the time to actually watch those performances? This actor who fully utilised his imposing presence to dominate the stage, and who cared deeply for his co-actors, will forever remain in the hearts of those like me who had the privilege of knowing him closely. But after we are all gone ... Time will inevitably consign us all to oblivion ... the sands of time will slowly bury all these legacies, leaving none to remember.

'Waqt ki dhoop mein yaadein bhi pighal jaati hain, mujhko bhi log bhula denge fasaane ki tarah' (Memories melt under the heat of the sun of time, people will forget me too like a tale). I have come to terms with the fact that I will also be forgotten eventually. When I realise this about other people, it hurts me. However, it comforts me to know that my beloved musicians and their music will live on, transcending time. Every day, at some point, their names are heard and revived—Kishori Amonkar's classical melodies, Asha Bhosle's playful or sorrowful notes, the timeless compositions of Jaidev-ji ... All of this will endure, like the priceless shells, pearls and conches left behind by the receding waves of the sea. Hopefully, future generations will continue to gather and cherish this treasure.

When Jaidev-ji passed away in 1987, someone wrote, 'Jaidev lived to suffer and suffered to live.' That's exactly how I felt about his life. It was heart breaking to see a talented music director like Jaidev Verma, who gave us over three hundred exquisite songs, living in a small room sans basic amenities. When I first saw this with my own eyes, I was shocked. He was living in the ground-floor apartment of a building in an alley near K.C. College in Churchgate. It seemed as though the industry had cast him aside. There was not even a phone in his house; a car was out of the question! He followed a strict routine, spending his mornings composing with lyricists and singers, while afternoons were spent in recordings.

My first meeting with him was when two songs of *Gharaonda* were to be recorded with Runa Laila, who had gained considerable fame in Bangladesh. Rehearsals for '*Do diwane sheher mein*' with Bhupinder Singh began. Gulzar saab had shortened the word 'aasmani' to fit the metre. So I proposed adding a conversational tone to the lyrics to acknowledge and play with that creative liberty. Both Jaidev-ji and director Bhim Sain Khurana liked the idea so much that they incorporated a similar interrogatory tone into the second verse with the line '*Jab tare zameen par*'.

Despite the commercial failures of films like *Wohi Baat* (earlier titled *Sameera*), *Amar Milan* and *Solva Sawan* (the music for which was composed by Jaidev-ji), the experience of witnessing his creative journey catapulted my own artistic evolution. Jaidev-ji, the maestro, had granted me the unique privilege of visiting him during the early hours of the morning, a time he usually reserved only for himself. One morning, he shared with me a tune he had composed for the song *Zindagi Mere Ghar Aana* for the film *Dooriyaan*. I had been offered a lead role in the movie. The song was beautiful, and his spontaneous joy in creating that melody was infectious. But it created a dilemma in my mind. I had refused to sign *Dooriyaan* due to a disagreement with its producer-director, Bhim Sain. When I broke this news to Jaidev-ji, he sat quietly, reflecting for a while. He looked disappointed. Eventually, he reassured me, 'No worries, Maharaj, But do keep visiting.'

Over time, I made frequent visits to Jaidev-ji's house, working on various projects. Many evenings were spent with him, as he poured his heart out over his favourite whiskey. He shared stories of being sidelined in the industry, how he had been removed by his mentor from projects, how many had taken advantage of him by offering meagre payments, and how he had often been denied credit for his compositions. He allowed me into the deep recesses of his emotional world, where his pain was palpable. I often wondered why he endured all this. Perhaps this suffering was what fuelled his creativity. Stories kept trickling in from the outside—stories like how he was replaced in the film *Guide* or how he had left the film *Umrao Jaan* despite having composed ten songs for it.

I vividly remember working with Jaidev-ji and director Kantilal Rathod on the film *Ram Nagari* (1982). One day, Jaidev-ji excitedly introduced me to a young singer with the name Hariharan, saying, 'He's very talented; he'll make a name for himself.' The young man blushed at the praise. Kantibhai requested my help in filming the song that was sung by Hariharan. We had a blast shooting it in various styles: some scenes in traditional mythological costumes, some in a round trolley shot favoured by Dev Anand, and some with my co-actress Suhasini Mule riding pillion on a motorcycle. The beautiful bhajan '*Main toh kabse teri sharan mein hoon*' was recorded with Hariharan and a new female singer. However, Jaidev-ji was visibly upset because the female singer couldn't match the magic that Hariharan had brought to the tune. Later that evening, Jaidev-ji confided his displeasure in me, admitting that he had only allowed her to sing at the insistence of his close friend. His eyes welled up slightly as he handed me his empty glass, asking, 'What should I do, Maharaj?'

During the making of *Ankahee,* Jaidev-ji and I spent hours having long discussions. Instead of composing new songs, I suggested that we use traditional songs for certain scenes, to which he agreed. He immediately quoted Kabir's '*Kaun thagwa nagariya lootal ho*', and said, 'But, I'll give it a completely different form, Maharaj!' We agreed that Asha Bhosle would also sing the other song, '*Mujhko bhi Radha bana le Nandalal*'. When I approached her, she readily agreed, but on two conditions—there would be at least three rehearsals before the recording, and that she would personally visit Jaidev-ji for those rehearsals.

We decided to record at the Western Outdoor Studio across from the Coffee House in the Fort area. On the morning of the recording, Asha-bai's secretary called to inform me that Asha-bai was running a fever of 102 degrees and couldn't come for the recording. Since Jaidev-ji didn't have a phone, I rushed to the studio to inform him. He heard the news but continued working silently. Pandit Hariprasad Chaurasia, Pandit Shivkumar Sharma and Vidushi Zarin Daruwala had already arrived and were tuning their instruments. According to the rules of the Musicians' Association, even if the recording didn't happen, the musicians had to be paid if they had marked their attendance. After two rehearsals with the orchestra, Jaidev-ji asked me to check on Asha-bai's health. I quickly scribbled a note to her: 'Cancelling the recording would be too costly. Please advise.' Chitra took the note to Prabhukunj, Asha-bai's residence. An hour later, Asha-bai arrived at the studio, wrapped in a shawl. She went straight to the booth, stood before the mic and said, 'Shall we start?' I stood there, holding my breath. As the immortal words of Kabir

Ankahee (1985), with Asha Bhosle

merged with Jaidev-ji's heart-wrenching tune, I saw tears streaming down his face. He entered the booth and hugged her. She bowed and took her leave, but not before pausing at the door to tell me, 'Bring the cassette home this evening'. That evening, I visited her, and she listened to her song sitting in her bedroom, eyes closed. After a while, I broached the subject of payment. She held my hand, made me sit and said, 'I was fortunate to get such a song, Amol. It came to me because of you; the matter ends there.' I sat there, speechless and humbled.

I later realised how much Asha-bai revered Jaidev-ji. One morning, the doorbell of my home Chirebandi rang. I opened the door to find Asha-bai standing there. 'Jaidev-ji had recorded a song for you in my voice, I remember,' she said, humming the tune. I reminded her of the lullaby *'More naina, jage saari raina'* from *Footpath*, and she was pleased to hear that. She didn't have the original recording, so I immediately offered her my cassette. Years later, when she recorded the song for a tribute album to Jaidev-ji, she graciously acknowledged my contribution.

While working on my film *Ankahee*, Jaidev-ji suggested we approach Pandit Bhimsen Joshi for two bhajans. When I called Pandit-ji, he said he would be in Bombay on a particular day and suggested to meet him at the airport. Standing in the parking lot, he mentioned he wasn't particularly interested in singing for films anymore. But he agreed to sing when he learnt it was Jaidev-ji's wish. He touched his earlobe in reverence and asked for more details regarding the film. Jaidev-ji too was thrilled. A few days later, he invited me over and played a soulful bhajan based on Tulsidas' '*Raghuvar tumko meri laaj*'. I was overjoyed and held his hand, but he stopped me, saying, '… and the second one is ready too, Maharaj. Listen to this.' He then played '*Thumak thumak pag dumak kunj madhu, chapal charan Hari aaye*'. He added that he had finalised the lyrics with Bal Kavi Bairagi, and asked me to complete the formalities with him.

A few days later, in the most humble manner, Pandit-ji sat down with Jaidev-ji at Chirebandi to rehearse the two bhajans. Soon after, the bhajans were recorded at the studio, one in the morning and the other in the evening. A rather amusing incident took place when Pandit-ji, finding himself unable to sing comfortably within the confines of the recording booth, apologised for the inconvenience. This led to some last-minute scrambling on our part. However, Jaidev-ji, remaining calm as always, arranged for the session to be held in the larger room used for the orchestra. Esteemed musicians like Hari-ji and Shiv-ji contributed, helping us set everything up. They even refused any overtime pay for the delay. I was deeply grateful to all of them.

In 1985, both Jaidev-ji and Pandit-ji were honoured with the National Award for *Ankahee*. When I visited Jaidev-ji's home to congratulate him, he fed me sweets with his own hands and blessed

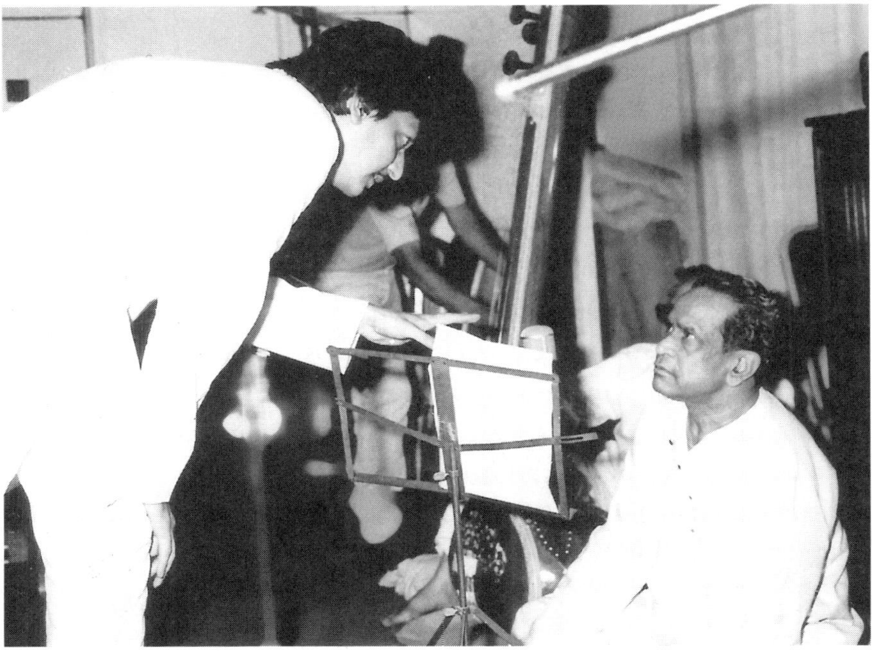

Ankahee (1985), with Pt. Bhimsen Joshi

me with the words, 'May all your wishes come true.' That blessing has stayed with me forever.

However, just two years later, I had to bid farewell to that extraordinary individual who affectionately called me 'Maharaj'. That jinxed genius left this world in 1987. I continue to take pride in my unwavering decision to work with Jaidev-ji as the music director for my first directorial film *Footpath*. I steadfastly refused to replace him despite pressure from the producer. In fact, I did walk away from that film later.

कभी ख़ुद पे कभी हालात पे रोना आया,
बात निकली तो हर इक बात पे रोना आया।
किस लिए जीते हैं हम किस के लिए जीते हैं,
बारहा ऐसे सवालात पे रोना आया।

We weep sometimes for ourselves,
sometimes for our circumstances
Now that the conversation has started,
we end up crying over everything
What do we live for, and for whom do we live
These eternal questions have often moved me to tears.

Every time I hear these soulful melodies, I hear the echoes of Jaidev-ji's own sorrow, as if his personal pain was distilled into the notes. The same overwhelming feeling grips me when I immerse myself in the poignant notes of Raag Basanti Kedar, Huseini Todi, Rageshri, Bhimpalasi, or any other soul-stirring raga sung by Tai (the legendary Kishori Amonkar). Eight years have passed since she left us, yet I have not become fully accustomed to her absence, because even now she remains deeply ingrained in my consciousness, forever rooted in my awareness. The day she passed away, I was in the hospital for my own surgery. The wound from the surgery has long since healed, but the pain of her absence can only be soothed by listening to her immortal recordings.

This extraordinary artiste, decorated with honours like the Padma Vibhushan and Gaan Saraswati, and blessed with a divine voice, expanded her inheritance from Maai (her mother, the great Mogubai Kurdikar) using her own intellect. Rumours and gossip about her life may have swirled within our Marathi art circle, but they never managed to tarnish the profound bond I shared with her music, which remains unblemished and pure. Thanks to Sandhya, I was able to grasp the intricate nuances and details of the grammar of Tai's music. Perhaps Tai sensed my deep love for her music, which is why, once, with tears in her eyes, she took my hand and made me promise, 'You must not leave me until the very end.'

I first met Tai in person in the 1970s at Khopoli, while on the way to Pune. As we were enjoying some batata vada, she asked, 'Who is Mohanrao Palekar to you?' I quickly replied, 'He is my uncle.' I learnt then that Maai had sent Tai to study under him. Perhaps it was this connection that forged a bond between us. Another time, Tai lovingly invited me, 'Would you compere Maai's eightieth birthday celebrations?' I immediately agreed.

With relentless passion and dedication, Tai navigated the challenges of her career in music. Undeterred by criticism, she continued to push boundaries, offering fresh perspectives through her craft. Even though she often searched for the perfect notes, to her listeners, her voice was a gateway to bliss, effortlessly evoking feelings of euphoria and transcendence.

One morning, I got a call from her. She asked, 'Would you be interested in making a documentary on my life? I would actually prefer it if you were the one to do it.' I was taken aback; I had never imagined receiving such a proposal. Before this, many, including her friend Vijaya Mehta, had tried to make a documentary on Tai, but all efforts had remained incomplete. Knowing her strong-willed and demanding nature, before agreeing to collaborate, I put a condition that except for financial assistance, she would provide me with all the necessary resources and support to ensure the project's successful completion. True to her word, she stood by me and Sandhya. She joined us for the filming wherever we requested, even allowing us to record special renditions of a few ragas. We captured Tai singing bhajans in the small stone temple in Kurdi village, singing Raga Bhoop inside the ancient black stone temple of Tambdi Surla in Goa, and sitting in the dilapidated courtyard of her ancestral home, remembering with tears in her eyes her mother, Maai, who had been a strict disciplinarian. We were also able to use some rare audio-visual footage, although Tai herself did not offer any rare or exclusive photographs or recordings to us from her personal archives.

For Tai's eightieth birthday, Sandhya planned a unique tribute, 'Sahela Re'. Inspired by Tai's lofty concept of uniting different musical styles to pay homage to the massive ocean that is Indian classical music, we brought together nearly thirty-two maestros of Hindustani classical and Carnatic music on one stage in an unprecedented event. This performance was a novel experiment in seeing how one raga could be sung or rendered differently across different gharanas, even while retaining its essence. On behalf of the overflowing audience at Pune's Ganesh Kala Krida Manch, we presented Tai with a gift of five lakh rupees through the hands of Ustad Zakir Hussain.

After the completion of the documentary on her life, *Bhinna Shadja* (Note Extraordinaire), a private screening was held at Tai's residence first. It was attended by her children, grandchildren and a few disciples. After watching the entire documentary, Tai rushed to the kitchen, her eyes filled with tears. Afterwards, she lovingly served us a homemade dessert. When Sandhya bent down to touch her feet, Tai stopped her and hugged her tightly, while gently caressing both my cheeks.

Tai's magnificent legacy spanned over sixty years. Sandhya and I are fortunate that she allowed us to express our deepest gratitude for the countless moments of bliss and fulfilment that her art had given us.

Sandhya and I will forever cherish this opportunity that fell into our laps.

We had kept Marathi as the original language of the documentary, while also dubbing it in Hindi, in the melodious and soothing voice of Kalapini Komkali. This allowed viewers to watch the documentary in Marathi or Hindi, along with English subtitles. With Tai's fan base spanning the globe, we prioritised language accessibility to guarantee that cultural and linguistic differences didn't hinder the connection between her music and her diverse audience.

Throughout the time I spent with her while shooting the documentary, I was aware of her restlessness, and of a certain bitterness she carried within her. Her fiery personality, pragmatic nature, cautious approach and sceptical outlook were incongruous with the sublime music that flowed from her. I had a certain degree of difficulty in understanding this paradox between her art and her persona. Sandhya, however, saw these traits as a natural defence

Bhinna Shadja (2011), with Gaan Saraswati Kishori Amonkar and Sandhya Gokhale

mechanism, a protective armour that Tai had developed as a result of her tough life experiences, to shield herself from further pain and vulnerability. Despite our differing perspectives, Sandhya and I worked in tandem. Compiling Tai's interviews was very challenging. All our attempts to persuade Tai to deposit her extensive collection of concert recordings with a trusted organisation dedicated to preserving cultural heritage remained unsuccessful, leaving the long-term fate of these valuable recordings uncertain. We could have digitised and shared those recordings online. But she remained steadfast in her decision, saying, 'I will not do this for free.'

The documentary ends with an image of ripples being drawn in sand, accompanied by a poem recited by me and written by Sandhya. The lines aimed to express her inner conflict, the inner anguish she constantly struggled to conceal.

उद्या मी गेले की एक नक्की म्हणा -
तिने स्वरांची कूस कधी सोडली नाही,
त्या अस्पर्शी 'सा'ची आसही सोडली नाही,
आंदण मिळालेल्या क्षणांची प्रतारणाही केली नाही.

Tomorrow, when I am gone,
Let it be known -
She never strayed from the path of music.
She never let go of her yearning for the purity of the note "Sa",
Nor did she ever betray the moments gifted to her.

Even those who were Tai's critics would agree with this description of her.

After weathering many storms, I have arrived at this juncture in my life, having endured numerous chapters. But the reflections from these memories continue to shine brightly within me.

Time has taken its toll on my close friends, leaving only one still by my side: Haider Ali. But even he has grown a bit weary now. Throughout his life, Haider has had to fight many battles. Despite only being educated up to the eighth grade, he possesses a sharp mind. And his heart is full of compassion. His mother, Pramila, was a renowned actress and producer in the male-dominated film industry of the 1930s. In 1947, she was honoured as India's first beauty queen. She had great affection for me. She would often proudly remark, 'He is a blue-blooded boy.' She even played a small role, of a grandmother, in my film *Thaang* at the age of eighty-nine. Sadly, she passed away just a few months later.

Haider's father, Kumar, was a famous actor of his time, but he moved to Pakistan after the Partition. Pramila stayed behind. Haider grew up as the odd one out among three brothers and a sister. During his formative years, Haider struggled with impulsiveness and aggression, leaving a number of people with physical injuries. Once, when some local thugs tried to harass his sister, Haider jumped straight from the first floor to confront them. His combative nature has somewhat mellowed over time, and he has managed to maintain many friendships, thanks to the inherent kindness that resides within him. His wife, Uma, has played a significant role in preserving and nurturing that kindness.

Uma, a Tamil Brahmin by birth, grew up in a household steeped in orthodox traditions. Yet, when it came to her marriage with a Muslim, there was surprisingly little opposition. What was the reason? Haider, driven by his deep love for her, not only gave up eating meat but also vowed to honour her religious beliefs—a promise he has faithfully kept to this day. Even now, Uma (a renowned paediatrician in Mumbai, known for her quiet demeanour and calm presence), relying solely on her own accomplishments, bears the entire financial responsibility of their household. Looking back, it seems as though she effortlessly took on the daunting challenge of living with someone as eccentric as Haider. But it goes beyond that: she didn't just live with him, she transformed him. She taught him to think deeply, to reflect. Calming a volcano would have been an easier task, yet she succeeded in doing it. The fact that Haider did change is a testament to the power of her influence. Throughout their life together, Haider has cherished Uma and their two daughters with extraordinary tenderness. From cooking meals to braiding his daughters' hair and seeing them off to school, he has embraced every household responsibility with alacrity. Haider embodies a true feminist spirit, and that fills me with pride.

Our nearly five-decade-long friendship began around 1975, when one day out of nowhere, Haider turned up at my home in Gamdevi. He wanted to direct a Marathi film called *Brahman, Kshatriya, Vaishya, Shudra.* The concept seemed interesting to me—it wasn't about the hierarchy of the caste system but about the four stages in every person's life. Before this, he had made a short film and a Hindi movie as well. Since I have always been eager to work with new directors, I agreed. After just four or five days of shooting, Haider had to shut down the shooting due to financial difficulties.

Then in 1985, Haider and Dilip Dhawan (the lead actor from the popular television series *Nukkad*), decided to co-direct a Hindi film called *Kal.* It was the Indian adaptation of Hollywood's *To Sir, with Love*. During the shooting, I had a major disagreement with Haider. A romantic song sequence was being filmed at Bandstand. In the sequence, my co-star and I were supposed to be walking, deep in conversation, while a song played in the background. After five or six takes, Haider came up to me while I was preparing for the next one. He suggested, 'Kiss her without telling her that you will do it.' He wanted to capture her reaction at this unexpected gesture. I insisted that such things should only be done with the full consent of the co-actor. In the end, Haider had to agree with my point. The film was completed, but due to differences that had arisen between the producers and directors, it was never released. After that, my friendship with Haider deepened even further. But Haider's attempts to do something different outside of the established norms of the industry continued to fail. Years later, he experienced some success with the movie *Jodhaa Akbar*, which was written by him and Uma and directed by Ashutosh Gowariker.

Actually, he had always wanted to be an actor. He had acted in *Nukkad*, but other than that, he hadn't found much success. I frequently grappled with feelings of guilt and unease, knowing that Haider's tireless efforts hadn't yielded the success he deserved, while I, with relatively little effort, had been bestowed with abundant opportunities. Perhaps that's why I continued to overlook his eccentric behaviour and included him in my projects. Eventually, to avoid conflict, I made a pact with him that we would not work together anymore.

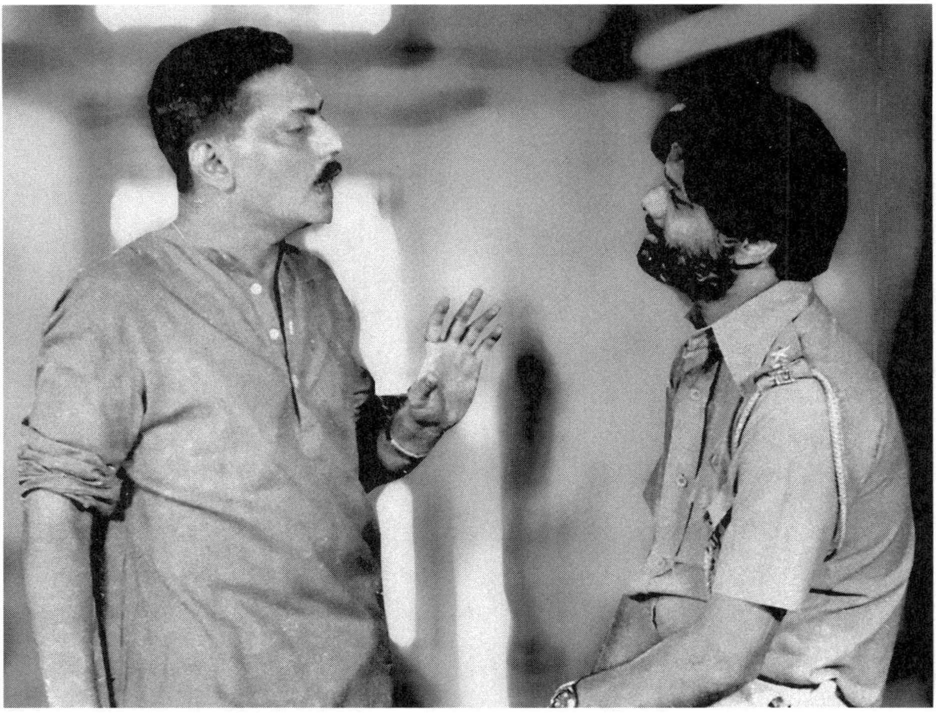

Akriet (1980), with Haider Ali

I often call Haider, with admiration, an encyclopaedia of the film industry. He knows the history of the industry down to the smallest detail. He can recall who the producer, director and actors were for any film, who wrote the songs, who sang them, and what eventually happened to the film. He animatedly shares these details, along with stories and gossip, in our conversations. As a result, even a casual visit to his home Pramila Nivas in Shivaji Park for a cup of coffee often turns into a two to three hour long conversation. Even today, whether on the phone or in person, Haider always begins our conversations with a loud 'Paleeeeeekar!', his unique way of calling me. His warmth shines through his eyes and voice, always making me feel good.

I've always been hesitant to put labels on relationships, preferring to let them unfold naturally without definition. Similarly, I've never been comfortable categorising artistes based on their caste, religion or gender, instead allowing their work to speak for them. I've sought to distil the beauty and spirit of relationships and art, preserving their integrity and fragrance. In turn, my life has remained grounded and vibrant, unhindered by the superficiality of the digital world.

José Saramago's novel *Death at Intervals* is based on a fascinating idea. In some unknown country, on the first day of the new year, people stop dying. Saramago starts and ends his book with—'No one died the next day'. What if that unthinkable really happened and no one died anymore? I would be reunited with all those loved ones I thought I had lost forever. I would once again feel their warm embrace, bask in their warm presence and be immersed in their love.

However, if the act of dying ceased, I would also become immortal, which isn't something I desire. Perhaps I should propose a revision to Saramago's novel: the freedom to opt for death. If one chooses to die, it should be honoured.

After all, I'm not seeking to escape death … I'm ready.

Beyond the Horizon of Dalí

As I reflect on this extensive series of experiences, I am increasingly mindful of its immense scale. I am reminded of everything I did during that time—all that I encountered, endured and overcame …

Lived … Lived in a waking state.

People might think that, given all I've lived and done in a short span, I must have been deprived of good sleep over the years; but that isn't true. It is known to many that I can fall asleep anytime, anywhere, for any length of time! I love to sleep. I avoid early morning flights for this reason. However, if I don't get sufficient sleep, I never experience issues like acidity or headaches, nor do I become irritable, even on mornings with early shoot-shifts. My sleep is thick and rich like dense and well-fermented yogurt; it's so deep that I rarely remember my dreams. People often remark that I wear a 'cloak of happiness' due to my excellent sleep habits. After a gruelling twenty- or thirty-day stretch of non-stop shooting, I would indulge in a rejuvenating two- to three-day sleep marathon, stirring only to satisfy my hunger with a light snack and to perform essential routines like using the toilet or brushing my teeth, before surrendering to sleep again. It was sheer bliss to skip taking a bath on those days.

When deep in slumber, my mind conjures up visions, ideas, or thoughts, which I often recall upon waking. Sometimes, only colours flow before my mind's eye. I can trace the origins of most of my abstract paintings back to my sleeping state. These nocturnal musings form the foundation of my abstract paintings, which I later bring to life on canvas. Occasionally, while reading, a concept or an idea may not immediately resonate with me, but later, its meaning unfolds and lingers in my mind.

Another advantage of sleeping for long hours was that I didn't smoke during that time. My only break from chain smoking came when I was asleep! I'd light up as soon as I woke up and put out my last cigarette just before going to bed. From age sixteen to fifty, my habit grew to a whopping seventy-two cigarettes a day. Even during film shoots, I'd smoke right up until the moment the camera rolled, handing the cigarette to my assistant, and then resuming as soon as the take was over. However, I cut down on smoking during shoots after realising its potential harm to others. Thankfully, this realisation came early on. What still puzzles me is how my body, despite its acute nicotine addiction, never craved it while I slept.

If I were to create an advertisement for a cigarette company, I'd stage it with my own body lying face down on the ground, surrounded by countless cigarette butts forming an eerie outline, like the chalk sketch of a murder victim. Slowly, the outline would get filled in as my body would gradually fade in, and I would gaze directly at the camera, flash a sly smile and casually reach for a cigarette from the pack lying next to me. I'd light it right there on the ground, and as the smoke curled upwards, the name 'Dunhill' would appear in the rising haze. The preferred brand in the industry then was 555; I alone was loyal to Dunhill. I would order heaps and heaps of cartons from Calcutta; twenty cigarettes in a pack, ten packets in one carton. I stockpiled cartons upon cartons to avoid running out. And still, there was one time when I found myself without cigarettes, at the onset of filming *Akriet*. As a result, I was forced to switch to an Indian brand for a few weeks, which left me with a nagging sore throat.

Many in the industry consumed drugs. But I never fell into that trap. In hindsight, I'm consumed by regret for the harm I have inflicted on the environment, on the innocent bystanders who have inhaled my second-hand smoke and on those who may have been inspired to pick up a cigarette because of me. These thoughts fill me with remorse. Perhaps I'm facing the consequences now, living with the fragile lungs of a 136-year-old man. My COPD (Chronic Obstructive Pulmonary Disease) diagnosis oddly feels like a kind of redemption to me.

When I turned fifty, Shalmalee encouraged me to quit smoking, and I overcame my decades-long addiction without any struggle. It's been thirty years since I last smoked a cigarette. Now, the mere smell of smoke is unbearable to me. Quitting also revived my appreciation for diverse culinary flavours.

The fragments of my life, accumulated over decades, lie dispersed in a state of chaos, much like the cigarette butts I carelessly littered for thirty years. I'm now faced with the daunting task of figuring out how to piece together the scattered remnants of my past, where to begin, and which direction to follow. Perhaps I should categorise my work into distinct groups, like the films and plays I acted in and directed, unfinished projects abandoned after a few scenes were shot, completed films that remained unreleased, and guest appearances in films made as a gesture of goodwill. Despite my best efforts to unearth all the memories, many will remain forever lost. Conversely, the memories of some events, despite being from a very distant past, remain remarkably vivid, as if they occurred just yesterday, refusing to be erased by the passage of time.

Childhood memories of the annual circus trips with my parents and sisters to Churchgate still mesmerise me. While the joker's tricks and aerial feats were thrilling, the motorcyclist in the 'well of death' held me spellbound. I'd be utterly captivated, my heart racing, as he performed his death-defying stunts. The memory of him riding in circles would haunt me long after the show ended. The sound of the motorcycle's engine would echo in my mind even in sleep. Astonishingly, the thrill of that experience still lingers, even at my advanced age. Similarly, my years of smoking has left a lasting trail of smoke that refuses to dissipate.

Another environmental transgression I must acknowledge is the significant carbon footprint left by my extensive global travels with Sandhya and Samiha. With air travel emitting around 90 kilograms of carbon dioxide per hour per passenger, our journeys have undoubtedly contributed to the growing problem of greenhouse gas emissions. Considering that air travel accounts for 2-3% of global environmental damage, and car travel contributes around 10%, our travels may have played a sizeable role in this ecological harm. This realisation weighs heavily on me.

The stream of consciousness takes you on such a joyride through life … where did I begin and where have I ended up!

Speaking of carbon footprint, as a family, we travelled extensively throughout India, both for work and leisure. In fact, there are hardly any places in the country that I haven't explored. Our global travel, spanning around forty countries, has been a fantastic source of refreshment for me. We spend at least five to twelve days in a country, depending on its size, to truly immerse ourselves in its culture. Every trip is curated with careful attention to detail while picking accommodations and culinary experiences. We research and seek out the best local eateries to ensure an authentic taste of the region's flavours.

The moment we land at the airport, we rent a four-wheeler. Sandhya and I share a passion for driving and are both skilled drivers, easily navigating roads anywhere in the world. After just an hour or so of observation, we usually mange to grasp the local traffic patterns and conventions. Self-driving allows us to experience the true pulse of a place, revealing its peoples' discipline, temperament and attitudes. Interestingly, we often hear comments from locals, such as 'you don't seem to be from India'. This remark, though meant as a compliment, can be disheartening, as it perpetuates a negative image of Indians abroad.

I've always valued the freedom of being able to travel on my own terms, untethered from the constraints of group tours. I've always declined enticing proposals from Indian tour operators seeking a brand ambassador and offering substantial compensation for promotional cruises and excursions. The prospect of being tied to a rigid itinerary, surrendering control over my schedule and compromising personal preferences holds no appeal for me. Many travellers consider it a triumph to have access to familiar Indian staples like rice-daal every day even when they are thousands of miles away from home. It saddens me that they remain unaware of the rich gastronomic experiences of the places they visit. On leaving India, we make a conscious effort to venture beyond Indian cuisine. Planning our own travels has allowed us to embrace the thrill of navigating uncertain situations, a thrill we've relished for the past twenty years. The roar of the motorcycle in the 'well of death' remains an unforgettable soundtrack in all our travels, encapsulating the essence of our daring adventures. At all the stops on our itinerary, we're consistently surprised by unexpected experiences, and it's these unplanned delights that make our trips memorable.

Once in Norway, we decided to take the train from Oslo to the city of Bergen. On the way, the train stopped at a cute little station with a single platform. The moment we saw it, we fell in love with the small hamlet at the foothill beyond the station. In winters, many tourists would have come here to ski on the pristine snow-covered slopes. But since it was September, there was hardly a soul in sight. We immediately deboarded the train, and the train left the station. It was getting dark. We could not see a single lamp-post anywhere. But after walking for a while, we saw a lovely little hotel made of logs. Initially, we couldn't see anyone inside, but soon, two people approached us with a sense of urgency and ushered us into a room with a large fireplace. Talking to them, we learnt that one of them was an internationally known chef and that we were in a 120-year-old Michelin hotel, which had to be booked two years in advance for a booking during the season. They insisted that since no guests were staying at the hotel at that time, we could stay in any room we liked and that they would cook any dish we wanted. We stayed there for three days. I will never forget the feasts we enjoyed there—we ate excellent reindeer meat, cakes, breads, fresh fish preparations, and so much more. In fact, we were so enchanted by the place that we nearly bought a log cabin there for thirty lakhs! But then we prudently changed our minds and let go of the idea. Could a conventional guided tour have ever offered such a magical experience?

South Ireland, Iceland and Bolivia stand out as the most unforgettable destinations in my travel history. These places with their extraordinary geological terrains and landscapes, have a mesmerising quality that sets them apart. Each location boasts of a distinct geographical setting that has infused the local environment with a touch of magic. Ireland's traffic rules are famously idiosyncratic, with each of the twenty-six counties having its own set of regulations. The country's stunning natural setting, with the Atlantic, Celtic and Irish oceans never more than a few miles away, makes for a spectacular place to explore. Yet, the need to constantly adapt to changing traffic rules can be unsettling for a traveller. Perhaps it was this spectacle that led to my accident while walking one day, which resulted in a permanent shoulder injury.

Iceland has a peculiar car insurance law. Car insurance is essential there because the road surfaces are rough, with stony sand spread on either side and sometimes in the middle of the road, making driving hazardous. Moreover, windstorms are so strong there that when you open the car door, the doors and even the roof are at risk of being blown away. Due to these reasons, car insurance premiums are quite high there. We experienced the terrific speed of the Icelandic wind once; caught in the storm, we huddled together, desperate to reach safety which lay just ten feet away.

The country boasts of live volcanic lakes, which emit sulphur with a rumble. Iceland's picturesque landscapes, with their turquoise lakes and glacial ice formations, have been showcased in Justin Bieber's music videos, captivating a global audience on YouTube. Additionally, the filming of Shah Rukh Khan's hit song '*Rang de tu mohe gerua*' on the dramatic black sand shores has further boosted Iceland's popularity, making it a coveted destination for travellers worldwide.

The salt pads and the deserts of Bolivia offer an entirely different, one-of-a-kind experience. Bolivia's high altitude of over 12,000 feet above sea level, often poses a challenge to tourists who might end up suffering from acute mountain sickness or AMS. Despite being rich in natural resources like cocoa, coca, lithium and other minerals, the country struggles with poverty. Many residents travel to the notoriously hilly capital city of La Paz in search of livelihood. Interestingly, Swiss companies have donated buses to the city, known as Mi Teleférico or Gondola, which run on aerial cables, providing a unique transportation solution.

Covering over 10,000 square kilometres in Bolivia, the Uyuni Salt Flats are a breathtaking sight, with their brilliant white salt stretching as far as the eye can see. Formed thousands of years ago through the evaporation of lake water, this natural phenomenon is aptly named 'the world's largest mirror'. During the rainy season, the salt flat transforms into an otherworldly landscape as collected water creates a reflective surface that perfectly mirrors the sky, giving one the illusion of walking on clouds. Visitors can even stay in hotel rooms constructed entirely from salt.

The cacti region spanning twenty-four hectares is a marvel, with majestic cacti reaching heights of two to eleven metres, seemingly defying odds by flourishing on the salt flats. This fantastical landscape immerses you in a surreal world, preparing you for your next spellbinding experience. As you journey deeper, you enter the Salvador Dalí desert, a realm that pushes the boundaries of imagination. Set against the backdrop of a desert born from volcanic eruptions, the vibrant colours of Laguna Verde and Laguna Colorado—the green and red lakes—are a sight to behold. Without a guide, it is easy to become disoriented in these parts. The occasional sighting of long-necked llamas, roaming in small herds, sparks wonder at their ability to thrive in this unforgiving environment, devoid of grass, trees, or bushes.

For those like me, who are drawn to Salvador Dalí's Surrealist art and the dreamlike desert landscapes he depicted in his work between 1929 and 1940, Bolivia is a treasure trove of inspiration. Dalí's paintings, such as *Persistence of Memory* and *Swans Reflecting Elephants*, famously breathed life into desolate scenes, and Bolivia's own surreal desert-scapes offer a similar canvas to the imagination.

As the COVID-19 pandemic raged on, my thoughts frequently wandered back to Bolivia, seeking refuge in its dreamlike, surrealist landscapes that are captured in the masterpieces of Salvador Dalí. Amidst the global chaos, I found solace in recalling the golden phase of my past, particularly between 1971, when I acted in the Marathi film *Bajiravcha Beta,* and 1982, when I worked in the Hindi film *Ram Nagari*. Memories from that phase prodded and urged me to reflect on my past and pen these memoirs. They offered me a tranquil refuge from the pandemic's turmoil, enabling me to gaze beyond the surreal landscapes of my mind, and embark on a cathartic journey of introspection.

I still marvel at the sheer breadth of experiences I packed into that decade, from 1971 to 1982. I juggled a 9-to-5 job with my art exhibitions, theatre shows and a steady flow of films. I wore many hats: of an actor, producer, director and a devoted family man. It's a wonder how I was able to sustain such a pace.

Some theatre critics accused me of abandoning theatre for Hindi cinema, but I was too engrossed in my work to bother refuting such claims. Now, I realise that I should have spoken up. To succeed in this field, self-promotion is crucial. If you can't do it yourself, hire someone to sing your praises or join networks where mutual admiration is the norm. Having devoted followers can help too. Otherwise, unsubstantiated rumours, half-truths and exaggerations can become the established narrative. But I wasn't fazed by it then, nor am I affected by it now.

In this context, I remember two incidents that took place eight to ten years ago. In 1986, Kamalakar Nadkarni had played a role in my theatrical production *Julus*. In 2017, he asked me if I would write a preface to his book in Marathi in which he had reviewed my productions—*Julus* and *Gochi*. While speaking informally, Kamalakar suddenly said, 'Despite your significant contributions to the theatre, your unconventional approach towards mainstream theatre has regrettably resulted in a lack of acknowledgment.'

Since Kamalakar's tone was a little apologetic, I shared with him a surprising development—a senior theatre director, Rajinder Nath, had nominated me for the Sangeet Natak Akademi award, unexpectedly, at that late stage in my life! I had dissed this news given the political climate and my anti-government stand. Earlier, Sandhya had received an email from Girish Karnad, expressing his dismay that despite my significant contribution to theatre, I had not been given the Akademi award. He wrote, 'We have erred in overlooking Amol's achievements … a grave injustice has been done to his art. Hopefully, we can rectify this oversight now.' Just a few months before his passing, I visited Girish at his Bangalore home. He held my hand and said with regret, 'I failed you, Amol. The system is unjust.' I was shaken by his words, spoken despite his frail condition. His wife, Saras, had to console me since it took his words for me to understand just how deep my wound was.

The second incident relates to my career in cinema. I served as the president of Prabhat Chitra Mandal for several years, frequently interacting with Sudhir Nandgaonkar, a veteran film club activist. A heated debate between us once turned personal.

'As jurors, we must set aside our biases and assess films based on artistic merit,' I said. This sparked controversy, since he disagreed with me and believed that 'objective evaluation is impossible'. The discussion took an ugly turn when I exclaimed, 'After *Sant Tukaram*, my film *Akriet* was the first Marathi film to receive an international award. I'm surprised a seasoned film historian like you didn't acknowledge that.'

Nandgaonkar fired back. 'As the producer, it was your job to inform us about the award. Why didn't you do that?'

'Your thorough research should have uncovered this fact. Why should I sing my own praises?'

Nandgaonkar was visibly surprised. 'If your achievements haven't been properly recorded, it's you who is at fault, no one else.'

I accepted his point and concluded the debate right there.

Unfortunately, seniors like Girish Karnad, Sudhir Nandgaonkar and Kamalakar Nadkarni are no longer alive. I'm still around, which is why these memories have resurfaced. But when I'm gone, countless memories like these will vanish with me.

What Kamalakar said was indeed true. I never found commercial, mainstream theatre attractive, perhaps for two main reasons: one, it involved doing the same thing again and again, and two, it lacked experimentation. It was confined within the boundaries of 'realism', leading to the stagnation of creative vision, which left both the production team and the audience apathetic to the lacklustre props and poor visual quality.

In the Gujarati adaptation of *Natasamraat* (King of Theatre), titled *Bahut Naachyo Gopal*, the final act included a breathtaking cyclorama featuring the iconic Bharatiya Vidya Bhavan, complete with its numerous steps and towering pillars. This visual masterpiece was unforgettable. The set designers, Chel and Paresh, had meticulously recreated the era and the building where modern Indian theatre had been born, without any concern about commercial viability. They might have asked themselves these questions while designing the set: Why hold back on effort and expense even for a scene that lasts mere minutes? What prevents Marathi commercial theatre from exploring such innovative approaches? Why don't we witness set designs comparable to the spectacular ones seen in the American Broadway or British West End productions? Not just international theatres, but even within India, theatres in other states or languages showcase remarkable visual richness in their props. Then what hinders mainstream Marathi theatre from achieving similar excellence?

Ebrahim Alkazi's productions at the National School of Drama; the Bengali play *Kallol*, which envelops the audience in a dramatic scene of an underground mine flooding; and Ratan Thiyyam's Manipuri play, which vividly captures the moment when Arjun shares the secret of piercing the Chakravyuha with Subhadra, who then passes it to Abhimanyu in her womb—all showcase the power of theatre as a multisensory art form. These visual experiments have raised the bar for theatrical storytelling. I ask myself why has Marathi mainstream theatre failed to deliver such immersive experiences?

The staging of Girish Karnad's *Flowers* was remarkable, leveraging the vertical and horizontal dimensions of the theatre to create an immersive experience for the viewers. Seated at the base of a deep metaphorical well, the audience received the priest's words from high up, elevating the experience beyond mere sound to a visually stunning and immersive encounter. The aroma of camphor, divine incense and jasmine enveloped the audience, transporting them to a sacred realm. Mohit Takalkar, from the younger generation, is pushing the boundaries with fresh experimentation in presentation styles. His play *Ajab Kahani* was a spellbinding experience, boasting of exceptional performances from its talented cast and stunning visual aesthetics. But these are exceptions!

Mainstream Marathi theatre relies on extensive touring throughout Maharashtra. As a result, productions often prioritise efficiency and adaptability over set design. Typically, a new play opens in Shivaji Mandir Theatre in Mumbai, followed by shows at the Rangayatan Theatre in Thane and then immediately at the Balgandharva Theatre in Pune. The need for portability has led to a reliance on foldable props that can be quickly set up and taken down, that allow for swift transportation on top of a bus. This approach restricts creative possibilities and production values. The 'realist' framework has become so entrenched that even a slight variation, like swapping a hall for a bedroom in the opening scene, is greeted with applause. This creative stagnation is compounded by producers who prioritise star power over innovative storytelling and visual design. The underlying assumption is that audiences are primarily drawn to celebrity actors rather than to the artistic merit of the production.

The story of the play *Mata Draupadi* (Mother Draupadi) is noteworthy here. During one performance, the actor playing one of the Pandavas was unexpectedly absent. Vijaya Mehta, the director and actor in the titular role, suggested cancelling the show. But the producer persuaded her to proceed with the remark, 'The audience comes to see you; manage with just four Pandavas today.'

Even while staging plays designed to meet the expectations of the audience, there should be an effort on the producers' part to elevate their aesthetic taste. Unfortunately, this has been completely forgotten, leading to very little change in the expectations of viewers. Although Marathi theatre had experienced a resurgence in the 1960s, echoing the golden age of Balgandharva, and reached new heights by the 1980s, a crucial aspect—the visual dimension—was always neglected. The emphasis on nostalgia over innovation was disheartening. Furthermore, a disregard for punctuality in stage performances turned into a habit that was hard to shake off. Delays of up to ten minutes becoming commonplace, even at the experimental theatre hub of Chabildas Hall in Dadar. As an artiste striving for excellence in all aspects of stagecraft, I found these developments very troubling.

In the production of my plays such as *Pagla Ghoda*, *Avadhya*, *Rashomon* and *Vasanakand*, I experimented with set design in many different ways. In *Gidhade*, Dr Lagoo presented me with a chance to break free from conventional theatrical visualisation. I proposed a Surrealist approach, inspired by Dalí's paintings, to temper the underlying violence in the script. Unfortunately, my sketches were rejected by Dr Lagoo and Dubey. The production ultimately opted for Bapu Limaye's realist props, which looked like vulture nests.

For all the three shows of *Pagla Ghoda*, I adhered to the principle that props should be suggestive instead of simply being realistic or representational. By framing a room in a village crematorium with varied dimensions and omitting traditional door and window frames, I created a minimalist space. The entries and exits of the four male characters defined the boundaries of the crematorium, liberating the 'young woman' (the female protagonist) to move unfettered across the stage. This deliberate design choice infused her presence with a metaphorical quality, seamlessly integrating Surrealism into the narrative. The audience perceived this as an organic aspect of the performance rather than a gimmick.

In my 1971 production of *Avadhya*, I broke away from conventional set design, using ornate pillars to evoke a small village guest house.

Rather than explicitly showing the peephole allowing residents to spy on adjacent rooms, I decided to use lighting to suggest its presence on the imaginary fourth wall separating the stage from the audience. The erotic scenes were illuminated only by the soft glow of light peeking from behind the pillars.

When I reflect on the parallel or experimental theatre scene of that era, my scope extends beyond the Chabildas movement to encompass productions created for inter-collegiate competitions, state theatre competitions and *kamgar* (workers) theatre. These experiments had a ripple effect, their influence spreading beyond the boundaries of Mumbai and Pune. Institutions like Mumbai's Bharatiya Vidya Bhavan, Avishkaar, Rangayan, Indian National Theatre, Mumbai Marathi Sahitya Sangh, Goa Hindu Association, Roopvedh, Aniket, Bahuroopi, Theatre Unit, Unmesh, Sutradhaar, Abhivyakti, Ya Mandali Saadar Karu Ya and Antarnatya; Pune's Theatre Academy, Jaagar and Samanway; Kolhapur's Pratyay; Solapur's Natya Aradhana, and many others dedicated to theatre contributed significantly to the evolution of this art form.

In 1975–76, Dilip Kolhatkar produced *Rajacha Khel* (King's Play) written by Vrindavan Dandavate for an inter-bank theatre competition in Bombay. This production was a testament to the power of group theatre, with Vrindavan's script offering a searing critique of the contemporary socio-political landscape. Notably, the banks' management respected the artistic freedom of their employees, refraining from controlling their creative expression. This liberal spirit defined the theatre practices of that era, allowing for uncompromising artistic voices to flourish. In the same competition, the one-act play *Mhaa* (The Call of the Buffalo) was presented. It was written by Ramesh Pawar who performed it with Ashok Saraf. It was one of the greatest productions of the time by far, capturing live moments in an experimental manner. Able actors such as Usha Kalbag and Ravindra Divekar worked with great energy in the competition.

In the state theatre competitions, a new generation of playwrights emerged—namely S.N. Navare, Suresh Khare and Ratnakar Matkari. Smaller towns witnessed theatre productions based on H.M. Marathe's novel *Nishparna Vrukhaavar Bhar Dupaari* (On the Leafless Tree in the Scorching Sun). *Paacholaa Jalat Naahiye* (Fallen Leaves Are Not Burning) by S.N. Navare and *Lokakatha 78* (The Folktale of '78) by Ratnakar Matkari both debuted on the same platform.

The younger generation of theatre practitioners remains oblivious to the pioneering work that emerged from the three playwright workshops conducted in 1970, 1980 and 1990. In 1970, Dubey hosted an innovative workshop, gathering promising young playwrights of the time in one place. His sole stipulation was that each participant share a fresh, previously unperformed play and read it aloud to the group. This fostered a dynamic exchange of ideas and creative energy. Satish Alekar's *Miki Ani Memsaheb* (Miki and Memsaheb), Mahesh Elkunchwar's *Vasanakand*, Achyut Vaze's *Chal Re Bhoplya Tunuk Tunuk*, Dilip Jagtap's *Ek Ande Phutle* (One Egg is Broken), G.P. Deshpande's *Udhvasta Dharmashala* (A Man in Dark Times) and Shankar Shesh's *Ek Aur Dronacharya* (One More

The great master of theatre, Satyadev Dubey

Dronacharya), were all first read out in Dubey's workshop. Dubey had anticipated that the workshop's focus would be on critiquing the shortcomings of the plays. The three decades were characterised by a surge in scripts that broke away from traditional storytelling and embraced abstract theatrical techniques instead. An entire new crop of playwrights like Ajit Dalvi, Shafaat Khan, Premanand Gajvi, Prashant Dalvi, Jayant Pawar, Rajeev Naik, Chandrashekhar Phansalkar, Tushar Bhadre, Chetan Datar and Makarand Sathe emerged from these workshops.

Have these groundbreaking theatrical movements received the recognition they deserve? Has the Akhil Bharatiya Marathi Natya Parishad undertaken a comprehensive study of parallel theatre, or even a thorough examination of Marathi theatre as a whole for the matter? Unfortunately, I too haven't documented my own experiments in theatre. If we consider experimental theatre to be plays that challenged conventional theatrical language, is there a comprehensive list of such Marathi plays available? Given that the entire trajectory of experimental theatre remains undocumented, lamenting the lack of individual contributions like mine seems futile. There is an urgent need to extend the narrative of Marathi theatre beyond commercial productions and nostalgic accounts of a particular era, and create a more inclusive and diverse record that encompasses various theatrical approaches and perspectives. I am told that a list of plays featured in Maharashtra state theatre competitions over fifty years, titled *Suvarnarang*, is now available. It is essential that the newer generations of theatre enthusiasts, spectators and researchers be acquainted with these pioneering efforts. Ultimately what's vital is that young playwrights keep breaking new ground and that the spirit of theatre remains vibrant and ever changing.

I have always believed that in addition to set and lighting design, costume and make-up design should also be reimagined from a fresh perspective. In 1980, I produced and directed the play *Rashomon*. I had written an elaborate introduction to the play, titled 'A

Transformation for the Discovery of Truth', which has never been published. An extract from it is reproduced here:

> While many of my contemporaries in theatre were drawn to producing plays by Western masters like Shakespeare, Shaw, Miller, Sartre and Brecht, I made a conscious choice to focus on Indian playwrights. I was committed to translating dramatic scripts from other Indian languages into Marathi and exploring new theatrical dimensions. The only exception was *Rashomon*, a theatrical adaptation of Akira Kurosawa's iconic film of the same name (Prof. Anantrao Bhave had translated the play from English). I was captivated by the complex theme of Truth. In the play, four characters claim responsibility for a murder, leaving the audience with a profound question: what is the ultimate truth? The fact that the story offers no clear resolution, and that the truth itself may be subjective, fascinated me. I was eager to tackle this depth and complexity on stage.

I knew that Marathi audiences struggled to connect with foreign characters and settings. Even then, I deliberately chose to present

Rashomon (1980): Chitra Palekar & Manohar Tawade

the *Rashomon* story in its original Japanese setting, preserving its cultural fabric and maintaining the integrity of the narrative seen in Anantrao's script.

This inspired me to explore the world of Japanese miniature paintings, enabling me to accurately depict historical characters. I chose to enhance the characters' eyes with intricate designs and assigned a specific colour to each of their foreheads, mirroring their personalities. The traditional Kimono-style attire harmonised beautifully with these elements. To add depth to the production, I curated an authentic Japanese soundtrack to accompany each scene, immersing myself in the NCPA library in Mumbai for this purpose. During rehearsals, I sought help from special trainers to ensure that the duel between the samurai and the dacoit appeared realistic and intense.

When I began exploring the dimension of sound in theatre, I realised that merely understanding the meaning of words was insufficient. I needed to tune into the rhythmic resonance, the sonic textures and the unique authorial voice that defined each writer's style. This understanding dawned on me through the works of two masters, Mohan Rakesh and Vijay Tendulkar. In *Aadhe Adhure*, Mohan Rakesh had written a sentence in Hindi—'*Uljhe hue haathon ka gijgija paseena*'. It was only Tendulkar who could translate it so marvellously into Marathi as '*Ritya talhatavaracha chikchikit gham*'. I realised that creative translation must encompass not only the literal meaning of words but also onomatopoeia, or sound similarity, to truly capture the essence of the original text.

My off-beat approach to theatrical sound design, which began with *Gochi* (1972), continued to evolve and refine itself through subsequent productions like *Chal Re Bhoplya Tunuk Tunuk* (1973), *Party* (1976) and *Aprakaashit Divakar* (Unpublished Divakar, 1975).

In *Gochi*, I experimented with nonsensical words that would convey a sense of outrage through their sonic quality and rhythmic patterns.

By breaking free from conventional theatrical norms, we can unlock a new realm of artistic expression, where colours and sounds converge to create a fresh language. This liberating approach allows sound to emerge in a bold, new dimension. Theatre critic Pushpa Bhave has made special mention of *Gochi* in her book *Ranga Natakaache* (The Colours of Plays), published in 2012.

> Sunday evening theatre outings have become a comfortable habit for middle-class spectators, who arrive dressed up, relaxed, and ready to be entertained in an air-conditioned setting. They assume the role of patrons, expecting to be pleased by the performers. However, both the audience and the entertainers often neglect the true essence of theatrical art. For them, theatre is merely a vehicle for presenting the playwright's words and the director's interpretation, rather than a dynamic, immersive experience that challenges and engages. Last month, a Sunday evening in Mumbai's Ruia College witnessed a transformative theatrical experience. The unconventional setting, where spectators sat on the floor in traditional Indian style, blurred the lines between the audience and the performers. Amol Palekar's innovative direction of Sadanand Rege's *Gochi* transcended the script, making it a collaborative creation of the director, the actors and the playwright. This groundbreaking performance, hailed by critics as a 'liminal theatrical experience', revitalised the experimental theatre movement and marked a milestone in Marathi theatre. Palekar's bold vision and the actors' improvisational genius infused new life into the production, rendering it a testament to the power of collaborative creativity.

One evening in 1972, Baburao Chitre (editor of *Abhiruchi* magazine and father of writer Dilip Purushottam Chitre) visited our Coffee House haunt and handed me the latest issue of the magazine. 'Read the script of *Gochi*,' he urged. As I delved into the pages, I was mesmerised and intimidated at the same time. The words leapt off the page, conjuring vivid images, a cacophony of disjointed sentences, and a surreal theatrical experience unlike any I had encountered. The script probed the intense mysteries underlying a deceptively simple narrative; its poetic language and absurdist nature leaving me fascinated yet apprehensive. Could I do justice to this complex dramatic work on stage? My trepidation grew, but so did my captivation with the script. I was under the sway of its enigmatic power.

My exploration of *Gochi* revealed that it was more than just a play; it was the symbol of a new, timeless experience. This abstract theatrical experience required a radical approach, one that abandoned traditional stage settings in favour of using the actors' bodies as dynamic props. As rehearsals commenced, I was still uncertain about the play's genre and direction. Our daily readings brought together a talented ensemble: Jayram Hardikar, Chitra, Juili Deuskar, Dilip Kulkarni, Dilip Gangodkar and Bal Karve. I'd sit quietly, absorbing their myriad interpretations of the script. Gradually, I began to sense the interplay between voice and silence, envisioning the vital relationship between body and sound. Inspired by this synergy, I opted for live, human chorus sounds instead of pre-recorded effects, leveraging the actors' own vocalisations, like the haunting *dhitaang*. The creative process unfolded organically, defying traditional roles. I didn't just direct; the actors didn't just act; Mangesh Kulkarni didn't simply design music. The performance of *Gochi* was a collective expression, a harmonious fusion of theatrical artistry.

We introduced a new format of staging shows called 'double billing', where two plays were presented back-to-back, with a brief interval in between. This novel move not only provided our audiences with a three-hour experience but also optimised production costs by consolidating advertising and ticketing expenses. Our production of *Gochi* would run for ninety minutes, followed by *Aajacha Karyakram*

Yashasvi Karanyasathi Aaplya Sahakaryachi Garaj Aahe (We Need Your Cooperation to Make Today's Event a Success), directed by Achyut Deshingkar and produced by Mumbai's vibrant Bahuroopi theatre group. I had the pleasure of performing in that second play. This new format paved the way for many future productions, including Vijaya Mehta's presentation of Mahesh Elkunchwar's *Sultaan* and *Holi* in a similar double-billing format.

Typically, the dialogue and language used in a play are evaluated using the same criteria as in literature. That was challenged by the inventive performance of *Chal Re Bhoplya Tunuk Tunuk*. It delved into the unexplored possibilities of absurd conversations, the musicality of language and the extremities of physical movement. By incorporating repetitive chanting of poems, the script pushed the boundaries of conventional storytelling, paving the way for a new kind of theatrical experience that prioritised sound, rhythm and movement over traditional notions of meaning and narrative. The playwright Achyut Vaze effectively used lines such as the following:

First character: The bus has come, the bus has come, the bus has come.
Second character: Where is the bus? It's not our bus.

The repetition of such words and sentences served as a form of rhythmic punctuation, mirroring the thrill of reaching the *sam* point in Indian classical music, where the cycle of *taans* and songs (*aavartan*) converges in a moment of sonic fulfilment. The debut performance of *Chal Re Bhoplya Tunuk Tunuk* at the Maharashtra State Theatre Competition in Bombay's Ravindra Natya Mandir was a resounding triumph. Encouraged by this response, we took the play to diverse venues beyond Bombay and Pune, including non-traditional spaces like community grounds, private homes and public areas. Notably, the play's effectiveness persisted even without sound amplification. The Hindi adaptation *Chal Mere Kaddu Thummak Thummak*, translated by playwright Shankar Shesh, enabled us to reach a broader audience, culminating in two highly acclaimed performances in Delhi, which I directed and in which I also performed the role of the *sutradhaar*.

I had another opportunity to experiment with sound while staging *Aprakaashit Divakar*. It put my ability as a director to the test. Sometime between 1974–75, I received a phone call from Kumudben Mehta. 'Please go and meet Prof. Sarojini Vaidya at the University of Bombay; it's quite close to your workplace,' she said. When I met Sarojini-bai, she enthusiastically shared with me her doctoral thesis, which was centred around Shankar Kashinath Garge, who wrote under the pen name 'Divakar', a pioneering writer of the unique genre known as 'Natya Chhata', meaning monologue. She described him as a visionary, akin to a Sufi saint, whose ingenious approach far surpassed his contemporaries. Sarojini-bai's eyes sparkled as she spoke about the treasure trove of unpublished works by Divakar that she had discovered.

I was astonished by the compilation Sarojini-bai shared with me. Unlike other playwrights who wrote lengthy plays with elaborate dialogue, Divakar's works were remarkably spare, lasting around twenty-five minutes, with only seven to eight scenes. Inspired by Nobel laureate Maurice Maeterlinck, he wrote a thirty-minute play about visually challenged individuals, featuring intentionally unfinished sentences and poignant ellipses. Divakar's wish to remain unpublished during his lifetime suggested that he knew his works would not be digestable to the contemporary audience who welcomed three hour-long, verbose plays. I found this truly dazzling.

I created a comprehensive stage script combining three to four of Divakar's unpublished works and some unknown dramatic monologues. Before rehearsals began, we conducted a week-long workshop where actors spent an hour blindfolded, then gradually moved around the room. This exercise helped us understand the diverse experiences of visually challenged individuals as portrayed by Divakar. We gained insights into the worlds of those born blind, those who faintly recalled sight and those who recently lost sight but still sensed light. Through sound, the actors developed a nuanced understanding of these differences.

While directing *Aprakaashit Divakar*, I discovered an entire universe of sounds that the visually challenged navigate: the unique timbre of each white cane, the sound of a cane falling, the rustling search for it, and other sounds like the eerie wail of a mad woman and the scraping screech, as Divakar's stage directions so vividly described in his script. Our production adopted the simplicity of 'intimate theatre', shunning ornate costumes, props and lighting.

This production had a run of twenty-five to thirty performances, each one presented in non-traditional spaces. The response was overwhelmingly positive, with my team at Aniket receiving widespread acclaim for our inventive approach. By transcending spatial and temporal boundaries, we had managed to transport the audiences into the distinctive world of Divakar.

As the creative mind evolves, new ideas arise and past decisions may seem flawed or inadequate in retrospect—as I experienced with *Rao Jagdev Martanda*, which reminded me of the classic French play *Cyrano de Bergerac* (1897) by Edmond Rostand, adapted for the Marathi stage by Mangesh Patki. The protagonist, Cyrano, relies on his sword to navigate social hierarchies, yet harbours a poetic soul. He cherishes a lifelong love for one woman but remains silent due to his insecurity about his large nose. Ultimately, he meets his end in battle. The renowned theatre company Kalavaibhav planned to stage the adaptation of *Cyrano de Bergerac* with the title *Rao Jagdev Martanda* on the commercial stage, with Dr Lagoo set to play the lead role. Dr Lagoo approached me to direct the play, offering complete creative freedom to select my team. In a meeting with the producer, Mohan Tondvalkar, I stipulated that the opening show's date would be announced only after sufficient rehearsal, which was agreed upon. However, Mohan had a condition of his own: Dr Lagoo would be credited alongside me as co-director. Dr Lagoo clarified that he would focus solely on acting, while I would bear the complete responsibility for direction. I accepted this condition, recognising the potential box office draw of Dr Lagoo's name. We commenced rehearsals in 1972.

While working on the Marathi adaptation of *Aadhe Adhure*, I had the privilege of witnessing Dr Lagoo's acting prowess up close. I saw how he masterfully reinterpreted the five roles originally played by Amrish Puri in the Hindi version, particularly that of Singhania, the female protagonist's boss. With subtle restraint, Dr Lagoo conveyed the boss's lascivious nature through a mere gaze and the deliberate rolling of his tongue over his lips, transforming the character without altering the script. I was also in awe of his performance as the villain Ramakant in *Gidhade*.

However, during our rehearsals for *Rao Jagdev Martanda*, I realised that he lacked the agility and force required in a historical play. The swordfight scenes, in particular, suffered from his weighed-down movements, coming across as comical rather than elegant. We brought in a specialist trainer for fencing lessons and the sword duel scenes, but I knew I had to address the issue with Dr Lagoo directly. One evening, over tea and cigarettes, I tactfully demonstrated his movements and their unintended effect. He listened thoughtfully, then rose, patted me affectionately, and said with a tinge of regret, 'I should have met someone like you fifteen years ago, my boy. It's too late now.' In the subsequent rehearsals, I focused on enhancing Dr Lagoo's movements to make them appear more graceful. I modified the choreography and enlisted the help of the younger actors in the crew to facilitate faster-paced scenes. However, in doing so, I inadvertently neglected the script's word-oriented nature, due to which the play eventually suffered. Additionally, I realised that actors accustomed to commercial theatre were resistant to exploring new styles, preferring to stick with the familiar tropes. Consequently, my vision of reimagining the historical play through radical dialogue presentation, body language and movements slowly faded away.

Following the opening performance at Ravindra Natya Mandir, the producer Mohan Todvalkar invited Dr Lagoo and me for a drink, where he candidly acknowledged the play's failure. But he refrained from criticising anyone involved. Dr Lagoo graciously accepted responsibility for the flop, but as the director, I should have taken ownership of the failure. In retrospect, I recognise that the production's shortcomings were entirely my own.

For months, I faced ridicule and snide comments, such as 'The play flopped, but the nose continues to remain in the air'—an allusion to the infamous prosthetic nose worn by Dr Lagoo in his portrayal of Cyrano. Others quipped, 'The echoes of this play's failure in Bombay's Ravindra Natya Mandir can be heard as far as Thane and Pune.' My friends were subjected to jibes like, 'Only a select few, like Palekar, can manage to turn a globally acclaimed play into a flop'. Initially, these remarks stung, but eventually I learnt to laugh them off. However, this experience marked the end of my journey in commercial theatre.

In hindsight, I realise that directing *Rao Jagdev Martanda* and *Chal Re Bhoplya Tunuk Tunuk* simultaneously led to an unintended overlap in artistic approaches. I inadvertently imposed experimental elements, such as minimalistic set design, on *Rao Jagdev Martanda*, a commercial play that demanded a distinct vision. Meanwhile, my passion project, *Chal Re Bhoplya Tunuk Tunuk*, received meticulous attention, distracting me from refining the dialogue delivery of characters in *Rao Jagdev Martanda*. I acknowledge that this lapse in focus was unprofessional and unjust to the commercial play. However, I acknowledged the error and made a conscious effort to avoid it in my future endeavours. Following this failure, I made a crucial decision, as a director, to approach each script with an open mind. The wise words of veteran director Raj Khosla became my guiding principle from thereon: *'Bahuteri filmein josh mein banti hain lekin yaadgaar filmein hosh mein!'* (Many films are made in a fit of passion, but the memorable ones are made after a great deal of thought.)

Satyadev Dubey had urged me to attend a performance of *Evam Indrajit* at Birla Matoshree Theatre in Bombay. It was directed by the renowned Calcutta-based theatre practitioner Shyamanand Jalan. Witnessing this production early in my career had a profound impact on me, broadening my understanding of theatre. Some key elements from the play that still resonate with me are the clever use of abstract shapes as props, the absence of a traditional box-setting, a non-linear narrative and a profoundly optimistic conclusion. Shyamanand Jalan's production of *Evam Indrajit* floored me with its understated, non-theatrical approach.

In Dubey's adaptation of *Evam Indrajit*, the focus shifted entirely to the character of Indrajit, played by Dubey himself, while Puri saab took on the role of the writer. Although not as peripheral as the characters Amal-Vimal-Kamal, Dubey skilfully relegated the writer's character to a secondary role. Dubey's mastery of verbal histrionics shone in his delivery of the poetic and prose dialogues. His use of minimal props, simple black back-curtains and a rear stage platform blending into a large black screen, created an intimate setting that drew the audience's attention to the actors' words and body language.

I had the privilege of witnessing two vastly different interpretations of *Evam Indrajit* in my formative years, both of which were equally successful. This exposure became the foundation of my understanding of theatre. The two versions of *Evam Indrajit* left such a lasting impression on my mind that coming up with my own production of the play proved to be an insurmountable challenge. It remains an unfulfilled aspiration, a creative endeavour yet to be undertaken.

In 1969, Dubey entrusted me with the task of translating Badal Sircar's play *Ballabhpurer Roopkotha* from Hindi to Marathi. After completing the first draft, I sought inputs from Puri saab, Abdul Shakoor and Dubey. As I began explaining my translation choices, including the change of the title to *Vallabhpurchi Dantkatha*, Dubey interrupted: 'Let's begin rehearsals. You'll play Bhoopati and you will also direct the play.' I was stunned by his announcement, having worked at the time on only three plays: *Chup! Court Chalu Hai* (1967), *Suno Janmejay* and *Aadhe Adhure* (1968). Theatre Unit was a revered company, acclaimed for its productions of Ebrahim Alkazi's English plays and Dubey's Hindi plays. The sudden responsibility of directing its third Marathi production, following Dr Lagoo's *Gidhade* and Dubey's *Aadhe Adhure*, left me feeling daunted and pressured.

In the entertaining tale of *Vallabhpurchi Dantkatha*, Bhoopati, a young dentist, seeks to sell his ancestral property to fund his Calcutta clinic. However, the property has two major drawbacks: the ghost of an ancestor and extensive damage to the construction. Bhoopati teams up with a few shopkeepers and a friend to hide these flaws from the prospective buyer, the idiosyncratic Haaldaar. Their pathetic attempts to deceive him ultimately lead to a successful sale. Eknath Hattangadi delivered an outstanding performance as the eccentric businessman, Haaldaar. I had initially approached Ashok Saraf, impressed by his inter-bank competition performances, but he declined the minor role, prioritising mainstream theatre. This ended up working in my favour, as his acting style wouldn't have been a good fit for the play's subtle, situational humour.

Our production of *Vallabhpurchi Dantkatha* dominated the Maharashtra State Theatre Competition, securing awards for the Best Play, Best Director (shared by Dubey and me) and Best Actors (Eknath Hattangadi and Rekha Sabnis). Its sold-out performances at Tejpal Auditorium, a non-Marathi playhouse, were a testament to its commercial success. However, after twenty shows, I shared my concern with Dubey that the audience's responses had become too predictable, with laughter, applause and disappointment being expressed at the same moments each time. I felt like the production had lost its edge. Dubey swiftly agreed, and we brought the curtain down on *Vallabhpurchi Dantkatha* I hadn't yet grasped the importance of injecting spontaneity into rehearsed performances, a key element in keeping the audience engaged and ensuring that the show didn't feel stale or predictable.

Later, a commercial production of the play, staged by Sahitya Sangha of Bombay, brought together a star-studded cast, including Daji Bhatavdekar, Kamlakar Sarang, Laalan Sarang and Lalita Kenkre, under the direction of Damu Kenkre. Unfortunately, the show fell flat with the audiences. It took me some time to understand that the vulnerability and imperfections of the characters in my production were the secret to its success. I made it a point to carry this insight forward, aiming to strip away artifice while bringing vulnerability in my future performances, in order to make them more relatable and engaging for the audiences.

Following the success of *Vallabhpurchi Dantkatha*, a theatre company called the India Culture League invited me to direct a play of my choice under their banner. Dubey encouraged me to take up projects outside of his own theatre group. He also handed me a bunch of scripts that were sent to him, including *Draupadi* by Surendra Verma, which resonated with me. As it was intended for the Maharashtra State Theatre Competition, I translated the Hindi script into Marathi. The play poignantly portrayed the struggles of women in middle-class families, featuring a strong female protagonist who juggled domestic and financial responsibilities. However, the male characters were somewhat naïve and one-dimensional. In my translation, I preserved these characters as they were, avoiding the influence of Mohan Rakesh's *Aadhe Adhure*. I shared my observations with Surendra Verma, who presented me with a new, Hindi script,

Surya Ki Antim Kiran Se Surya Ki Pahali Kiran Tak, assuring me that I wouldn't find a similar issue in it. My production of *Draupadi* in Marathi received acclaim from all corners of Maharashtra.

In 1970, Dubey announced plans for Theatre Unit to produce Badal Sircar's play simultaneously in Hindi and Marathi, with me directing and acting in both productions. We had Pratibha Agrawal's Hindi translation of *Pagla Ghoda*, which I needed to translate into Marathi. As I began work on the translation as well as the rehearsals for the Hindi production, I faced a dilemma: should I translate or adapt? It wasn't just about changing the names of the characters or their attire; I had to ensure that the Marathi version retained the essence of Badal Sircar's original Bengali script, right from its title to its very core. Badal Sircar's metaphoric use of a children's song symbolising a liberated horse and the layers of human life, posed a challenge. What if I failed to capture these nuances accurately in Marathi? This fear hindered my progress. Ultimately, I decided against adaptation, opting for a faithful translation instead. I have mentioned earlier how C.T. Khanolkar gave solutions to my concerns relating to this translation.

In 1992, *Pagla Ghoda* was revived on the Marathi stage under the banner of my company Aniket. On the day of the Babri Masjid demolition, we performed in Chandannagar near Calcutta. Amidst the ensuing chaos, our team was escorted back to the city under police protection; we remained stranded in Calcutta for four or five days. Fifteen years later, in 2007, I had the opportunity to present *Pagla Ghoda* in Bengali, under the banner of Epic Theatre in New Jersey, USA, featuring local actors.

Pagla Ghoda unfolds in a crematorium, where four men await the cremation of a young woman with no family. As they drink, play cards and gossip, the deceased woman's spirit symbolically embodies the various women who have impacted their lives, as well as the oppressed and marginalised women in society at large. The play's strength lies in its ability to seamlessly blend the realism of the men's existence with the surreal presence of the young woman. It is an enduring testament to the power of theatre as an artform and Badal Sircar's masterful storytelling.

The printed Marathi translation of *Pagla Ghoda*, published by Popular Prakashan in 2004, is essentially an adaptation of my directorial script used in the play's production. As the copyright holder, I frequently receive requests for permission to stage it. But I worry that these theatre groups will be influenced by my interpretation, which will limit their own creative vision. In my opinion, the original script, the translation and the director's script should be published together, allowing for a more comprehensive understanding and diverse interpretations. Unfortunately, this is not common practice in our theatre tradition.

In 1971, Rajabhau Thakur offered me the lead role in his Marathi film *Baajiravacha Beta*. Prior to this, I had played a minor role in Dubey's film *Shantata! Court Chalu Aahe*, for which I received film acting tips from Govind Nihalani. The film's shooting was wrapped up in about five or six months. During the outdoor shoot, director Rajabhau Thakur, advised by doctors to abstain from drinking, would join me for long walks after the shoot. It was during one of these walks that he shared the story behind the creation of the Marathi play *Ashi Paakhare Yeti* (How the Birds Come).

When Rajabhau Thakur was between projects, he considered producing a commercial Marathi play with the star Marathi actor Arun Sarnaik in the lead role. Rajabhau approached Vijay Tendulkar with a printed script from an American cinematographer and asked him to adapt it into a play. However, Tendulkar's busy schedule delayed the writing process, and by the time he finished, Rajabhau was occupied with directing another film. Moreover, Rajabhau was dissatisfied with Tendulkar's adaptation, feeling that it had watered down the strong female lead from the original script. To make matters worse, Tendulkar had offered the play to another theatre company without Rajabhau's permission. I had sensed Rajabhau's lingering hurt when he said, 'Surely, Tendulkar would not have forgotten that he had written the play specifically for me!' Later when I saw the play, I realised why the protagonist was named Arun Sarnaik in the play. Sadly, Rajabhau did not live to see the publication of the fourth edition of *Ashi Paakhare Yeti*, in which Tendulkar has elaborately described Rajabhau Thakur's efforts behind the play.

After wrapping up *Baajiravacha Beta*, Rajabhau Thakur invited me to join his next Marathi film project, a biographical love story on Kumar Gandharva. S.N. Navre's script aimed to harmoniously blend Gandharva's musical prowess with his romantic journey. Jitendra Abhisheki came on board as the music director. I was thrilled to attend a song-recording session, where I observed Abhisheki expertly guiding Asha Bhosle through the songs. Asha-bai's rich voice left me spellbound. However, months later, Rajabhau regretfully informed me that the project had been shelved, bringing the chapter to a close.

In 1972, Dubey decided to produce Girish Karnad's *Hayavadan* with Theatre Unit, casting Puri saab and me. However, a significant event was unfolding in my personal life at the time—Chitra was expecting. As rehearsals began, I found it challenging to balance my time between the play and supporting Chitra during her pregnancy. I would often receive urgent calls from a sympathetic neighbour during the rehearsals at Walchand Terrace, prompting me to rush to Chitra's side at her parents' home in Colaba. Observing my distraction and frequent mid-rehearsal departures, Dubey kindly offered a solution: 'Let's schedule the play's premiere for the week after Chitra gives birth and Amol becomes a father.'

Dubey envisioned the production of *Hayavadan* with a minimalist set design, strategic lighting and live singing by the actors on stage. The cast was exceptional, featuring Puri saab as the rugged Kapil, myself as the poetic Devdatta and Sunila Pradhan as the alluring

Padmini who captivates both Kapil and Devdatta. Priya Tendulkar and Kalpana Lajmi were chosen for the roles of the two dolls. A special attraction was Dina Pathak's guest appearance as 'Kali-mata' in a single scene. Dubey masterfully directed a pivotal scene in which Kapil and Devdatta exchange heads without using wigs or masks, relying solely on body language and verbal expression. This play pushed my acting ability to its limits.

Performing in *Hayavadan* was a Herculean challenge for me, as I had to portray three distinct roles—that of the assistant of *sutradhaar* in the supporting role, of Devdatta until the midpoint, and finally, of Kapil with Devdatta's head, showcasing a transformative behavioural change. Dina Pathak's performance as Kali-mata, who was irritable because of sleep deprivation and was supportive of Padmini's calculating nature, was enthralling. Her ease and skill on stage left me—and sometimes Puri saab too—speechless. So engrossed would we be in her performance that we occasionally forgot to change costumes and prepare for our own entries, earning us Dubey's reprimand.

In *Hayavadan*, Dubey broke new ground by introducing live music, a departure from his previous reliance on pre-recorded film scores. He entrusted me with the music direction, acknowledging my 'better than his' understanding of music. My friend Vijay Kelkar conducted intensive music sessions, striving to refine our vocal performances. Those evenings at Walchand Terrace were filled with the resonant sounds of our rehearsals, which drew zealous complaints from neighbouring residents about the noise disturbance.

Shalmalee was born on 2 May 1972. The triumphant premiere of *Hayavadan* followed soon after. The play's subsequent performances in Bombay, Thane, Pune, Delhi and Calcutta were met with resounding success. Audiences loved the production; critics universally praised the play, lauding its every aspect. Theatre Unit

Hayavadan (Hindi, 1972) after the performance at Delhi with Amrish Puri, Sunila Pradhan & Shalmalee Palekar

Hayavadan (Hindi, 1972) with Amrish Puri, Bapu Kamerkar, Sushma Tendulkar & Dilip Gangodkar

Hayavadan (Hindi, 1972) with Sunila Pradhan

Vallabhpurchi Dantkatha (Marathi, 1969) with Eknath Hattangadi & Rekha Sabnis

Aadhe Adhure (Marathi, 1968) with Deepa Basrur & Bhakti Barve

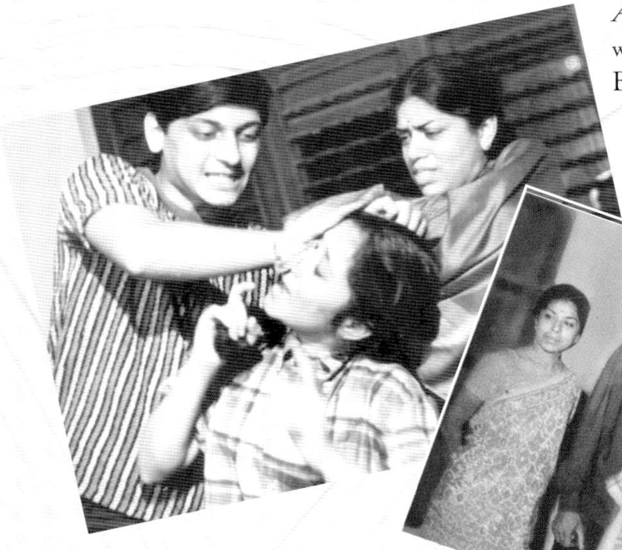

Aadhe Adhure (Hindi, 1968) with Amrish Puri, Jyotsna Karyekar, Bhakti Barve & Deepa Basrur

Aapla Buwa Asa Aahe (Marathi, 1978) with Dilip Kulkarni & Chitra Palekar

Pagla Ghoda (Marathi, 1992) with Hemu Adhikari

Gochi (Marathi, 1973) with (from left to right)
Dilip Kolhatkar, Bal Karve, Dilip Khandekar, Dilip Gangodkar, Achyut Deshingkar (seated) Dilip Kulkarni, Chitra Palekar, Jairam Hardikar & Juilee Deuskar

Kusur (Hindi, 2019)

24 November 2019, the director duo, just before the first show of *Kusur*, at NCPA, Mumbai

achieved a respectable financial gain; however, in keeping with the tradition of parallel theatre, the actors didn't receive a single penny.

The shows in Thane and Delhi stand out in my memory. En route to Thane, our bus suffered a flat tire, but a kind-hearted truck driver offered us a lift; we arrived an hour and a half late. Despite the delay, a crowd of three thousand welcomed us with thunderous applause. As we hastened to prepare for the stage, the local organisers expressed their disappointment over the minimalist set, mistakenly believing that we had left the props on the stranded bus. But Puri Saab's words alleviated their concerns. 'Please disregard the blank stage setting. We perform this play everywhere without props, and I assure you, the experience will be just as impactful.' The audience's standing ovation at the end of the performance validated his words.

Upon arrival in Delhi, we were informed that an array of cultural luminaries, ministers and even Prime Minister Indira Gandhi would be gracing our show. We were told that she would only be able to attend part of the performance, but to our surprise, she stayed until the very end. I later found out from Dr Narayana Menon, the director at NCPA, that she had fondly remembered my performance.

Prior to our production, B.V. Karanth had already adapted *Hayavadan* in the traditional *Yaksha-gana* style, captivating audiences with his powerful, high-pitched singing as the *sutradhaar*. The production masterfully incorporated an energetic dance style and stage masks into the performance, but I felt it didn't fully convey the playwright's modern themes, such as the woman's quest for an ideal partner and the nuanced aspects of femininity.

Following our production, Vijaya Mehta adapted *Hayavadan* in Marathi in 1975, but the translation done by C.T. Khanolkar fell short. It failed to capture the poetic essence of the original play struggling to convey the content through the traditional *Bhaarud* verse form, a metaphoric style often used by Maharashtra's saint poets. Vijaya-bai's production opted for a decorative approach, lacking the raw, vibrant energy of folk expression seen in Karanth's version. I was slightly disappointed as Vijaya-bai's rendition prioritised a polished, refined theatricality over the unbridled spirit of the original.

However, the opportunity to witness one script being interpreted by three distinct directors was a stupendous opportunity for theatre enthusiasts. For me personally, this experience marked a significant leap in my artistic growth and maturity.

Satyadev Dubey's encouragement led to the inception of my own theatre group, Aniket, around the same time. Vijay Tendulkar graciously served as our first president, remaining with us until the end. Under Aniket's banner, we produced around eight to ten Marathi plays. We adopted a collective financial strategy: we would stage at least five ticketed shows for each production, with me personally covering the initial costs; if the play generated enough profit to sustain further performances, we would continue; otherwise, we would discontinue the shows once the profits were depleted. While I was immersed in film shoots, Chitra, Dilip Kulkarni and Vijay Shirke adeptly managed the company's affairs, ensuring seamless operation. This company enabled me to utilise my film acting earnings into experimental play productions and other creative pursuits.

My primary objective behind setting up Aniket was to provide Chitra with a productive outlet for her creative energy, especially when I was so busy during my stint in cinema in the 1970s and 1980s, I urged Chitra to leverage Aniket for producing, directing and acting in innovative plays. Although Dilip Kulkarni directed two plays featuring Chitra, and we produced notable works like *Ani Mhanun Konihi* (And So Anyone) in 1977 and *Nagamandala* (The Serpent Ritual) in 1990, earning awards at the Maharashtra state drama competitions, Chitra's involvement with Aniket remained limited. As time passed, her disappointment grew, and I noticed a lingering sense of unfulfillment in her.

I adapted and directed the shorter version of the play *Suryastachya Antim Kiranapasun Suryodayachya Pratham Kiranaparayant*. An amusing anecdote from this show comes to mind. The inter-bank competition had devolved into unsavoury practices like sabotaging performances and causing commotion. Undeterred, my team of young actors took the stage, and as the curtain opened, the balcony audience began singing bhajans while playing instruments, attempting to disrupt our show. I recognised their ploy and instructed my team to power through, which they did with remarkable focus. The judges, Arvind Deshpande and Neelam Prabhu, were so impressed that Arvind publicly lauded the team's determination, awarding them a special prize.

In 1973, the shooting for *Rajnigandha* got over, and the film wasn't released for about a year and a half. But I was so engrossed in my theatre activities that I wasn't worried about it in the least. I took up *Vasanakand*, rehearsed with Chitra for a couple of months and did three performances at a go in August 1974. After a month, *Rajnigandha* was released. I was still working at the bank. Now, with my energy levels waning, I sometimes wonder how I managed to pack so much into such a brief period.

While designing *Vasanakand* for the stage, I faced the daunting task of translating the text's vivid visual descriptions into a live performance. The story unfolds in a grand, isolated palace surrounded by barren rocky terrain, devoid of any greenery. The protagonist, Hemkant, is a sculptor who brings Lalita to life through his sketches and sculptures. Their journey together is ignited by Lalita's sensual inspiration. To convey these evocative visuals, I relied on fresh lighting techniques to transport the audience to this desolate yet enchanting world. I had approached the brothers, Pramod Guruji and Vinod Guruji, who gave me sculptures made with plaster of Paris. To convey the palatial setting, I opted for subtle, suggestive props—a grand wooden door frame, a small window-like gate at the back and an embossed pillar in the front. For the climactic scene where a mob gathers to condemn the couple, I chose not to physically stage the crowd. Instead, I leveraged audio-visual elements to evoke its presence: a cacophony of instruments and flickering torchlight. By suggestion rather than spectacle, I aimed to intensify the focus on the couple's emotional entrapment, their desperate struggle against the crushing weight of societal expectations.

The play's central theme of an incestuous brother-sister relationship was undoubtedly shocking and taboo for the middle-class theatregoers. I was also dissatisfied with the original play's verbosity, so we distilled it into a concise ninety-minute stage script. However, we were drained by the exhausting legal battles to preserve artistic freedom. I have previously written at length about these struggles.

Sandhya has a knack for catching me off guard with incisive questions. She fired away, asking: What drove you to stage *Vasanakand*? Considering the script's emphasis on dialogue, wouldn't an audio drama on the radio be a more suitable medium? Didn't the script's depiction of sexual inequality, objectification of women, and adherence to traditional gender norms raise concerns for you? These fiery questions left me reeling. They prompted me to revisit my thought process. I have to admit, I don't analyse art with sharp objectivity like Sandhya does. Instead, I rely on my 'theatre instinct' to evaluate scripts, classifying them as good, bad, classic or ordinary. After eight to ten performances of *Vasanakand*, we reluctantly ceased planning further shows due to the unavailability of suitable theatres. The exact reason for our abrupt decision to halt our production eludes me now. Mahesh Elkunchwar hadn't witnessed the play's staging; his silence on our censorship battles and the freedom of expression debate was unexpected.

The Pune show of *Vasanakand* was memorable for a peculiar reason. After the play ended, many spectators lingered in the hall, disgruntled that the play had only lasted for seventy-five minutes. They felt misled, as the advertisements hadn't specified the duration.

Some requested a refund, while others sought to meet the film hero Amol Palekar. The amusing aspect is that this post-show turmoil extended over a hundred minutes. In hindsight, I could have countered that they had, in fact, received a three-hour entertainment package worth the price of their ticket!

In 1974, the Chabildas High School hall was inaugurated as a theatre venue with the performance of C.T. Khanolkar's play *Pratima* under the banner of Aavishkar. This atypical play, written entirely in free verse, was directed by Arvind Deshpande. Bhaskar Chandavarkar was its music director, and the cast included Dr Lagoo, Kumud Powar, Deepa Basroor and me. Besides the actors' impressive memorisation skills, the production ultimately fell short of expectations. The disappointment of investing time and effort without achieving the desired result can be overwhelming, but fortunately, a serendipitous incident often emerges to lift the spirits and rekindle hope.

Anamika, a pioneering theatre company in Calcutta, had been tirelessly promoting Hindi plays in a region dominated by Bengali culture. To mark their silver jubilee, they organised a national theatre festival, featuring an experimental project called 'One Script, Many Expressions' for young directors. Dubey recommended me for this exciting opportunity, which brought together directors from across India. We were to spend ten days in Calcutta, conducting workshops for local artistes and staging a performance of about half an hour or more. About six weeks before the festival, we received the script for a one-act play written by Ashokamitran, which would be the basis for our creative interpretations at the festival. Alongside the dialogue-free script, we received the playwright's prefatory note, which offered insightful guidance. Ashokamitran expressed a desire for his play *Bayaan Ek Buddhu Ka* (The Account of a Dumb Fellow) to be performed for an intimate audience with passion and dedication. He encouraged us to think beyond the conventional proscenium stage, inviting directors to take creative liberties in deciding on the performance space, including audience-seating arrangements.

His play aimed to capture the inner world of the everyday person, their turbulent surroundings, and their struggles with their environment—all without relying on words or dialogue. The script eschewed traditional narrative structures, instead opting for abstract scenes, fragmented incidents and characters without sharply defined personalities. Before heading to Calcutta, I delved deeply into the script and resolved to honour its spirit by forgoing dialogue altogether. I envisioned a performance in which the actors' physicality, their collective body language and live sound would conjure the dramatic impact, creating a unique theatrical experience.

Upon reaching Calcutta, I began the selection of actors from a pool of unknown talent. Relying on my instincts, I quickly identified eight to ten individuals with potential. I structured our rehearsals in such a way that I focused on vocal and physical expression in the morning, and explored the script's theatrical possibilities in the afternoon. Two actors stood out: Ajit Bannerjee, with his striking physique and agility, and Yama Agrawal, with her expressive face and melodious voice made their's a compelling presence. I began to craft situations centred around these two in the script, encouraging the entire cast to push their boundaries and tap into latent artistic depths. This marked a continuation of my exploration of the primordial man-woman relationship, which began with *Avadhya* and evolved through *Bayaan Ek Buddhu Ka* and later *Gochi* with Jayram-Juili—each iteration revealing new layers and levels of expression.

Six directors transformed various spaces within Shri Shikshaayatan School into unique performance venues. Vimal Laath utilised the empty swimming pool, surrounding it with seating for the audience on all four sides. I opted for the ladies hostel veranda and the adjacent staircase, arranging the spectators on three sides. Satyavrat Sinha chose the conventional proscenium stage, while Vibhu Kumar set up a central stage on the grounds, encircled by the audience. This unconventional format, in which viewers moved from one stage to another, eagerly anticipating each new performance, was a novel experience for all. As a young director, I was particularly thrilled to have esteemed theatre personalities from Bengal and Delhi appreciate my work.

Throughout my career, I've been blessed with the affection and admiration of Bengali artistes and spectators from the world of drama and cinema. My trio of Bengali films, *Mother* (1979), *Kalankini* (The Defamed) (1981) and *Chena Achena* (Known Strangers) (1983), managed to leave an impact on Bengal's cultural landscape, with a loyal fan base that endures to this day.

Once, during a busy shoot in Bombay, I received an unexpected visit from Narayan Chakraborty from Calcutta. He offered me a lead role opposite Sharmila Tagore in a poignant love story titled *Mother*. Language wasn't a problem as I had learnt Bengali in my college days. Chakraborty came with a recommendation letter from none other than Manik-da (Satyajit Ray), which sealed my decision to join the project. However, upon commencing the shoot in Calcutta, Sharmila and I quickly realised that the director lacked fundamental filmmaking knowledge. Further investigation revealed that the producer, a renowned jeweller, was more interested in establishing himself as a music director than in the film's technical aspects. Undeterred, Sharmila, the cinematographer and I pooled our experience to bring the film to life. Our collective efforts paid off as *Mother* became a massive hit, its songs remaining popular even today, especially during Durga Puja celebrations. My bond with Sharmila, 'Rinku' as I call her fondly, has stood the test of time.

I shared my misadventure of working with Narayan Chakraborty with Manik-da, expressing surprise at his endorsement. Manik-da chuckled and clarified, 'You might have missed the nuance in my letter … I described him as someone who worked hard in the film society movement.' He pointed out that it was my responsibility to dig deeper and not just rely on his recommendation. Indeed, I had overlooked the details of the letter once I saw Manik-da's signature.

Two years later, I received a visit from another elderly gentleman from Calcutta. His grey beard and moustache, paired with his rumpled kurta and pyjama and a cotton bag slung over his shoulder, gave him a distinctive appearance. Cautious due to my experience with Narayan Chakraborty, I engaged him in conversation and discovered that he was none other than Dinen Gupta, a renowned cinematographer who had worked with Ritwik Ghatak on classics like *Ajaantrik* and *Meghe Dhaka Tara*. He proposed that I play the lead role in his upcoming mainstream Bengali film *Kalankini*, which he would both direct and cinematise. The prospect of working alongside Mamata Shankar, already on board as the heroine, sealed the deal. Though the film's story has now faded from my memory, the experience remains etched in my mind.

As the shooting began, I was shocked to discover that the esteemed cinematographer, Dinen Gupta, struggled as a director. He seemed more focused on managing the cast's egos, and orchestrating the set, rather than grasping the film's artistic vision. In one song sequence, he asked me to dance with Mamata Shankar, a skilled dancer, which was a daunting task for me. Before this, I had danced only in two films, *Baton Baton Mein* and *Damaad*. With no guidance available on set, I relied on Mamata's expertise, moving my body in time with her steps, and hoped for the best. To my utter surprise, Mamata praised my efforts, saying, 'Oh, you're being modest, you danced quite well!' Despite my disappointment in Dinen Gupta's direction, I completed the film as a professional obligation. *Kalankini* achieved financial success, and Shyamal Mitra's music became a hit.

In 1983, I had a similar experience with Pinaki Chaudhuri, a director from mainstream Bengali cinema, who approached me for the film *Chena Achena*. The prospect of working with beloved actors Soumitra Chatterjee and Tanuja convinced me to join the project. The shooting took place entirely in Calcutta, requiring me to make multiple trips. The highlights of my experience were the literary discussions with Soumitra at his residence after our daily shoots, and sharing drinks with Tanuja while indulging in gossip about the Hindi film industry. Unfortunately, these were the only positives; and the fact that the film did surprisingly well at the box office despite my reservations.

After this trio of successes, I eagerly joined Asit Sen's Bengali film *Prarthana* (1984), expecting a valuable learning experience. Unfortunately, I found him struggling with alcohol addiction. Nevertheless, the dedicated cast, including Moushumi Chatterjee, Debashree Roy, Victor Banerjee and I, pushed through and completed the film. Back in Bombay, I was shocked to discover that the producer had dubbed my role using another actor without my consent and even short-changed me on payment. Disillusioned by this unprofessional conduct, I decided to step away from commercial Bengali cinema, with a few cherished exceptions that sadly remained unfinished.

Shankar Bhattacharya's promising film *Ashwamedher Ghoda* (The Ashwamedh Horse), starring Smita Patil and me, was unfortunately cut short due to financial issues after just four days of shooting. We had arrived in Calcutta with high hopes, and one scene, in particular, stands out—a scene outside the Grand Hotel on Chowringhee Road, where Smita and I were to walk amidst the crowd while talking. However, as we began filming it, the crowd recognised us, and people started closing in on us, leaving Smita terrified. She clutched my hand, urging me to leave, but I persuaded her to stay until the shot was completed. The resulting scene was terrific, and I loved it so much that I recreated it in my own film *Ankahee*, in Bombay's crowded Fort area, with Dilip Kulkarni and Devika Mukherjee. This poignant scene highlighted the human ability to find solitude amidst chaos.

In 1981–82, I had the privilege of working in Pijush Ganguly's film *Britta* (The News), alongside esteemed theatre personalities Tripti Mitra and Anil Chatterjee. The story follows the journey of a newly appointed labour officer as he becomes involved with the lives of jute mill workers. I vividly recall the sweltering heat in which we shot on the bank of the Ganga, surrounded by massive machinery, labour colonies and the officer's picturesque bungalow. After each day's shoot, we'd gather in the evenings, sharing poems in Bangla and Marathi. Despite the promising start, *Britta* remained incomplete due to insufficient funding, leaving only memories of a powerful narrative and the camaraderie the crew shared on the location.

Though I gave up acting in Bangla films, I enthusiastically acted in two Kannada films, *Kanneshwara Rama* (The Legendary Outlaw) (1977) and *Shringaramas* (Paper Boats) (1978), and one Malayalam film, *Olangal* (Waves) (1982). Moreover, I deliberately accepted three big commercial Hindi films with south Indian producers and directors: *Solva Sawan* (1979), *Shriman Shrimati* (1982) and *Jeevan Dhaara* (1982). The real reason for this decision was rooted in my dispute with B.R. Chopra over unpaid remuneration for *Agni Pareeksha* (1981). He had tauntingly said, 'Let's see how you survive in the film world!' Determined to prove him wrong, I seized every good opportunity to show that I was in demand in not just Hindi but regional language cinema too. My foray into south Indian cinema was a refreshing change, as I encountered respectful, disciplined professionals who provided actors with the next day's shooting schedule, complete with scenes and dialogues, the evening before. I appreciated their honesty in financial dealings, the generous remuneration they offered, and the delicious, clean food they served the crew.

M.S. Sathyu, acclaimed for his groundbreaking Hindi film *Garm Hava*, was set to produce *Kanneshwara Rama* in Kannada. Following the success of Shyam Benegal's *Ankur*, the lead pair of Anant Nag and Shabana Azmi was a sought-after pair. Anant was cast as the titular 'Kanneshwara Rama', a Robin Hood-like figure in Kannada mythology, with Shabana as his heroine. I was thrilled to be offered the role of 'Chennira Daakoo', the hero's close friend. Sathyu transformed my look with a thick moustache, dark eyebrows and a cheek-wound mark. We travelled overnight by train to Bangalore and arrived at the outskirts of Shimoga, where the team was stationed in a tent.

The evening before shooting began, the assistant director handed me my Kannada dialogues. Through just a few rehearsals, I committed them to memory. I've found that when it comes to memorising dialogues in Indian languages, oral repetition is more effective than relying solely on the script. Using this method, I quickly grasped the lines. Impressed with my diction, Sathyu exclaimed, 'You'll be doing your own dubbing.' It was indeed a vote of confidence. I arrived at the shooting location, ready to tackle the scene. It was a question-answer exchange between Chennira, seated in the old castle, and Rama, entering through the broken gate opposite the castle. Sathyu aimed to capture the magical atmosphere of dusk, so we began the preparations around 5:30 p.m. However, I realised that in my excitement, I had memorised only my own lines and not the other character's dialogues, my response cues, and so on. I quickly sought out Anant, asking him to read out his lines so I could grasp the dialogue flow and respond accordingly. I listened intently to Anant's lines, identifying the cue words 'station' and 'police' to respond with my lines. With a deep breath, I returned to my mark, and Sathyu asked, 'Amol, are you ready?' Though I nodded, my heart raced with the fear of mistimed cues. Knowing the fleeting nature of the dusk hour, I focused solely on Anant's words. As he began, I zeroed in on 'station' and ignored everything else. As he spoke, I responded fluidly, executing a series of subtle actions—taking out a beedi, tucking it into my lips, producing a matchbox, lighting the beedi and extinguishing the match—all in perfect sync with my lines, and delivered my second line upon hearing the next cue. The unit erupted in applause as Sathyu called 'Cut!'

This experience reinforced a fundamental principle I had learnt from Dubey: 'First, listen carefully to what the person in front of you is saying.' I also realised the importance of rehearsing not just my dialogue but also those of my fellow actors when working in unfamiliar languages. This lesson proved invaluable in my future film projects, allowing me to deliver more nuanced and responsive performances.

In 1978, Pattabhi Rama Reddy, the well-regarded producer of the award-winning film *Sanskaar* starring Girish Karnad, met me in Bombay. He proposed to simultaneously produce two films—*Shringaramas* in Kannada and *Paper Boats* in English—based on a single story. The narrative focused on a husband's efforts to help his wife overcome depression. The montage-style, non-linear script with minimal dialogue featured only two characters. Drawn to this complex exploration of the man-woman relationship, I immersed myself in the lead role. The wife's character was to be played by Deepa Dhanraj, who had no prior acting experience. Pattabhiram asked me to guide her through the process, adding an extra layer of challenge to this ambitious project.

A small hut was constructed on a farm near Bangalore, serving as the setting for our scenes. The script called for experimentation; we enacted each scene in two or three different ways before selecting the final version for the actual shooting. I appreciated this flexible approach, which allowed for creative exploration. Because the location was quiet, we used the lip-sync recording technique to capture high-quality sound. However, since we did not have to dub, I never got to see the film's final cut. Later, I learnt that the Kannada version *Shringaramas* was released after a significant delay, leaving me wondering about the final product.

After the shooting had been wrapped up, I was waiting to catch my flight back to Bombay at the Bangalore airport, when I was surprised by a friendly pat on the back. It was Mehmood, the

Shringaramas/Paper Boats (1978), with Deepa Dhanaraj

legendary comedian. Despite it being our first meeting, he was very warm. When he discovered that we were both headed to shoot for *Bin Baap Ka Beta*, he insisted that I go along with him directly at S.L. Studio in Chembur, rather than going home first. I noticed Mehmood frequently taking handfuls of tablets, a habit that seemed to be a part of his daily routine.

The shoot commenced with a scene featuring the sensuous dancer Helen's bewitching performance, which Mehmood and I were supposed to watch sitting at a table. However, Mehmood spontaneously got up and joined Helen, prompting the director to shout 'Cut!' I assumed the shoot was halted due to the actor's unexpected move. But when he returned to sit beside me, his face was drenched in blood. Blood was streaming from his eyes. He was rushed to a hospital. Over the next few days, I completed my scenes with Simple Kapadia. Months later, the second leg of shooting took place at Vrindavan Garden in Mysore, where I worked alongside Bhagwan Dada and Shashikala. Mehmood was noticeably absent, and I learnt that his health had declined drastically due to his struggle with drug addiction.

The director of *Bin Baap Ka Beta*, Mukul Dutt, tried to plan a couple of films with me. One of them was *Ankush*, starring Shabana Azmi as well. But the film was abandoned after just three or four days of shooting.

I owe my involvement in *Solva Sawan* to Kamal Haasan, who personally called and urged me to recreate his role from the Tamil original, *16 Vayathinile*. After watching the highly acclaimed Tamil film, I suggested to the Telugu producer, Anjaneyulu, that they should consider casting Sridevi in the remake as well, who I believed was exceptionally talented. Her performance alongside Kamal in the Tamil version had looked remarkably effortless. Although her mother was initially concerned about her lack of proficiency in Hindi, Sridevi eventually agreed to take on the challenge.

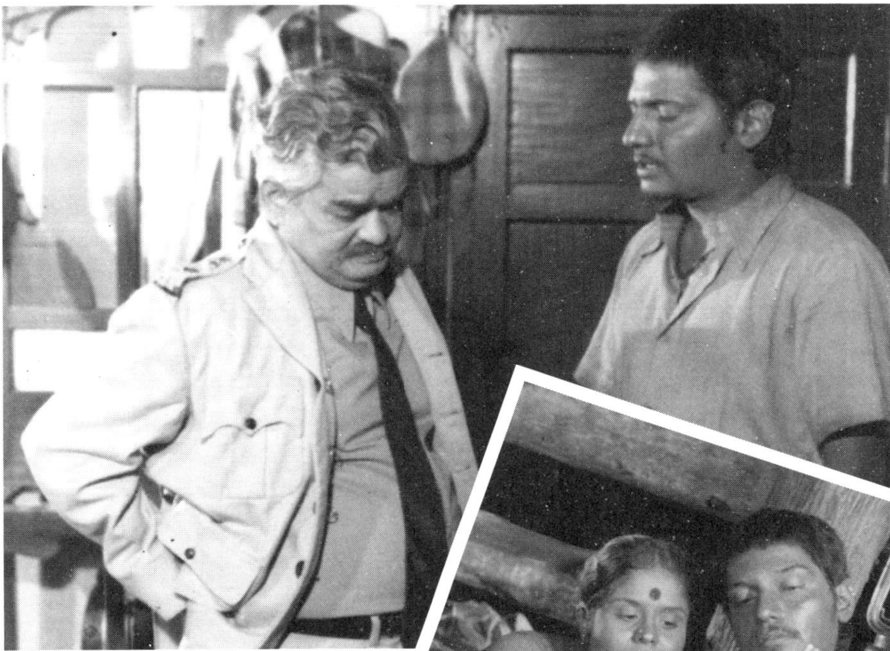

Agantuk (1978),
with Datta Bhat, Chitra Palekar

Bin Baap Ka Beta (1978), with Mehmood, Simple Kapadia

Ankush (1977), with Shabana Azmi

Solva Sawan (1979), with Sridevi

Solva Sawan's narrative followed a familiar triangular structure: a pure-hearted boy deeply in love with a charming village girl, and a villain seeking to exploit her. I wanted to bring a fresh spin to the role of the innocent boy, diverging from Kamal's portrayal. I engaged in extensive discussions with the director, Bharathiraja, sharing my thoughts on how to make the character more believable. I suggested that the boy's innocence might sometimes appear unconvincing and proposed an alternative approach. We agreed that depicting the boy as mentally challenged would add depth and originality to the character.

I underwent a complete transformation for the role—getting curly hair and a downward-sloping moustache, and altering my body language so that it conveyed a subtle deformity. Through extensive rehearsals, I honed my demeanour to perfect the character's unique physicality. The shoot spanned a month and a half, traversing various locations along the Andhra Pradesh–Tamil Nadu border. During the shooting, Sridevi would occasionally allude to Kamal's performance in the Tamil original, but Bharathiraja, would promptly remind her that our version had deviated from the original. I had the privilege of witnessing Sridevi's raw talent and spontaneity up close, but unfortunately, I didn't see that same spark in her subsequent Hindi film career. Her trajectory was remarkable though, beginning with our film and including her iconic performance in Shekhar Kapur's *Mister India* in 1987. When Kulbhushan Kharbanda's understated portrayal of the villain diverged from Rajinikanth's iconic style in the original, the team, including Sridevi, the director and producer, grew uneasy. As I had advocated for Kulbhushan's casting, the issue fell to me to resolve. During a meeting on the third day of shooting, we debated whether to replicate the original style of the villain or infuse our version with a new creative vision. Ultimately, we decided to eschew imitation, embracing instead a distinctive approach for each character. This allowed us to complete the film without any delay.

Following my usual practice, I detached myself from the film after completing my work. I ignored rumours about Sridevi's dialogues being re-recorded or the film being suppressed by a popular Hindi film hero. After its release, the film unfortunately didn't fare well. However, our performances, particularly Sridevi's and mine, received positive reviews. I couldn't help but feel a tinge of sadness that Sridevi's subsequent success was largely attributed to her sensual image, rather than to her remarkable talent for conveying emotional depth and sensitivity.

The esteemed South Indian producer–director duo, B. Nagi Reddy and Vijay Reddy, helmed *Shriman Shrimati* with precision and discipline. The entire film was shot in three sessions at the AVM Studio in Madras. It featured an ensemble cast of three couples: Sanjeev Kumar–Rakhi, Rakesh Roshan–Deepti Naval and Sarika–I. The schedule was meticulously planned, ensuring that no time was wasted. Scenes featuring Sarika and I were filmed in the morning, while those that involved Sanjeev, Rakhi and the two of us were shot in the afternoons. In the final session, I even completed my dubbing in the afternoons, after the morning shoot.

On the first day of shooting, Sanjeev Kumar invited me to his room, saying, 'Join me tonight. Let's have some fun.' After his evening shoot, he returned to his room around ten, where Rakesh Roshan was already waiting. Sanjeev pulled out a bottle of Black Label whisky and poured us each a glass. I was curious to discuss about his time at the IPTA (Indian People's Theatre Association), but they had other plans. They regaled me with stories of actors' antics abroad, leaving me with the feeling that my own misdeeds were tame in comparison. This impromptu gathering lasted till three in the morning and my early morning shoot loomed over me. I quickly understood why Sanjeev preferred starting work in the second shift in the afternoon. Disinterested in late-night drinking and gossip about things like 'who gets their laundry done at the producer's expense', I politely declined any future invitations after that first night.

During the shoot of *Jeevan Dhaara*, I once again got an opportunity to appreciate the disciplined approach of South Indian filmmakers. This film, inspired from Ritwik Ghatak's classic *Meghe Dhaka Tara*, starred Rekha and boasted of an ensemble cast that included Raj Babbar, Kanwaljeet Singh, Simple Kapadia, Sulochana Latkar, and many others. Laxmikant–Pyarelal's music added to the film's charm. One song, *'Gangaram kuvaaraa reh gayaa'* was extensively filmed on me, and, although I found it monotonous, it surprisingly became a hit. A memorable moment during the rehearsals was when the director felt my understated acting wasn't enough for a scene in which I had to mimic comedy legends like Mehmood and Johny Walker. I pointed out that if he wanted exact imitations, a professional mimicry artiste might have been a better fit.

To shoot this film, we used the sprawling, air-conditioned studio owned by Telugu superstar Akkineni Nageswara Rao. Interestingly, our film's shooting occupied only one floor; the remaining five floors were dedicated to various projects with Jeetendra in the lead role. On my first morning, I arrived at 9 a.m. to find Jeetendra filming a song in the outdoor area. He warmly greeted me in his authentic Marathi accent, enquiring about my stay. After exchanging pleasantries, he invited me to join him for lunch. Throughout the day, Jeetendra efficiently moved between the floors, simultaneously working on a whopping six or seven films. This starkly contrasted with the often lackadaisical Bombay film culture, which allowed for delays and unprofessional habits, sometimes even taking pride in them.

At lunch with Jeetendra, I expressed my surprise at his ability to juggle multiple roles and shooting schedules. He chuckled and said, 'I simply change clothes and keep presenting the same beloved "Jeetendra" image.' He then added with a mischievous glint in his eyes: 'And I often don't even need to change out of my white trousers and shoes!' I was struck by his candid response, which inadvertently also revealed the key to success in mainstream cinema: sustain the star system, repeat what the audiences like, and maintain a consistent image. When I remained silent, he playfully remarked, 'Besides, I've left the actual acting to talented folks like Sanjeev, you, Karnad and Naseer.' It is impressive that his daughter Ekta Kapoor replicated this disciplined approach in television production as well, achieving unparalleled success for many decades.

When I was offered a role in the Malayalam film *Olangal*, I eagerly accepted it. The team boasted an impressive lineup: co-stars Poornima Jayaram and Ambika, renowned composer Ilaiyaraaja and the inventive director-cinematographer Balu Mahendra. Balu was adapting Dick Richards' film *Man, Woman and Child* for the Malayalam audience, while Shekhar Kapur was working on its Hindi adaptation, *Masoom* with Naseer, Shabana and Supriya Pathak. I was curious to see how Balu would interpret the same theme. However, both Balu and Shekhar chose to remain faithful to the original story.

For the first session of *Olangal*, we headed to the picturesque surroundings of Ooty for the outdoor shooting. Balu's mastery of visual storytelling was evident, and his shooting style was equally exemplary. He leveraged the soft, natural light of early morning and sunset, putting aside lighting and reflectors. We shot for just two hours in the morning and an hour and a half in the evening. The atmosphere on the location remained calm and peaceful, without a single instance of unpleasantness among the crew. Balu was very supportive and made the time to help me memorise my Malayalam dialogues. Having learnt from past experiences, I made sure to remember by heart the dialogues of my co-stars as well.

The film industry's cultural aspects are fascinating. In Mumbai, I've seen people praise others to their faces, only to criticise them when they're not around. Hypocrisy was almost absent in the south.

The Bengali film industry's elitist attitude, claiming sole ownership of artistic knowledge, was also refreshingly absent from the south. Instead, it stood out for its polite and constructive exchange of ideas, at all levels of the pyramid. It is disheartening that the Marathi film industry has assimilated the worst traits of these cultures, despite having exceptional talent. Why we are consistently offered secondary or insignificant roles when we have the talent to pull off lead roles? That we have failed to showcase our potential and unique voice is a sorrowful reality. The Marathi film industry has a rich legacy to be proud of, thanks to pioneers like Dadasaheb Phalke, the founder of Indian cinema, and V. Shantaram, the visionary who revolutionised the industry. Shantaram-bapu created a self-sufficient empire, encompassing production, sound recording, editing, laboratory services, and distribution and exhibition facilities. He boldly introduced new faces and explored fresh themes, achieving great success. Unfortunately, his radical business model and contributions were not emulated or appreciated by the Marathi film industry. Instead, his use of Marathi-influenced Hindi and experimentation with a non-star cast were ridiculed. In contrast, I've witnessed greater respect and admiration for his achievements in Bengal and the south. It is sad to see Maharashtra failing to honour its own cinema legends.

A.V. Mohan, a prominent Tamil producer based in Mumbai, held me in high regard. He signed with me a three-year contract for a trio of mainstream Hindi films: *Taxi-Taxie* (1977), *Damaad* (1978) and *Meri Biwi Ki Shaadi* (1979). This contract proved to be a game-changer for me, offering a fantastic chance to establish myself in the industry.

Taxi-Taxie had several appealing elements. I was excited to work with the new director Irshad and debutant music director Hemant Bhosle. One song, *'Laai kahaan ae zindagi'*, remains unforgettable—it is a rare duet by Lata and Asha, its composition a masterpiece. I had the privilege of attending Asha-bai's recording session with a full orchestra, an experience I'll always treasure. However, the film's fast-cutting editing style diminished the song's haunting beauty. Jalal Agha's attempt to emulate R.D. Burman's style fell flat, and his acting left a lot to be desired. It pained me to see a beloved song ruined in the film. I wish I could have intervened in the shooting or the editing process, like other stars used to, to prevent this disappointment.

The film's core narrative had come together quite well, but A.V. Mohan was intent on keeping the first-time director firmly under his thumb, and that lack of freedom ruined the project in every possible way. The story was simple—a Mumbai taxi driver forms fleeting yet occasionally life-altering connections with his passengers. Much of the film was set in a moving taxi, but the poignant scenes and songs were shot in the studio using back projection. During filming, I often sat with the co-stars in the taxi, chatting about everything under the sun, laughing, sharing stories—heartwarming moments that remain vivid in my memory.

When it came to *Damaad*, I refused to let A.V. interfere. I adopted short hair, a thick moustache and glasses for the role as the director wanted. My heroine was Ranjeeta Kaur, riding high on her fame from *Laila Majnu*. Having worked with Rishi Kapoor before this, it took her a while to adjust to the restrained tone of my acting. For one of the supporting roles, I proposed the name of Ashok Saraf. Working with Preeti Ganguly was an entirely different experience. Owing to her heavy weight, she had often been typecast into comic roles, a fate she deeply resented. In truth, she was a very sensitive actress, and I was adamant on ensuring that her role didn't get reduced to exaggerated, farcical gestures. Preeti appreciated my support and, even after the film, maintained a close friendship with me.

During the song recordings with Hemant Bhosle, I had to record a few lines in my own voice. While sharing the same microphone as Asha Bhosle, my heart pounded so loudly that I'm certain not only could she hear it, but everyone else in the adjacent room could too. My throat was parched, and sweat soaked through my clothes. But Asha-bai, ever the professional, calmly guided me through the ordeal, helping me overcome my nervousness. In the end, *Damaad* proved to be a financial success, a silver lining in an otherwise tumultuous experience.

For the third film proposal, A.V. Mohan constantly suggested different stories and casting options. After turning down most of them, I finally mentioned Vishram Bedekar's play *Vaje Paul Apule* (The Sound of our Footsteps) to him. The story revolved around a man consumed by an irrational fear that he is suffering from a terminal illness, and in his desperation, he embarks on a search for a new husband for his wife. Mohan immediately set things in motion to produce *Meri Biwi Ki Shaadi*. He was getting an excellent Indian adaptation of the 1964 Hollywood classic *Send Me No Flowers*. The heroine, director and technical crew from *Damaad* were retained, and Usha Khanna was brought on board as the music director. A.V. Mohan also accepted my suggestion to cast Dilip Kulkarni, whose performance in the play *Aapla Buwa Asa Aahe* had impressed him. Because Dilip and I both were shooting in Goa, we would shoot during the day and perform *Aapla Buwa Asa Aahe* on the stage in the evenings.

One evening, after wrapping up a scene on the beach, we were relaxing when Ranjeeta came and sat beside me. Out of nowhere, she asked, 'Vidya Sinha was your first heroine; after that, you chose to work with actresses like Zarina, Shabana and Rameshwari—all from FTII. I'm also an alumna of the same institute, so I'm puzzled why you seem hesitant to work with me.' Her directness took me by surprise.

'Who told you that? That's completely untrue. The selection of actors is always the producer's prerogative, and I don't interfere in that. I do, however, offer suggestions for supporting roles when I'm asked. I think there's been a misunderstanding. While it's true that some actors wield their influence to get their way, I've never been one to throw my weight around. Lastly, I am not from the institute myself, and am certainly not in awe of its alumni,' I said.

Despite my efforts to reassure her, I could sense that the question continued to linger in her mind throughout the shoot. However, in a delightful turn of events, we reunited years later in Pune, and we had a great laugh about that very incident. Today, our interactions are free from any remnants of awkwardness or reserve. We wonder now why the film didn't resonate with audiences. Perhaps because the story revolved around a middle-aged couple, or maybe Usha Khanna's music wasn't as impactful as it should have been.

Even after A.V. Mohan moved to Chennai, he would periodically call me, enthusiastic about new ideas and projects. Each time, I'd tell him, 'I'm no longer interested in acting,' but he never seemed to accept it. Monument Valley, nestled in the Utah desert, served as the iconic backdrop for Clint Eastwood's legendary Westerns. Just as the Valley's awe-inspiring rock formations have been shaped by time and wind, the landscape of my life has been moulded by its own monumental figures. A.V. Mohan was undoubtedly one of them.

While *Taxi-Taxie* was in production, I was simultaneously shooting for a Hindi film called *Agar* (1977) and a Marathi film called *Tuch Mazi Rani* (1977). Mohan Rao, the producer of *Agar* was banking on the successful trio of Zarina Wahab, Vijayendra Ghatge and I from *Chitchor*, and was hoping to replicate the same magic with *Agar*. Playing a high-society character in *Agar* was a departure from my typical middle-class roles. The fact that it marked the debut of a promising new director, Ismail Shroff added to the excitement. However, the film's uninspired music and the jarring performances of supporting actors like Kader Khan, Gulshan Bawra, Jagdeep and Kishan Dhawan—each trying to outdo the other in their own over-the-top way—ultimately left me disenchanted with the final product.

Boredom, which has never once afflicted me while working on plays, had started creeping in during film shoots. I didn't have many expectations from *Tuch Mazi Rani*, in which Jayshree T. played the heroine. Even so, I couldn't pass up the opportunity to do another Marathi film after *Bajiravcha Beta*. The dialogue for *Tuch Mazi Rani* were penned by Rajesh Mujumdar, known for his work in Dada Kondke's hit comedies. I had assumed his humour would have a different texture. What I didn't expect, however, was a complete absence of humour! While shooting, it became glaringly obvious that not only was there no comedy, there was also nothing even remotely amusing. I was at a loss. My co-actors were freely improvising, inserting their own lines and changing the script to suit their style. This wasn't my approach. I was never one to change direction mid-take without a proper rehearsal—it wasn't in my nature to do this nor was this how I was trained. The experience became suffocating, yet I pushed through, relying on my work ethic to complete the film.

Fortunately, 1977, Shyam Benegal's *Bhumika* and Bhim Sain's *Gharaonda* were offered to me. They proved to be a lifeline, helping me shake off the dust.

One day, Shyam invited me to his office in the old Jyoti Studio at Gowalia Tank. 'I'm making a film based on Hansa Wadkar's autobiography *Sangtye Aika* (Listen to Me),' he said. I said I was familiar with Hansa-bai, the celebrated Marathi dancer-actor, who had lived next door to me in Shivaji Park, and that her three daughters were my friends. He asked me if I'd be interested in playing the male lead in *Bhumika*. Before I could respond, he added, 'But I think you'd be far more impactful in the darker, more nuanced role of Keshav Dalvi—there's a grey shade to it that would suit you better. However, Dubey and the others are opposed to my suggestion.' Without a moment's hesitation, I replied, 'If you asked me to choose, I'd pick Keshav Dalvi's character myself.' Shyam clapped his hands in delight and announced our decision to the team, and thus, my fate as the 'villain' was sealed.

Working on *Bhumika* with Shyam was not only a joy for me as an actor but also a masterclass in direction. His punctilious approach to framing scenes, his seamless collaboration with his cinematographer, Govind Nihalani, and his impeccable sense of rhythm, which the narrative demanded, left a deep impression on me. I often arrived on set even when I had no scenes to shoot, just to observe him work. The efforts he put in to recreate the atmosphere of a bygone era were especially remarkable. Everything that was missing from my work in mainstream cinema, I found here—my learning curve in direction owes much to Shyam.

In *Bhumika*, I was surrounded by an extraordinary cast: theatre stalwarts like Amrish Puri, Sulabha Deshpande and B.V. Karanth, and my contemporaries—Anant Nag, Smita Patil and Naseeruddin Shah. Vanraj Bhatia's music added to the magic. Most of my scenes were with Smita, and my part was shot over the course of three to four months.

Keshav Dalvi in *Bhumika*

There was one particular scene with Smita that wasn't quite working out as Shyam had envisioned it. We did two or three takes, but something still felt off to him. He felt that I wasn't tapping into Keshav Dalvi's violent streak. 'Just hit her for real. There's no need to tell her beforehand,' Shyam instructed. I objected, but he stood firm: 'This is an order, Amol,' he said, before calling 'Action'. Improvising something unrehearsed went against how I was used to working, and the idea of hitting a woman—no matter how staged—was something I couldn't stomach. My mind was in turmoil as Shyam called, 'Action!' again. Smita, completely in character, delivered her lines with seething intensity. Then, at an unanticipated moment, I grabbed her arm and slapped her hard across the face. The look of shock, pain and slow-building fury on her face was so captivating that I couldn't look away. I was completely enthralled by her brilliance.

After Shyam finally called 'Cut!', I immediately rushed to apologise to Smita. 'Don't say sorry, Amol,' she said, pulling me into a tight embrace. We both sobbed together, overwhelmed. Shyam joined us, offering his congratulations with a hug for us, while the entire crew broke into applause. When preparations began for the next scene, I sat in a corner, feeling conflicted. Smita came and sat beside me. Holding my hand tightly, she whispered, 'Thank you.'

Using violence or springing undiscussed surprises on fellow actors to outmaneuver them, is totally unacceptable to me. For me, professionalism and respect are paramount, and I strive to maintain open communication and mutual understanding in all my working relationships. A similar situation arose years later during the shooting of *Kal* (1989), when I firmly refused the director and producer Haidar Ali's demand that I kiss the heroine without her consent. Upon reflection, I acknowledge that my inexperience and intimidation at working with Shyam may have led me to compromise my values during *Bhumika*. I am certain that Shyam sensed my discomfort and guilt, which likely strained our working relationship. Furthermore, I suspect that Dubey's influence in Shyam's circle—who had by then blacklisted me—led to Shyam not considering me for future projects. But our interactions remained cordial when we met at events like the MAMI festival. Neither of us ever addressed the elephant in the room.

However, my unease regarding Smita lingered for many days. Perhaps it was our close personal bond that made me feel guilty of my actions while shooting *Bhumika*. I was also anxious about others taking advantage of her emotional vulnerability, a fear I couldn't shake off. Smita seemed to feel safe with me, and I sensed that she trusted me more than she did other men. I did not wish to breach her faith under any circumstance. In my presence, she appeared completely at ease, but this brought a peculiar sense of responsibility on my shoulders.

One evening, Smita came to Chirebandi, visibly disturbed. 'I've been offered a role in *Chhinna* (Broken), but the prospect of being on stage for two hours fills me with dread. What should I do?' I admired her willingness to work in theatre despite her success in parallel cinema. I reassured her, 'INT is a prestigious group, and with Sadashiv Amrapurkar's direction and his talented cast, you will have support

With Smita Patil

every step of the way. Waman Tawde's script is outstanding. Don't let fear hold you back.' After our talk, Smita seemed more relaxed. Later, their rehearsals began and soon, the word on the street was that leading men from the Hindi film industry were competing for a chance to meet her after rehearsals. It was rumoured that everyone, from stars to producers and directors, were vying for her attention and trying to win her over. After only a few shows of *Chhinna*, Smita went back to films again.

There was a widely known anecdote about her, about how she had broken down after shooting a rain sequence with Amitabh for the song *'Aaj rapat jaayein'* for the film *Namak Halal* (1982), in which she had to dance, soaked to the skin. When I asked her about it later, she said, 'I never forget Guru Parvati Kumar's advice: to leave the sacred thread of my convictions at home before heading to a shoot.' Her words made it clear to me that she hadn't mentally prepared herself to navigate the commercial film industry's harsh and exploitative environment.

Smita and Shabana's careers followed a similar trajectory. Both had carved out a name for themselves in parallel cinema. Shabana, however, managed to transition smoothly into mainstream cinema without compromising her identity. She never concealed her Left-leaning ideologies and continued to take firm stances against the government in the social sphere. This unwavering commitment is something I've always admired about Shabana. But unlike her passion for parallel cinema, Smita never fully embraced her work in commercial films. Perhaps a discussion with these two talented actresses, who navigated both art-house and mainstream cinema, would have clarified my own thoughts on the tussle between creative fulfilment and commercial success.

Once a mountain has been carved from the plateau of Dalí, its fate is sealed. It has no control over the shape it will take in the centuries that follow. Such is the truth of transformation, a reminder that once set in motion, change cannot be undone.

Several films that Smita and I were meant to work in together remained incomplete due to financial difficulties, much like the Bengali film *Ashwamedher Ghoda*. On the first day of shooting, we joked about whether the film would ever see the light of day! Over the years, we would often catch up on what was happening in the other's life, especially if we hadn't met for a while.

There is one other film that I did complete with Smita. Sometime in 1983–84, Kumar Shahani, a director of immense repute on both the national and international stage, approached me with the screenplay for *Tarang*. He offered me the role of a wealthy industrialist, quite different from my popular image. Smita was already on board. As he turned to leave, he paused, hesitant to mention the modest NFDC pay. I pre-empted it, saying, 'One rupee and twenty-five paise is fine.'

I had huge respect for Kumar's artistic integrity and his steadfast refusal to compromise. Supporting his singular vision felt important to me. He never bothered with calculations about whether people would like the film or if it would even be released. My only goal was to contribute, in whichever way I could, to the realisation of Kumar's dream. Just before he passed away, he spent about a year and a half staying in our vacant apartment in Pune. During that time, we had countless conversations on a variety of topics. He was determined to direct a play on the great mathematician D.D. Kosambi, with me in the lead. He'd joke about my 'one rupee and a quarter' remark from *Tarang*, urging me to say 'yes' to his new project.

The first morning of the shoot for *Tarang* is etched vividly in my memory. The Vashi Bridge, newly constructed at the beginning of the old Bombay–Pune highway, set the stage. The scene with

Smita and me was scheduled to begin just before sunrise, and to conclude as the sun rose in the horizon. I was dressed in a suit and tie, while Smita was adorned in ornate, mythological attire. Kumar intended to highlight the film's hyper-realistic tone through this stark contrast.

Smita, I, and the crew, including cinematographer K.K. Mahajan, arrived for the shoot at around 4 a.m. A massive six-foot crane stood ready on the side of the road, with a few police officers controlling the sparse traffic. Bhanu Athaiya, the renowned costume designer, had personally brought our outfits. Handing me my suit, she began to get Smita ready. But before she could leave, Kumar stopped her. 'This isn't the right shade for Amol's suit; it's too dark,' he said calmly, before announcing that the day's shoot would be cancelled. Watching Kumar's obsessive attention to every visual frame, the NFDC officials became visibly anxious. But as an artiste myself, I couldn't help but salute his dedication.

The cast of *Tarang* comprised stalwarts like Girish Karnad, Dr Lagoo, Om Puri, M.K. Raina and Rohini Hattangadi—each a

Tarang (1984), with Girish Karnad

seasoned actor in their own right. Kumar had asked all of us to perform in an understated, non-theatrical manner, with our natural tones subdued even further. His attention to detail extended to the locations as well, chosen to perfectly match the mood and texture of the film. The screenplay, which explored the intricacies of human relationships and the tensions within social hierarchies, fascinated me. His effort to make the narrative effective on multiple levels truly resonated with me. *Tarang* also gave me a chance to revisit Dubey's guiding principle: the smaller the audience, the better one should perform.

The wisdom I had gleaned from various directors over the years, both intentionally and intuitively, proved invaluable as I navigated my path forward. Their insights and approaches became an integral part of my creative DNA, guiding me as I continued to grow and evolve.

As Smita and I had hoped, *Tarang* was completed and released. But it hardly attracted any viewers. Even Vanraj Bhatia's music, though competent, failed to leave a lasting impression.

After *Tarang*, Smita and I never worked together again. Vijaya-bai had plans to direct a film titled *Mahasagar* with both of us in it. But that project, too, never materialised.

In the 1970s, during one of Dubey's workshops, budding writer Shankar Shesh had written two stories: *Gharaonda* and *Dooriyaan*. His friend Bhim Sain Khurana wanted to make films out of both the stories with me in the lead role. After hearing the plot of *Gharaonda*. I recommended Dr Lagoo to Bhim Sain, but he was hesitant to cast him. Although Bhim Sain had extensive experience in animation, he brought in Sushila Kamat as an assistant director for his debut feature film. To help them see Dr Lagoo's marvellous talent, I sent them tickets to the iconic play *Natsamrat*, starring Dr Lagoo in the lead role. After witnessing his power-packed performance, their reservations dissipated. It was a pleasure for Zarina and me to work with actors like Sadhu Meher, Dina Pathak, T.P. Jain and Sudha Chopra. Jaidev-ji's mesmerising music for *Gharaonda* was a true delight. Bhim Sain and I shared a wonderful rapport while filming at various locations in Bombay.

I, however, could not work smoothly with Sushila Kamat. One notable instance occurred during a shoot at a house in Vile Parle. At 5 p.m., she presented us with a complex scene which had extensive dialogue, intending to shoot till 10 p.m. I suggested postponing the scene until the next morning since I had to leave for my theatre rehearsal at six. She disregarded my suggestion and insisted on proceeding. I, however, left the set at six. The second disagreement with Sushila Kamat arose over a song. Jaidev-ji had invited me to the recording sessions for two songs: *'Do diwane'* and *'Tumhe ho na ho'*. He introduced me to a new singer, Runa Laila, and rehearsals with her and Bhupendra began. However, Sushila disapproved of replacing the word *'asmaani'*, used by Gulzar saab, with a more familiar term.

I have always adopted the philosophy of forward motion, recognising that sometimes it is wiser to move forward than to linger on irresolvable differences. When Bhim Sain initiated talks with me for Shankar Shesh's second story *Dooriyaan*, I declined, citing two major concerns. One was the prospect of collaborating again with Sushila Kamat, and second was Bhim Sain's questionable integrity. Having accepted a reduced compensation once for *Gharaonda* at Shankar Shesh's behest, I was dismayed when Bhim Sain again offered a low remuneration for *Dooriyaan*, citing financial constraints. Yet, when Zarina disclosed her substantially higher payment for both these films to me, I realised that Bhim Sain was taking advantage of my goodwill. It was disappointing to decline since I liked the story and had enjoyed the songs Jaidev-ji had composed for it. Eventually, *Dooriyaan* was made with the Uttam Kumar-Sharmila Tagore pair, who had already gained popularity in Hindi cinema through *Amanush*. *Dooriyaan* turned out to be a nice film too.

Meanwhile, *Gharaonda* received numerous awards; it also remains a personal favourite of mine as an actor. In reality, the role I played in it is that of a villain, though the audience might not immediately recognise it. Engaging in selfish acts—like advising a friend to marry her boss, continuing to cultivate a relationship with her even after her marriage, and secretly wishing for her husband's death—are all traits of a true villain. Yet, the way I portrayed Sudeep on screen evoked sympathy from the audience.

In hindsight, I realise that I was probably driven to explore roles with more depth and nuance, that sought to transcend the conventional 'boy next door' persona. I was drawn to characters with complexity, as can be seen from my roles in films like *Spandan*, *Aadmi Aur Aurat*, *Bhumika*, *Gharaonda* and *Akriet*, and later in *Khamosh*.

In *Ankahee*, I had specifically requested Vidhu Vinod Chopra to play a small but crucial role. At the time, he was working on the script for his film *Khamosh*. I was invited to a couple of meetings with his then-wife, Reenu Saluja, and his assistant, Sudhir Mishra. The idea of Shabana and I both being in pivotal roles was well received. I was thrilled at the idea of working with skilled actors like Naseeruddin Shah, Pankaj Kapoor, Sushma Seth, Ajit Vachhani, Sadashiv Amrapurkar and Soni Razdan. We all went through the script, which was praised for its tight narrative and unexpected twists.

During a discussion on the climax, I proposed a crucial change to the original script—replacing a melodramatic scene in which I was to kill Shabana in an open area with a more intimate and chilling scene. I suggested that there be a tense, whispered threat in a small, enclosed space, inspired from the contrast between a tiger's fierce attack and a cat's silent, stealthy kill. Vidhu loved this idea.

The scene was beautifully crafted by Vidhu and his cinematographer Vinod Pradhan using subtle shadows and lighting in the dimly-lit costume room in a hotel in Pahalgam. This added a distinctive layer to Shabana and my performances. Shooting for the last scene continued through the night, and it involved complex technical aspects like using the rain machine and creating a blood splatter after the final gunshot. By the time we wrapped up, it was dawn. The crew was exhausted but elated.

Shalmalee was present at the film's very first private screening. She couldn't have been more than fourteen at the time. As the plot thickened, her grip on my hand tightened. Even when the movie ended, and the lights came back on, and the auditorium echoed with applause, her hand remained firmly clasped around mine. I asked her, 'How did you find it?' She smiled and nodded, but in the next instant, she slipped away, releasing my hand. Even today, I can vividly recall the fear that flickered across her eyes—a fear that now stands as one of the greatest validations of my performance.

Khamosh was, to my mind, a perfectly crafted film, but it was rejected outright by distributors. After spending nearly two years running from pillar to post, only to find disappointment at every turn, Vidhu Vinod Chopra gutsily released the film in a single theatre in Bombay in 1986. It ran for weeks, becoming a much-loved movie. This was reminiscent of the boldness that Basu-da had displayed when he had personally brought *Chhoti Si Baat* to the audience after B.R. Chopra had refused to release it. Yet, the paths of Vidhu and Basu-da reveal an important contrast. Even when Basu-da worked with industry giants like Dharmendra, Amitabh and Rajesh Khanna, he never fully melted into the mould of the mainstream. He carved out a style that was distinctly his. Vidhu, however, shifted gears after *Khamosh*. He left the winding side roads for the fast lane, diving headfirst into star-studded blockbusters, planting his feet firmly in the commercial race. Naseer once made a pointed comment about him, saying something like, 'Vinod never bothered to look back at the people who helped him when times were tough.' This remark struck a chord with me, as I too had reasons to feel overlooked or underappreciated by certain individuals. However, I never had the inclination to lobby for roles by saying 'I can really nail this part; give me a shot.' That reluctance, no doubt, cost me dearly.

When it came to portraying villains, I was never drawn to the sensational, one-dimensional archetypes popularised by Jeevan, Ranjit or Prem Chopra. Instead, I was fascinated by more subtle and complex characters, like the villain Mama Pendse brought to life in the Marathi play *Duritanche Timir Javo* (May the Darkness of the Sinful End) which I'd had the privilege of watching as a child. Another inspiration was Nilu Phule's masterful portrayal in *Sakharam Binder*, where he delivered his dialogues in a subdued, whispery tone, with slumped shoulders and bound hands. Despite running the risk of repetition, I reiterate that I was never interested in simplistic, black-and-white roles.

Having said that, I usually was never approached for those conventional negative roles. The one exception was N.N. Sippy's *Teesra Kaun* (1994). I agreed to take on a role in which an otherwise unremarkable character is ultimately revealed to be the villain. I accepted this role primarily to explore different aspects of acting, without considering the specific nature of the villainous traits involved. However, by the end of the shoot, I realised that the role could be interpreted as a father committing sexual abuse against his daughter. This revelation made me extremely uneasy. The producer argued that no explicit wrongdoing was shown, and that the villainy was only implied through dialogue at the very end. Despite these justifications, I stood firm in my decision of not continuing with the role. The shooting was almost complete though. I reluctantly agreed to the suggestion to change the character's description from 'biological daughter' to 'stepdaughter' to avoid a substantial financial loss to the producer. In retrospect, I feel that I should have refused this compromise and should have insisted on returning his money instead. It remains a mystery to me how I overlooked such a significant issue, given my usual attention to detail. Thereafter, I banned myself from accepting roles that reinforced patriarchal stereotyping of women, or promoted regressive values in any manner. As a sensitive artiste, I believe certain principles must be adhered to. But by this standard, I probably should not have taken the role in *Khamosh* either.

Sandhya's blend of legal expertise and progressive values has profoundly impacted my thinking. As I declined various roles in numerous OTT series over the past decade, I grew increasingly mindful of my contemporary responsibilities as an actor. I have often turned down new offers due to their perpetuation of regressive values. However, I made an exception for two films, *200: Halla Ho* (2021) and *Gulmohar* (2023). In these cases, both directors agreed with my concerns and made a few changes in the dialogues or scenes. In 2020, I played a unique antagonistic role in the web series *Gormint* directed by Ayyappa K.M. for Amazon Prime. I suspect the role was crafted with politician Amit Shah in mind. However, due to the government having freedom of expression on a tight leash, the series wasn't released and may never be released anytime in the future.

I never got the opportunity to play a villain on stage, though. I console myself with the notion that my roles in three Marathi plays, *Vasanakand* (1974), *Garbo* (1978) and *Mukhavate* (Masks) (1983), which were tinged with shades of grey, were villainous in their own right. The theatrical depiction of villainy amplifies its intensity, laying bare the darkest aspects of human nature. The various facets of villainous behaviour—deception, betrayal, machinations and violence—assume a stark, unflinching quality that can be uncomfortable for the audience. Vijay Tendulkar's plays, with their bold exploration of taboo themes, pushed the boundaries of what was deemed acceptable, forcing middle-class audiences to confront their own hypocrisies. As spectators, we often inhabit a state of denial, shielding ourselves from the harsh realities of our society and our own inner turmoil.

Pushpa Bhave's insights in her book *Ranga Natakaache* resonate profoundly. 'The brutal violence in (the play) *Garbo* is a manifestation of the characters' frenzied quest for creative expression, which is rapidly slipping through their fingers. The playwright skilfully portrays the desperation that ensues, using a range of reactions to convey the anguish and frustration that accompany the loss of artistic vitality.' Reflecting on our past performances, I believe we merely scratched the surface of *Garbo's* complex theme under Dr Lagoo's direction. We didn't explore the murkier, more concealed layers of human relationships and inner lives, which were embedded in the script. Our portrayal of the violence born from stifled creativity in *Garbo* felt underdeveloped. In 1978, when we performed *Garbo*, we were unable to execute the raw and corporeal dimensions of the male-female relationships depicted in the script on stage. It might have been more fitting to present the play in a more intimate style or in the chamber theatre style rather than in the grandiose format of a conventional stage. However, I vividly recall how Dr Lagoo deftly conveyed the futility of the lives of the characters, Pansy, Intuk and Shrimant, using the games they played as an allegory. Given the star-studded cast, including Datta Bhat, Dr Lagoo, Deepa Lagoo and I, the expectations of the theatre-going audience were undoubtedly high. Each of us delivered our roles with dedication, yet the performance remained far from perfect. On a personal note, it was humbling to receive a letter from the great literary figure Purushottam Shivram Rege, praising my performance. I vaguely recall his comments appreciating how the portrayal of Pansy eschewed the stereotypical effeminate mannerisms.

Later, when I saw Mohit Takalkar's production of *Garbo*, it was a revelation. The way the actors' physicality brought to life the unspoken entanglements and conflicts was captivating, and it made me realise what we had missed. Compared to the drab set design in our version, the claustrophobic space crafted with plastic sheeting in Takalkar's version, offered a novel and evocative visual experience.

Only one time in my career have I accepted a play purely for earning profits: *Aapla Buwa Asa Aahe*. I recall a period when we could not make an ad-agency's payment for a considerable amount of time. Around that same period, I began to seriously consider making the leap from acting in films to directing them. In this context, the idea of leveraging my popular image from films to produce a commercially viable play on stage began to seem appealing to me.

In 1978, the playwright Manohar Katdare approached me with the proposal to act in his three-act play, *Aapla Buwa Asa Aahe*, under the direction of Damu Kenkre. We decided to proceed with it under the banner of my company, Aniket. With a cast that included Chitra, Dilip Kulkarni and I, Damu initiated the rehearsals. I learnt some critical lessons while acting for Damu. The chance to create humour through exaggerated and melodramatic gestures could have seamlessly fit into the play's presentation. Yet, Damu's discerning choice to resort to a more subtle style of acting was evident even during our post-rehearsal beer sessions. The distinction shown by Dubey in *Vallabhpurchi Dantkatha*, demonstrating the difference between farce and cheap slapstick comedy, was already deeply imprinted on my mind. The play *Aapla Buwa Asa Aahe*, narrating the simple story of how a young couple's first meeting goes awry, was presented in a comedic style. Its uniqueness lay in the fact that the first act was from the young man's perspective, the second from the young woman's, and the third act was dedicated to an unusual style of dialogue exchange. Despite its lack of thematic depth, our performances and the play's marvellous presentation pleased the audience.

The chemistry amongst us three actors was palpable, making it feel like we were sharing a collective experience rather than simply acting in a play. As we set out on a whirlwind tour across Maharashtra, our conventional box-set precariously perched on top of a bus, we felt like we were part of a travelling troupe. As soon as our bus rolled into a small village, a rickshaw equipped with a loudspeaker announced, 'He has arrived! He has arrived … the *chitchor* is here to entertain you!' The grand welcome, extended from the village gates to our accommodation, was memorable. We performed over a hundred and fifty shows, allowing me to amass a substantial fortune and erasing the red ink from our company's financial ledger. With what was left of those funds, we produced *Rashomon* and organised a festival of Badal Sircar's new plays at Chhabildas Auditorium.

After the resounding success of *Aapla Buwa Asa Aahe* on the commercial stage, my friend and fellow actor Madhukar Naik pursued me for almost a year to undertake another project in the same vein. This pursuit eventually led to the creation of *Mukhavate*. One of the landmark plays of my acting career was *Aadhe Adhure*, directed by Dubey in 1968. For many years, I harboured the desire to perform all the five male roles in that play. At the time, Puri saab played these roles in the Hindi version, while Dr Lagoo portrayed them in the Marathi adaptation. Dubey's decision to present both the original Hindi play and its Marathi adaptation simultaneously was groundbreaking. I played the son's role in both versions. Given the opportunity to revisit the play on the commercial stage nearly two decades later, I suggested the iconic *Aadhe Adhure* to Madhukar.

I made some minor alterations to *Aadhe Adhure*'s original Marathi translation by Tendulkar, replacing Delhi with Mumbai and substituting Punjabi–Hindi characters with Marathi names, among others. I chose the title *Mukhavate*. Over a span of a year and a half, we performed more than a hundred shows. Whether in plush, air-conditioned theatres or on makeshift stages erected in open fields, we managed to captivate audiences two- to three-thousand-strong. Two memorable anecdotes from our open-airfield performances stand out: at one show, as the curtain rose, I saw that beyond the footlights, there was a line of heads of small children, stretching from one end of the stage to the other. The thought of how these youngsters would react to such a serious play initially unsettled me. This was a novel experience for every actor who stepped onto the stage. However, the performance proceeded smoothly, with the children quickly getting absorbed into the experience. At another performance, occasional 'thchyuumm' sounds from a vendor selling *goti-soda* at the edge of the field would intermittently jolt everyone.

Mukhavate also brought me another kind of satisfaction. In the first ten minutes of the play, the audience realised that the 'boy-next-door Amol Palekar' they expected was not going to be present on stage. Despite this, the play's ability to hold their attention till the end reinforced my confidence in my acting abilities. I ensured that my portrayal did not entirely emulate the iconic performances of Puri saab and Dr Lagoo. I crafted a distinctive 'lecherous boss', employing quirks like spreading my legs, moving them slowly, and speaking while deliberately avoiding eye contact and staring at the female character's bosom. This portrayal earned high praise from discerning audiences.

Mukhavate's commercial success brought in significant revenue, leaving the producer delighted. To present an experimental play on the commercial stage was certainly a new experiment which proved to be very successful, I must say. On turning seventy-five, I thought I'd seen it all, but again my play *Kusur* brought in an unexpected windfall; earning a significant amount of money from theatre had earlier been a rarity in my experimental theatre days.

In 1979, our theatre company, Aniket, presented the Marathi adaptation *Ani Mhanun Konihi* (And Therefore Anyone) of Madhu Rai's Gujarati play *Koi Pan Phoolna Naam Bolo To* (To Tell the Name of Any Flower), directed by Dilip Kulkarni. Eleven years later, in 1990, we produced Girish Karnad's *Nagamandala*, also directed by

Dilip, marking Aniket's final production. My role in this production was limited to that of a producer. Unfortunately, Dilip struggled to do justice to *Nagamandala*. The rights acquisition was tumultuous, as Girish Karnad had earlier granted rights to Fritz Bennewitz for all languages except Kannada. Satyadev Dubey secured Marathi rights for Dilip but was denied Hindi rights. Dubey's response was characteristically defiant: 'Try stopping me! I am not a logical man; I am Satyadev Dubey.' In spite of the contentious negotiations, *Nagamandala* failed to impress when it was finally staged, leaving me genuinely disheartened.

One amusing incident from *Ani Mhanun Konihi* still remains quite clear in my memory. At Madhu Rai's insistence, we decided to perform a show in Ahmedabad. As we were about to board the plane, my bag was discovered to be containing a pistol. The local officer who stopped us was at first mollified when I explained that it was a prop for the play. However, when he pulled the trigger, the sight of sparks and a bit of smoke from the prop caused a minor panic. Two constables grabbed me from behind, and only after an extensive interrogation, were we allowed to leave. We rushed to the plane just in time. The real-looking toy pistol was handed over to the pilot and returned to me only upon landing. My insistence on using a realistic prop instead of a typical firecracker pistol had led to this dramatic episode.

By this time, I had resolved to dedicate myself completely to film production and direction. Yet, I was bound by prior commitments to several films, and I completed them all. *Aanchal* (1980), *Agni Pareeksha* (1981), *Plot No. 5* (1981), *Ram Nagari* (1982) and *Pyaassi Ankhen* (1983) were wrapped up. I also finished *Wohi Baat* (1977), later titled *Sameera*, and *Nirvaan* (1983), though they were never released by the producers. Despite the odds, each of these films somehow managed to cross the finish line, leaving behind a varied set of memories. The television serials *Ados Pados* (1984) and *Aa Bail Mujhe Maar*

(1987–88) made for Doordarshan were projects I eagerly embraced out of curiosity for the emerging medium.

The film industry's prevailing practices at the time were far from ideal. Completing a film took two to three years, with funding secured by casting a saleable star and a prominent music director. A rough cut and soundtrack would be presented to distributors, who would then purchase territorial rights, enabling further funding and shooting. However, this piecemeal approach often led to delays, exacerbated by actors' tardiness, which was tolerated due to their star power. I strongly disagreed with all these practices.

The multi-starrer *Aanchal* was no exception to these delays. With a star-studded cast including Rajesh Khanna, Rekha, Rakhi and Prem Chopra, and directed by Anil Ganguly, the successful director of hits like *Tapasya* and *Kora Kagaz*, and with music by the celebrated R.D. Burman, expectations from it were sky-high. A colossal set was erected at Rajkamal Studio, depicting a wealthy Bengali man's estate—my character's home. The cost of maintaining this enormous set for one or two years was equivalent to the budget for making two or three solid parallel cinema films!

I would reach the set at seven in the morning. Rakhi would arrive at around ten, and Rajesh Khanna around eleven-thirty. By the time the shift ended, at around two, we would have barely managed five or six shots. Time was of no value here. It was commonplace for actors to dictate terms, much to the director's dismay. In such scenarios, I would entertain myself by observing the antics of Rakhi and Rajesh Khanna.

In the film, I had been cast as Rakhi's husband and Rajesh Khanna's elder brother. To convey the age difference more convincingly, Anil-da and I engaged in a detailed discussion about my appearance. Following his guidance, I wore a wig with luxuriant white hair and a thick black-and-white moustache. Anil-da was visibly delighted with the transformation. We then proceeded to Rakhi's make-up room, where my new appearance seemed to shock her. Her outburst against the director was so fierce that I felt slightly uncomfortable. I completely understood her reprimand in Bengali. It wasn't just my aged look she found troubling, but the implication that my portrayal might inadvertently add years to her character's age as well. Unexpectedly Anil-da reversed his stance, completely surprising me. To maintain a semblance of composure and to deflect Rakhi's verbal blows, he continued to smile and asked me, 'Rakhi-ji has a point. Your natural hair is quite impressive; is the wig truly necessary?' Rather than responding to him, I chose to address Rakhi directly. 'The larger the age gap between the brothers, the more effectively will it highlight the emotional bond between the younger brother and his not so old sister-in-law. This contrast will naturally resonate with the audience. Therefore, while I need to appear older, it's essential that you maintain a youthful appearance.' My argument struck a chord with her, and she promptly agreed.

One evening, on the set of our studio mansion, we were preparing to film a scene featuring Rajesh Khanna, Rakhi and me. In this sequence, Khanna, playing the younger brother, was supposed to be slurring in a drunken state. As I, the elder brother, sat silently in the veranda, puffing on my hookah, his frustration was supposed to grow, culminating in a burst of anger, leading him to charge towards me. I would then calmly retreat to my room, locking the door behind me. After rehearsing the scene several times and capturing it in a few takes, Anil-da declared that it was a wrap. However, Khanna, ever buzzing with creative energy, suggested, 'Let's do one more take … but with a twist this time.' He proposed that, as he lunged towards me, I would suddenly leap up, and engage in a playful chase around the chair before dashing into my room. This impromptu suggestion would add a new layer of excitement to the scene.

I shot a quizzical look at Anil-da. With a nod of approval, Anil-da responded, 'Wow, great idea!' However, I felt compelled to interject: 'But it doesn't suit my character.' Khanna, unfazed, retorted, 'Forget the logic ... just think of how much people will laugh! Applause will follow! You're from the theatre, so your timing will be perfect.' By now, Rakhi had also warmed to Khanna's suggestion. He demonstrated his vision with a mock performance. It was as though Rajendra Nath and Mukri's style of 'comedy' was being invoked.

'Let's give it a try,' Khanna insisted. My patience wore thin. Meeting his gaze, I replied, 'Kaka, it's not about trying; my character is such that he would never act like a buffoon.' Khanna, taken aback by my resistance, paused for a moment, then turned away. Undeterred, Anil-da insisted, 'Let's try it once more,' and proceeded to shoot eight or ten more takes. I maintained the integrity of my role throughout, avoiding any antics. Eventually, the two of them relented, and the initial take we had deemed suitable made it into the final cut of the film.

As I returned home that evening, I had a nagging sense of unease. What could have possibly unsettled a superstar at the height of his fame, making him uncomfortable with my modest presence? I had uttered not a single word throughout the scene, nor had I attempted to upstage him with any attention-grabbing antics. I never tried to overshadow my co-stars, and my mere presence couldn't have threatened his dominance. And yet, the palpable insecurity from him was undeniable. This paradox left me pondering on the intricacies of human psychology and the complexities of fame.

The answer didn't reveal itself immediately, but I found some clarity later due to a different incident.

I had the chance to attend the six hundredth performance of the immensely popular Marathi play *Guntata Hriday He*, (An Entwined Heart) starring the superstar of Marathi theatre, Dr Kashinath

Ghanekar. Accompanied by a few colleagues from Aniket, I sat through the entire performance. His acting began with a high octave tone and ascended to an exasperatingly shrill pitch. I sat impassively in the front row.

Following the performance, I made my way backstage as per his insistent invitation. Before I could utter a word, Ghanekar launched into a verbal assault on my actor friend Dilip Kolhatkar, who had been seated next to me. 'Sitting with your feet up on the chair! Do you even understand the sanctity of this stage?' The barrage left poor Dilip visibly shaken. By now, the crew dismantling the set and eager fans awaiting their turn to meet Ghanekar had gathered around us. Turning his attention to me, Ghanekar said, 'Let me tell you, Amol, once at one of my shows, Vyjayanthimala was seated in the front row, munching away peanuts as she watched. "Would *you* like it if I sat in your dance performance tossing peanuts around?" I asked her directly, right from the stage!'

Remembering the teachings of my mentor, I took a deep breath and replied calmly, 'You're right, Doctor; the audience should indeed respect artistes. But artistes too must exercise restraint and not breach the fourth wall. We believe that even if there are only a few spectators, the show must go on. Regardless of who is seated in the audience, we stand by the discipline of adhering strictly to rehearsed actions. We are committed to preserving the sanctity of performance by ensuring that neither our own nor our fellow actors' portrayals are disrupted. There is a vast difference between your world and ours.'

An uneasy silence fell over us. The producer of the play, Anant Kane, stepped forward and said, 'Doctor, the taxi is ready downstairs.' Without glancing at Kane, Ghanekar fixed his piercing blue-tinged gaze on me and said, 'No, no, Amol, you will be the one to drop me today, won't you?' Kane attempted to explain, 'You're headed to Worli, and Amol is going to the opposite direction … to Juhu …'

Finally, with a smile, I said, 'Thank you, Doctor, for offering this golden opportunity for a small actor from the experimental stage to accompany a superstar of Marathi theatre. Let's go.' The drive from Shivaji Mandir to Worli passed in complete silence; neither of us spoke a word. As we arrived, he asked, 'Care for a drink?' I politely declined, mumbling an excuse that I had to head further, and departed.

As I continued the journey home and later, well into the night, my thoughts churned over the emotional insecurities of actors. The evening's performance had etched an indelible image on my mind: this superstar who commanded thunderous applause with the mere announcement of his name, had tried to distract the audience from the poignant soliloquy of his co-star Asha Kale. His exaggerated gestures, the incessant clinking of his ring on the armrest of her chair, and his relentless attempts to draw attention to himself were nothing short of melodramatic missteps. It was a textbook case of how not to perform in a play.

I couldn't fathom why a talented actor would feel compelled to belittle a fellow performer to boost their own status. It seemed illogical to think that insecurities about one's own abilities could lead them to diminish others. I thought, perhaps Ghanekar and Rajesh Khanna sensed the impending end of their reign, like sand slipping through their fingers. Was this behaviour a desperate attempt to cling to their fading stardom? As I pondered this, I felt drained, but also resolute: never to sacrifice my integrity for the sake of fame.

The next morning, while sipping coffee, I recalled a story the great actor Dutta Bhatt had shared with me about the formidable writer-director Vishram Bedekar. It was about Bedekar's last film, *Rustam Sohrab* (1963). The film, starring the legends Prithviraj Kapoor and Prem Nath, was shot on a gargantuan set that seemed neither Egyptian nor Islamic, offering no cultural context. Bedekar's son, having just returned from abroad, asked him, 'Father, which era is this set supposed to represent?' To which Bedekar calmly replied, 'Last phase of my receding career!'

The ability to observe one's work and surroundings with detachment is a rare gift. Even rarer is the capacity to adapt to an evolving environment, a trait found in only a select few exceptional individuals. I have had the privilege of sharing space with these giants, learning from them and absorbing their wisdom. The legacy of their experience and insight is, indeed, my most precious treasure.

At this stage in my life, I often feel that what has been lost far outweighs what has been gained. There's a persistent sorrow in a corner of my heart for the many people I once worked with who are no longer here. For the film *Paheli*, we had planned to shoot a scene around a pond used for cultivating water chestnuts. We had visited the location on earlier occasions and had photographed the pond thrice. Yet, when it came to the actual shoot, the pond was nowhere to be found. It came as a shock to us that in the six months between our recce for locations and the actual shoot, a canal had been constructed by the government, wiping out the small ponds in the area and displacing the local people. Similarly, we had planned to shoot a film in Nepal, and had secured locations and finalised local actors from small villages. But in April 2015, Nepal was struck by the worst earthquake it had ever suffered. Those villages and their inhabitants were gone. We had to shelve the film, but the memories of our recce are still captured on tapes stacked in our office.

In 1980, a young director, Yogesh Saxena, came to me with the screenplay for the film *Plot No. 5*, declaring his intention to make a Hitchcockian thriller. The cast included great actors like Pradeep Kumar, Dr Lagoo, Uttam Kumar, Viju Khote, Vidya Sinha and Sarika. Amjad Khan was to play the role of a secret agent. There wasn't a typical love triangle.

Although there were no songs in the film, the background score had been composed by Salil Chowdhury. The cinematographer was the highly-regarded G. Singh. The remuneration being offered was generous. I signed the contract, enticed by this grand offer. The friendship between Amjad and I grew during this project due to the free time we had. He was very open and playful. There was a scene in which I had to lift the temptress Komilla Virk. He teased me relentlessly. When I quipped back, 'I'm no novice in this field. I've had solid experience lifting Bindiya and Zarina before,' Amjad humorously detailed Komilla's measurements in front of everyone, adding, 'This case is different.' Even after the shot was approved, Amjad playfully requested additional retakes.

During shooting, I was pleasantly surprised to see Amjad rework his character, gradually adopting a more subdued and poised demeanour.

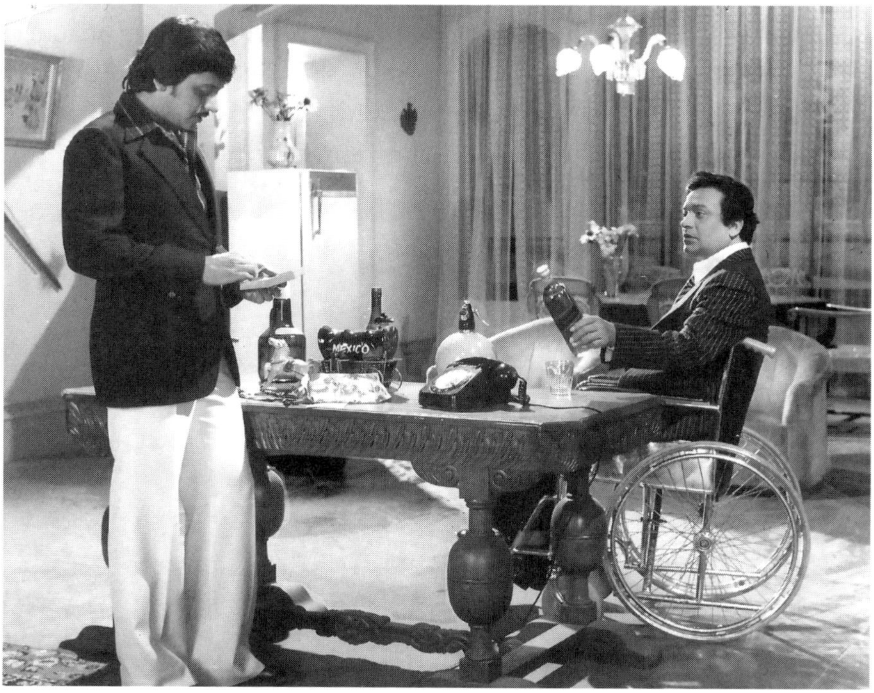

Plot No. 5 (1981), with Uttam Kumar

Unfortunately, the film met with disaster. Uttam Kumar had barely finished his dubbing when he passed away. It was released in 1981 but tanked. The director, overwhelmed by the failure, committed suicide. Amjad died of a heart attack at just fifty-one years of age. Despite the lively and successful shooting process, everything was lost by the end of the film.

When a film falls short of conveying its intended message, the entire endeavour can feel futile. Unfortunately, *Ram Nagari*, based on the autobiography of folk theatre actor Ram Nagarkar, suffered the same fate. Despite its potential, the film missed the mark in addressing caste and social hierarchy through a fresh, contemporary lens. It also failed to creatively amplify the voices of the marginalised Dalit community. Notably, Ram Nagarkar's personal story, as a barber and folk theatre artiste with Rashtra Seva Dal, was overlooked in the screenplay. Director Kantilal Rathod's lack of understanding of Nagarkar's social background was evident. When Rathod approached me for the film, I was juggling multiple shootings across Bombay, Madras, Hyderabad and Calcutta. With an existing production agreement with NFDC in place, the team was unwilling to delay

With Ram Nagarkar

the shoot, leaving me with no time to work on the script. Despite this, I was drawn to the project due to its talented cast, that included Suhasini Mulay, Sulabha Deshpande and Nilu Phule, and its music, which had been composed by Jaidev-ji.

My look was designed with precision. A clean parting was made in my hair in the middle, it was adorned with large *kalle*—decorative tassels—, and then topped with a tilted fur-cap . Kantilal Bhai was quite taken with this character's portrayal, one befitting the legends of the previous generation's Tamasha actors. Even Ram Nagarkar himself was pleased with my costume. My approach regarding the character's stance and movements, keeping my body slightly elevated rather than just grounded, also resonated with them. We agreed to steer clear of direct imitation or caricature of Ram Bhau's mannerisms and appearance, focusing instead on distilling the essence of his personality.

Despite completing the film, we faced a major setback when distributors' negative feedback led to the financiers withdrawing their support. As a result, we were left without crucial funds for publicity, which is essential before the film's release. Without publicity, the film failed to reach its intended audience, leading to poor earnings and earning the unfortunate label of 'failure', a common fate much of parallel cinema films suffered.

Numerous examples demonstrate that even a well-crafted story can fall short if the director lacks technical mastery or a grasp of the cinematic language. A case in point is *Pyaassi Ankhen*, which was the Hindi adaptation of the successful Marathi film

Ekati (Alone) (1968). Ram Kelkar's *Pyaassi Ankhen* had a stellar cast, including Shabana Azmi, Asha Sachdev and Waheeda Rehman. The narrative had two threads: the conflict between a newly-wed bride and her mother-in-law, and the unrequited love of a childhood friend for the protagonist. Ram Kelkar's casting choices were impeccable, no doubt, but the direction and music told a different story. Unlike *Ekati*, which was masterfully directed by Raja Thakur and featured memorable music by Sudhir Phadke, *Pyaassi Ankhen* suffered under Ram Kelkar's own direction and Usha Khanna's soundtrack.

As filming began, it became apparent that Ram Kelkar's attention was fixated solely on the actors' dialogue delivery, with scant regard being paid to camera placement, lens selection, or the actors' movements. His eyes would remain glued to the pages of the script after he called 'Action!', never once considering the visual elements. This oversight troubled me, so I shared my concerns with Om-ji. He dismissed my worries, saying, 'Don't worry, don't you know *Ekati* was a superhit? And look at our star-studded cast.' I chose to let the matter rest at that.

Shooting one of the songs was an entertaining experience, despite my initial reservations about my dancing skills. Shabana's initial awkwardness put me at ease. We engaged in playful banter, encouraging each other to improve. Dancing in front of the accomplished Waheeda Rehman seemed like an impossible feat, but my insistence on including her in the sequence led to a wonderful moment. Her brief yet dazzling *jhatkas* received an overwhelming response, becoming a highlight of the film. Unfortunately, its delayed release has faded my recollection of its details.

It still pains me that two of my favourite films were completed but never released: Jalal Agha's *Nirvaan* and Vinay Shukla's *Sameera*.

Filming *Nirvaan* in the picturesque village of Lohardaga, Ranchi, with Naseer and Sarika in the cast, was a unique experience. The film's visual beauty was enhanced by the consummate cinematography of Ashok Mehta. However, I had some disagreements with Jalal, the director, regarding his evening revelries and hunting excursions in the nearby jungle, which occasionally impacted the filming process. Despite these distractions, I cherished the moments in which I could fully immerse myself in the story and in my character. During an all-night shoot at a village festival, I became so absorbed in dancing while playing the drum that my fingers became swollen by morning. This unbridled performance was entirely uncharacteristic of me, but I was intent on portraying the character's simple, rustic persona with authenticity.

A pivotal scene required Sarika's character to reveal her sensual body, and my character to react with a subtle yet emotionally charged 'ney'. When we shot it, the unit's enthusiastic applause followed the director's 'OK'. I praised Sarika for her courage in appearing semi-nude in front of the large crew and for her authentic performance. She, in turn, thanked me for creating a safe space, saying, 'Your ability to convey complex emotions without words allowed me to let go and deliver the shot truthfully.' We shared a heartfelt hug, her body trembling briefly. The semi-nude scenes in *Nirvaan* generated significant buzz and curiosity within the industry. However, the film ultimately languished in the archives. I no longer recall the reasons behind its shelving. Possibly, the narrative's emphasis on the heroine's journey and the tragic love story didn't align with the conventional formulae for mainstream success.

Vinay Shukla, fresh out of FTII, was driven by a desire to do something different. With a cast featuring Parikshit Sahani, Shabana Azmi, Mithun Chakraborty and I, he embarked on making the film *Wohi Baat* (1977) The central theme of his screenplay was the frustration experienced by women in relationships, a bold and distinct subject that appealed to me greatly. Additionally, I was drawn to the character of the *'sutradhaar'* who takes the narrative forward. Setting aside considerations of remuneration, I immediately agreed to work with Vinay. During the shoot in Mahabaleshwar, I gained valuable insights into my fellow actors' perspectives and working styles. Parikshit's disillusionment after his Moscow Film School training, despite his sensitivity and talent, contrasted with Mithun's bewilderment amidst his international fame from *Mrigayaa*. I was particularly struck by Shabana's thorough research into her character. Although I maintained a distance from the central love triangle, I enjoyed portraying the nuanced shades of the 'sutradhaar'. A memorable highlight of the film was Bhupinder's soulful rendition of Jaidev-ji's song, *'Zeher deta hai mujhe koi dawaa deta hai'*, which mesmerised me.

{9}

The film was completed and screenings for distributors began. The original title was changed to *Sameera*. Gradually, the industry's negative feedback began trickling in. Shabana made considerable efforts to secure a release, but ultimately, Vinay, disheartened by the setback, turned his back on his directorial venture and blended into the industry as a dialogue and script writer.

Wohi Baat/Sameera (1977), with Parikshit Sahani, Mithun Chakraborty

One thing that wasn't immediately apparent at the time was how the landscape for parallel cinema changed when such films began to garner national and international awards. While this recognition was initially acceptable, the situation shifted dramatically when such films started receiving audience support, financial success and active investment as well. That's when the commercial film ecosystem began to resist parallel cinema in various ways. Attempts were made to run down Satyajit Ray and Mrinal Sen's films, claiming that they depicted national poverty before a foreign audience, tarnishing the country's image. In the Rajya Sabha, the esteemed actress Nargis expressed her dissatisfaction with parallel cinema. Ironically, *Mother India*, a mainstream film, which had elevated Nargis to a legendary status, had depicted rural poverty and the exploitation of women in a similar vein. It was paradoxical to see such criticism coming from an iconic heroine of a mainstream film that had celebrated these very themes. Slowly, efforts began to undermine institutions supporting parallel cinema, such as the NFDC, which had been established to promote and distribute films exploring alternatives beyond the mainstream. The appointment of mainstream figures like Hema Malini and Ramesh Sippy to helm NFDC seemed to undermine its original objectives, as if sabotaging its very purpose. Attempts to find alternatives to the entrenched system were systematically dismantled, though I lacked the insight to recognise this at the time.

While films like *Bhuvan Shome*, *Ankur*, *Ardh Satya* and *Jaane Bhi Do Yaaron*, which rejected the star system, were well received by audiences, the films that operated within the mainstream framework but showcased unique perspectives, such as *Saraswatichandra*, *Rajnigandha*, *Mere Apne*, *Chetna*, *Guddi* and *Chashme Buddoor*, also achieved notable commercial success. The pioneering efforts of parallel cinema to re-examine gender dynamics and social issues from unique vantage points struck a chord with moviegoers. Viewers welcomed the genre's commitment to honest storytelling and its willingness to confront complex problems.

Post-Independence, films like *Ek Hi Raasta*, *Bandini*, *Naya Daur*, *Sujata* and *Dhool Ka Phool* were made by stalwarts of mainstream cinema. However, this tradition was gradually set aside in favour of films that promised pure entertainment for the masses, such as the superhit *Amar Akbar Anthony*. As Indian cinema transitioned from films with a purpose to films that want to entertain for entertainment's sake, the unfortunate fate of movies like *Nirvaan*, *Spandan*, *Aadmi Aur Aurat* and *Wohi Baat* could have been foreseen well before their time, though this realisation is only clear in hindsight.

The emergence of Doordarshan in 1975 paved the way for innovative storytelling, with the series *Hum Log* (created by director P. Vasudeva and writer Manohar Shyam Joshi) cementing its place in the popular imagination in 1984. Naturally, I was thrilled to receive an invitation from Sai Paranjpye to work in her Doordarshan series, *Ados Pados*. I was eager to accept it for several reasons. Despite our close friendship, I had previously declined her film offer due to concerns regarding the producer, Basu Bhattacharya, who had a reputation for not paying actors. Additionally, after Sai's separation from my friend Arun Joglekar, she had distanced herself from me, while Arun and his young son Gautam had stayed with me at Chirebandi for a period of time. Therefore, her invitation felt like a gesture of reconciliation.

Sai had established a unique identity of her own beyond her illustrious connections as Shakuntala Paranjpye's daughter and Wrangler Paranjpye's granddaughter, which earned her my deep respect. This regard was further amplified by *Ados Pados*, in which her grasp of the television medium and distinctive directorial style were evident. The series, which aired in thirteen episodes, presented the struggles of a widower in his fifties raising a schoolboy, and the affection he develops for his son's teacher. The show instantly resonated with the general public; the viewers identified with the widower's stuggles. With Doordarshan reaching every corner of

India, the serials broadcast on it became the talk of every household. I experienced this firsthand during a trip to Manipur. While attending a meeting, I happened to be near a school. When the meeting got over, somehow news had spread that 'Robin's daddy' was nearby. In no time, a crowd of children, their parents and guardians gathered, making it impossible for me to leave without meeting them. During our conversation, I realised that they had no inkling of Amol Palekar or his celebrity status. To them, I was simply the 'Robin's daddy' from *Ados Pados*.

Recently, Naresh Suri, my co-star in *Ados Pados* and I watched an episode together while working on our play *Kusur*. The entire scene depicted us smoking one cigarette after another. Unlike today, where there are warnings about the effects of smoking on children, such considerations were non-existent back then. Reflecting on the past reveals how social norms and sensibilities have evolved over time.

As a director, I too was captivated by the allure of the TV medium. After I had directed *Kachchi Dhoop* in 1988 for Doordarshan, an assistant of Hrishi-da's, Vinay Bhatia, along with his brother, approached me with the proposal for the series *Aa Bail Mujhe Maar*. They suggested broadcasting it in the afternoon instead of the evening. Seeing my puzzled expression, Vimal Bhatia said, 'Amol-ji, your popularity spans across two generations, from mother to daughter. Considering that, we're confident that the afternoon slot is the right choice.' I had no reason to decline. Additionally, Jyoti Swaroop, known for creating the pure comedy film *Padosan*, was to direct the series. For the role of the nagging wife, the Bhatia brothers had chosen Bharti Achrekar.

Premiering at 3:30 p.m. on a Saturday in 1985, *Aa Bail Mujhe Maar* very quickly became a massive hit. It was often said in its reviews that 'mothers and daughters, mothers-in-law and daughters-in-law, sisters-in-law and their siblings, all watch this series because of their affection for Amol!' Doordarshan even enquired, 'Will you make thirteen more episodes?' In haste and amidst the frenzy, I declined the offer to continue shooting. Unlike these days, shows were not written and shot in multiple 'seasons' back then.

During the pandemic, when Doordarshan revived the airing of their classic series, I was delighted to see both *Kachchi Dhoop* and *Aa Bail Mujhe Maar* entertaining audiences once again. Knowing that my work provided solace to people during a difficult time filled me with immense satisfaction. Hearing viewers share how my films helped them cope with the challenges of the pandemic, saying things like, 'I lost track of time watching your films. Your work made the hardship more bearable,' brings me a profound sense of fulfilment.

The weight of responsibilities bears down heavily on my shoulders.

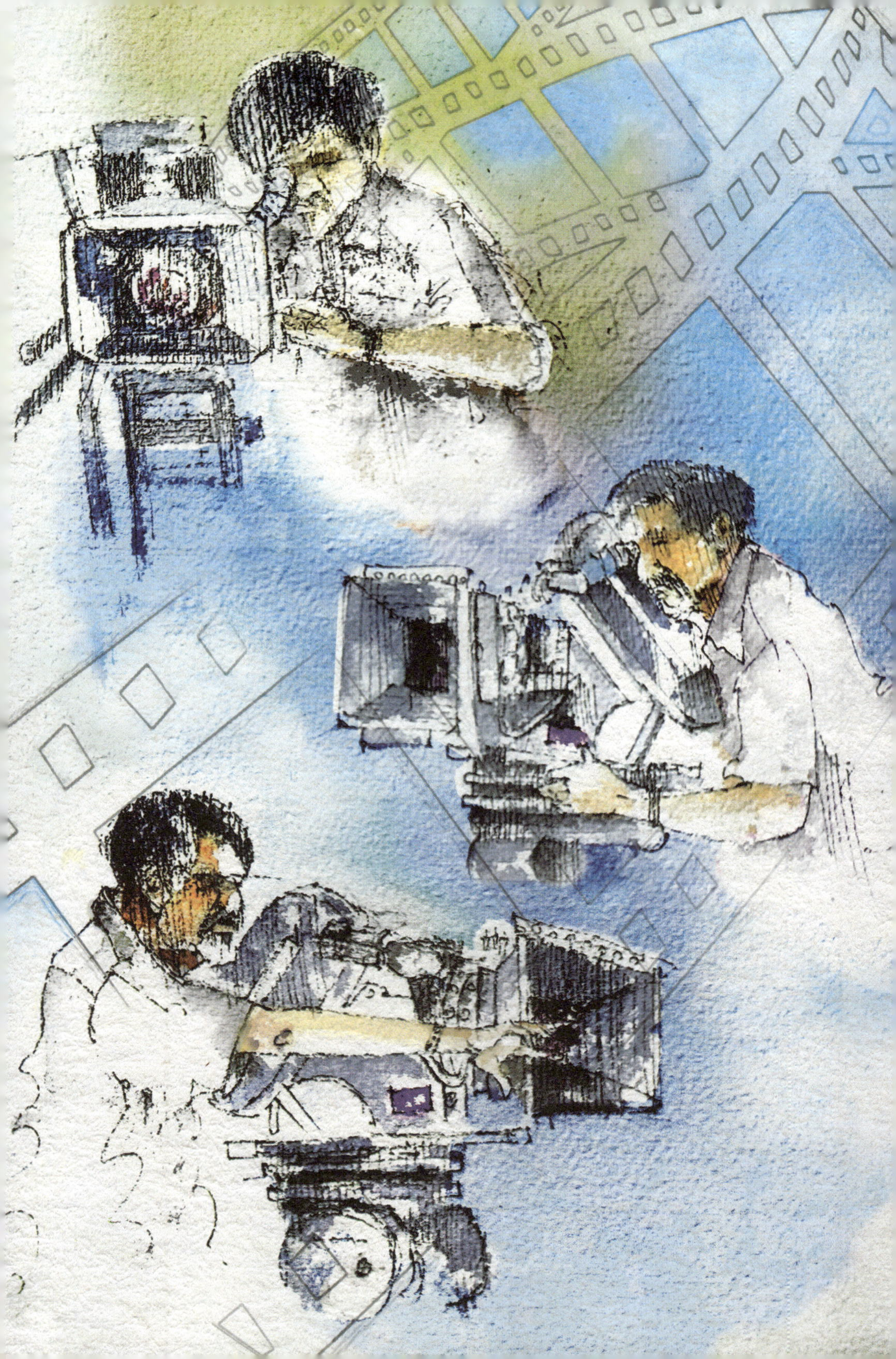

The Ultramarine Hues

It's been a few months now. I've been shedding my past like a worn-out T-shirt, letting go of memories, events and people that were once a part of my being.

What kind of exercise is this? Is it an excavation? Not really ... but many things are floating up to the surface and shining before me.

Is it *aakhyaan* or *bhaarud* (these are kinds of folk narration in Marathi)? Not quite, as these forms have metaphysical and religious contexts.

Or is it a biopsy? All of these have negative connotations. Can it be called contemplation? Or guarding?

Contemplation is a function of the past; guarding takes place in the present. But being perennially awake, one's relationship with elemental 'guarding' has no specific temporality. I instantly recollect two poetical references to 'guarding', each reflecting its class character.

The first is from a poem by Grace (the pen name of the Marathi poet Manik Godghate).

संदिग्ध घरांच्या ओळी, आकाश ढवळतो वारा
माझ्याच किनाऱ्यावरती, लाटांचा आज पहारा.

Original Marathi by Grace

मी माझ्या भविष्यावर रात्रभर ठेवला आहे पहारा
एखाद्या सकाळी मी पृथ्वीचाच रंग बदलून टाकीन!

(Original Marathi by Dhasal)

The lines of anonymous houses, the wind stirs the skies.
The waves guard my own shore today.

The second reference is from poet-social activist Namdev Dhasal.

I'm guarding my future through the night.
I'll change the colour of the earth some morning.

In surveying this chaotic spread, I'm revisiting my intimacy not only with people and events but also with science, aesthetics, philosophy, literature, music, criticism and psychology.

If I describe this in visual language, it is like a swimmer who is surfing on a three-metre-long board rising to the height of ten metres; a gigantic wave attacks him, he dives into it with tremendous energy, and the water splashes out of the screen. I'm thoroughly wet and satiated. (No reference to Freud, please.) Or, it is like a batsman on TV, hitting a reverse sweep beyond the fence, and the ball directly comes straight at me, and I catch it—or if I can't, it hits me hard somewhere. The ball, which appears in twenty-five frames per second, is suddenly captured in five hundred frames per second by a Hawk-Eye camera. All of a sudden, a thirty-year-old incident resurfaces, which then connects with another incident in the present, creating a semblance of continuity. Or, the movement between two stable points becomes visible, making the connection between two unrelated events suddenly apparent. The roots of these events can be traced back to an incident that occurred many decades ago.

'Persistence of Vision' led me to believe that I wasn't Not-Okay.

Kudos to the fathers of the Gestalt psychology: Max Wertheimer, Wolfgang Köhler and Kurt Koffka. It is they who told me that my initial instinct was right. Instead of baking a hotchpotch bread from small details, one needs to take a holistic approach to life and then draw conclusions about oneself. It is only then that you sense the pricks under the skin—your howlers, deep-rooted complexes and phobias that tie you down completely to the ground like the Patagonian Cypress tree from Chile. It is only when your gaze meets the horizon that you grasp the vast expanse of your life, like the 250-year-old banyan tree in Kolkata with its thousands of aerial roots spreading far and wide. If I had never trimmed my nails, perhaps the hidden pendulum's gentle arc might have been revealed, oscillating between the vibrant spectacle and the soft-solitary glow. But in this age of AI, why on earth should anyone make this futile effort?

The Hawk-Eye technology was first used in May 2001 during a cricket match between England and Pakistan, giving the very first glimpse of the use of AI. The high-speed video cameras were placed at six different locations around the ground, so even if only 25 per cent of the ball's movement was captured, it was possible to decide its location three-dimensionally. Thus, using any two cameras, it was possible to determine the direction in which the ball was moving and the point at which it touched the ground. This technology was used over the next six or seven years in tennis and international cricket tournaments. The trigonometric principle behind the technology is very simple: if you know one side and two angles of a triangle, you can map the remaining two sides. The Hawk-Eye technology has become an inalienable part of all sports today.

The Cairos system developed by German AI experts is equally effective. In this technology, a magnetic field is created by spreading thin wires near the penalty area and behind the goal post. The football is fitted with a microchip sensor, which sends location signals to the main computer throughout the game. FIFA (Fédération Internationale de Football Association) tried it first in 2007 in Japan. The footballs manufactured by Adidas were so tough that the chip stayed intact even when the ball was hit very hard.

Now, isn't it logical that if any sport is televised using such fantastic technology, one would remain glued to the television screen at home?

But then one would miss out on the fun of mixing with huge crowds and shouting oneself hoarse under a scorching sun or in torrential rain! It is perhaps this sense of joyous participation that inspires me to watch many live sports events, particularly football, badminton, cricket and hockey. And now, since my daughter Samiha is a part of the sports industry, she books our tickets in advance—a year in advance for the finals of the July 2024 UEFA European Football Championship and the 2024 Olympics. What more could one ask for at the age of eighty?

During my school days, I regularly attended the Kanga League matches at Shivaji Park Gymkhana, where I enthusiastically cheered from the boundary. I was especially impressed by Ramakant Desai, a diminutive bowler, who intimidated renowned batsmen with his incredible speed. His small stature belied his impressive skill, making him a compelling player to watch. I have even seen the legendary Vinoo Mankad teach precise bowling by placing a coin in front of the wicket.

Our neighbour, Mr Dharmadhikari, held an important position in a big cement company, where star cricketers, such as Polly Umrigar, Ajit Wadekar and Ramakant Desai, were employed as well. Often, Mr Dharmadhikari would take me to international matches, where I would experience live the cricketing environment. I watched my first international cricket match in 1960, and realised how deeply I had fallen in love with cricket, much before I fell in love with any girl! That love has simply grown over the last sixty-four years. Once, while I was travelling to watch a match between India and Australia, I met Ramakant Desai on the local train. Naturally, everyone recognised this star player. But nobody bothered him. Would this be possible in today's world?

At the stadium, I would follow every ball carefully, my eyes wide open. Once a tall and fair batsman strode out to the crease with his shirt collar turned up in a cocky, intimidating manner. It was burning hot that day. From the East Stand came a loud cry, 'Salim, we want a sixer!' and Salim Durani instantly obliged by hitting a six towards the stand. During the same match, on the last day, we also watched how a young woman ran onto the field and kissed Abbas Ali Baig on his way back to the pavilion during tea break. Mr Dharmadhikari also once took me to his office to show me the complete recording of the memorable 1960 'tied' match between Australia and West Indies.

How many debts do I repay in my earthly sojourn? This life's canvas is painted in vibrant hues of gratitude.

I tried to express my love for cricket and other field sports through my art twice. In one endeavour, I failed; in the second, I succeeded. In 2013, I made a Marathi film called *We Are On! Houn Jau Dya*, which fell in the comic genre and featured many senior artistes. The climax was a cricket match, the filming for which went on for a week. Both the artistes and the technicians thoroughly enjoyed the experience. Dilip Vengsarkar spent an entire day with us. This light-hearted subject had been on my mind for many years, but I had lacked the nerve to try my hand at comedy. It was the last film of my career, and it did not work. But, in life, you win some, you lose some.

The other opportunity came in 1988, when the Indian sports ministry launched a campaign, 'Fitness for Fun, Fitness for Everyone'. They invited me to make inspirational ads for it. There was a huge sports festival planned in Delhi, in which the international star sprinter Michael Johnson was going to participate. The stadium was packed to the rafters and we were ready. Michael Johnson ran a terrific race. We also filmed a small segment with him giving a brief message to the youth. I created a montage with sports luminaries like Milkha Singh, Zafar Iqbal, Prakash Padukone and P.T. Usha, as well as renowned film personalities like Dimple Kapadia, Aamir Khan and Nana Patekar, who were shown playing or working out. We also shot a segment with Gulzar saab, who surprised me by wearing a sports outfit instead of his usual white kurta-pyjama, while performing the *ardha shirshasana* or the half headstand yoga pose. Sharmila Tagore and Tiger Pataudi joined the campaign with their two daughters. I prepared short two-minute segments featuring each participant's unique voice and handed them over to the ministry. The next day, I received a phone call from the chief secretary inquiring about the remuneration. I explained to him my stand of not taking any compensation for such endeavours, also adding that none of the participants expected any remuneration because they had worked for me out of respect.

Before our marriage, Chitra used to participate in state-level table tennis tournaments. Our daughter Shalmalee was competent enough to participate in national-level badminton tournaments. Her daily practice, inspired by her role model, the great international player Ami Ghia, fuelled her journey to success. It was my responsibility to take her to the ground early every morning, even if I had gone to bed late at night. I took her for tournaments outside of Bombay as well. In 1988, a junior badminton tournament was held in Imphal. I paid for the airfare of all the players from Maharashtra. Shalmalee's playing style was very attractive and aggressive, and as a result, I came to be known on the badminton circuit more as 'her father' than as a popular film hero, and even today I'm proud of that identity.

Bringing Shalmalee home after a tough match, I would give her hot water in a tub to soak her aching feet in, and massage them. Even today I remember the decisive points in every one of the tournaments she won and the errors she committed in every match she lost. Shalmalee is now a professor of English literature in Australia. I cherish the memories of those special shared moments to ease the pain of our permanent physical distance.

My younger daughter, Samiha, has a solid athletic frame, and she plays football and rugby. One look is all you need to perceive her tremendous strength. We share a deep connection and often bond over late-night sports tournaments, indulging in plenty of food while we watch. Our first meeting with her now-husband took place at The Oval in London—together, we watched the 2019 Cricket World Cup final between India and Australia.

One memorable incident stands out. In school, Samiha would always play cricket with the boys. Once, our all-rounder cricket hero Kapil Dev visited her school and played with the kids. She was very proud that she took his wicket twice! Impressed by her, Kapil Dev invited her to take professional cricket training. She came home announcing, 'I have to join Kapil Dev's academy. He has invited me.' Mentally, she was already there! That day, she and I shared some fantastic dreams till her mother returned home. The entry of this villain transformed the entire scene. We had a family feud.

'You are not going anywhere until you finish college,' was the only remark addressed to Samiha. The rest of the attack was directed at me. It started with 'You agreed to her leaving school in eighth standard to run after cricket?' and escalated to arguments like, 'Behind every successful sportsperson, there are a thousand others who fail to reach the top'. References to the Third Wave of feminism were also thrown in. I was questioned on all fronts. Sandhya believed that completing her education and gaining self-sufficiency was crucial for Samiha's future. However, despite these arguments, Sandhya never imposed any career choices on Samiha, nor did she put any restrictions on her participation in sports tournaments taking place anywhere, anytime. When Samiha was seventeen, we encouraged her to go to Ukraine as a volunteer for the UEFA Euro championship. After finishing her education, this highly capable and independent daughter of ours made the decision to pursue a career in sports law in Switzerland.

My life has been full of various sports and sports personalities, and yet I have never played a single game myself. I have absolutely no interest in an exercise or yoga routine, or any sort of strength training. After a fall in Ireland, I refused surgery and physiotherapy, and have continued leading my life for the last five years despite a broken shoulder. Utter lack of interest and lethargy! Only once did I deliberately put on weight, for the role of Mukutrao in *Akriet*, and then reduced it with the same zest. Beyond that, I have never entered an actual sports arena or playing field, always remaining a spectator. By this logic, it would have been consistent with my personality to have remained a film actor. The director and the producer do all the hard work for the film; the actor has no load to carry as he is a temporary traveller. However, I took up the mantle of producer and director, completing five television serials, sixteen full length films and one documentary film between 1980 and 2013.

Kachchi Dhoop (1987), *Naqab* (1988), *Mrignayani* (1991), *Paulkhuna* (1993) and *Krishnakali* (2007) were the TV serials I made for Doordarshan. I had to master a different set of skills while making them. Unlike condensing a narrative into a few hours to make a film, I had to learn how to expand a story over thirteen parts. Of course, I could never acquire the expertise of those masters who managed to work within very restricted budgets and yet consistently churned out one episode in a day and a half. I never could follow the prevalent practice of using scattered bright light, or of making actors rattle away their dialogues facing the camera, and then inserting, in between, the close ups of other actors to show their reactions. I've found that delivering high-quality work without cutting corners might not yield immediate financial rewards, but it ultimately leads to a lasting sense of pride and fulfilment in one's work.

While raising Shalmalee, and then Samiha twenty years later, we realised that content, theatre and films that appeal to adolescents are scarce in Indian languages. In order to fill that gap, I made *Kachchi Dhoop* in 1987, and later, a fun-filled comic film called *Dumkata* in 2007 with Sandhya.

I have a deep regret that, despite my best intentions, I couldn't make a meaningful contribution to children's theatre. Additionally, my dream of hosting an international children's theatre festival remains unrealised. Between 2004 to 2008, Sandhya and I organised five theatre festivals in Pune (I have written about the Badal Sircar and Tendulkar festivals in previous chapters). Even though there are retrospectives of films, opportunities to see multiple plays by the same director in one place are relatively rare in theatre. Considering this, we worked to present the 'Chorus Festival' to showcase two trilogies (six plays) which allowed the audiences to see the artistic evolution of Manipur-based director and playwright Ratan Thiyam. His journey from formative works to more refined productions was evident. Through Ranga Shakti (also known as the Chorus Repertory Theatre), Ratan Thiyam had dedicated himself to empowering local youth, steadfastly producing plays with social and political significance for over four decades, a notable achievement amidst Manipur's volatile landscape. We provided him with financial assistance of Rs 5 lakh on behalf of Marathi theatre buffs—something that gave us immense satisfaction.

To pay tribute to the rich tradition of musical dramas in Maharashtra and Karnataka, we celebrated the 'Rang Sangeet Mahotsav'. From Karnataka, we invited Enagi Balappa, G.V. Malathamma, and from Maharashtra, renowned artistes like Chandrakant Gokhale, Jaimala Shiledar, Bhalchandra Pendharkar, Kanhopatra Kinikar, Sumati Tikekar, Narayan Bodas, Ashalata Wabgaonkar, Ramdas Kamat, Prasad Sawkar, Rajni Joshi were invited and felicitated.

We hosted the Theatre Beyond Words festival, which featured Irshad Panjatan's mesmerising pantomime as well outstanding performances by esteemed artistes, including Atul Kumar, Rajat Kapoor, Ranvir Shorey and Sunil Shanbag. The festival also included thought-provoking discussions with renowned theatre experts Veenapani Chawla, Neelam Mansingh Chowdhry, and Makarand

Sathe, among others. To share these extraordinary experiences

{24} with you and preserve them for posterity, we present a *compilation of recordings* from these festivals through this book, encompassing the essence of these events. Please overlook the flaws and immerse yourself in the experience.

The theme of *Dumkata* can be guessed from its English title, *A Tale of a Tail.* It tells the story of a small family with a young working couple, their two boys, the grandfather and a maid. Sandhya was inspired to write this story based on her own experience with Samiha when she was three years old. Some blood drops are found in the toilet as the younger boy has a polyp—a small growth projecting from the colon. After a medical examination, the doctor jocularly indicates to the elder boy that his younger brother is going to have a tail. The comic situation that arises in the family after this can arise in any family. Om Puri, Sachin Khedekar, Shernaz Patel, Anjana Basu, Khush Mullick and Asim Desai played memorable roles. Gulzar saab's delightful lyrics were set to tune by Shankar-Ehsaan-Loy. The film was intended for family viewing, so we opted to release it on a private channel rather than in theatres, allowing families to watch it together. The channel acquired the broadcast rights to the film but dilly-dallied over its release under some pretext or

{11} the other. Finally, we gave up. *Dumkata* neither reached the public nor could we send it to any children's film festivals in spite of receiving a number of invitations. Now accessible through this book, we encourage you to enjoy the movie in its entirety!

Doordarshan was in its heyday when we made the thirteen-part serial *Kachchi Dhoop* (1987). It reached even the smallest of villages. The central narrative theme of the novel *Little Women* by Louisa May Alcott was adapted into *Kachchi Dhoop* by Chitra. She wrote the screenplay and dialogue in English. *Kachchi Dhoop* allows a glimpse into the emotional world of four people—three daughters of a middle-class woman and the only grandson of a retired naval officer who lives in the neighbouring bungalow. We contacted the brilliant writer Kamlesh Pande for the Hindi dialogues. I mentioned Vijay Tendulkar's *Kovli Unhe* (Tender Sunrays) and Kamlesh instantly composed the title song.

(Original Hindi Poem)

कच्ची धूप, गुनगुनी धूप, अधखिली और चुलबुली धूप,
जिंदगी के आंगन में, उम्र की दहलीज़ पर
आ खड़ी होती है इक बार, कच्ची धूप

Tender sunlight, soft sunlight
Half-open and bubbly sunlight
In the front yard of life, at the threshold of life
It arrives ... once in a while, tender sunlight

Our neighbour Vijay Singh Patwardhan set it to a lovely tune. It was sung by Shalmalee, Bhagyashree and Pinky Patwardhan along with Anuradha Paudwal. People still talk about the title song with fondness. We had tried to structure the entire serial as a musical.

As an actor, I made it a point to work with new directors who struggled to cast other popular actors in their films. I also consistently shaped raw talent in the younger generation, introducing new faces to the industry. I can mention at least twenty-five to thirty names that I introduced to the industry and who later became celebrities. Our star cast in *Kachchi Dhoop* comprised Ashutosh Gowarikar, Bhagyashree Patwardhan and her two sisters, and Shalmalee—all of them young and inexperienced. Still the entire serial was completed in record time.

As per the convention of that period, we created a pilot consisting of two episodes and sent it to Delhi. We received a prompt and positive reply saying that Friday evening prime time had been fixed for the release. I politely rejected the proposal. I had made a serial to be watched by the entire family together, maybe on Sunday mornings, and I was confident that it would start a new trend. The approval came very soon, and *Kachchi Dhoop* became an instant success. As a result, the Sunday morning slot became the most expensive 'prime' slot on Doordarshan, and was later used to air the immensely popular series *Ramayan* produced by Ramanand Sagar.

In 1988, I directed *Naqab*, which was produced under the banner Dnya Films owned by Chitra.

This time we came up with an emotional story. The story of an actor struggling to hide his disability following a paralytic attack and a nurse trying to save him from depression. Through this story, we sought to shed light on the all-pervasive casting couch culture in the industry. Anil Chatterjee played the lead role with finesse. Believing a Western-style soundtrack would better suit the theme, I reached out to versatile music director Vannraj Bhatia. He composed a symphonic background score in just three days, which added a unique dimension to the serial. *Naqab* was received very well by viewers.

It was filmed mainly in a bungalow in Khandala. The final part of the shooting took place over three or four days in Chirebandi. We finished the shoot at ten in the night and then threw a party for the entire unit that lasted into the wee hours. Since the crew had decided to pick up the equipment the next day, the camera, sound equipment, lights and other material were left in the hall overnight. When we woke up in the morning, we realised that there had been a break-in. And it's possible that we might have been drugged as well. The burglars appeared to have moved through all the bedrooms too. The drawers and cupboards had been ransacked and emptied on the floor; stuff worth lakhs of rupees was thrown out onto the lawns of the bungalow. But nothing was actually stolen. I tried to trivialise it by saying, 'The world of thieves and burglars must have received the news that this fellow is a pauper; no point in looting him.' The police commissioner was surprised at the way I dealt with the situation.

Around that time, Achyut Vaze approached me with a project: a serial based on the novel *Mrignayani*, written by renowned Hindi author and Padma Bhushan awardee Vrindavan Lal Verma. The story was set in the sixteenth century, with Raja Mansingh Tomar falling in love with 'Ninni', a girl belonging to the Gujjar tribe that was fighting bravely against Ghiyasuddin Khilji's army. The news of their love reached the royal palace. Ninni also had to tactfully handle the politics within the king's inner circle of queens. The renowned court singer Tansen composed the raga 'Gurjari Todi' in Ninni's honour.

This multi-layered story required elaborate costumes and costly set design. Mohan Bhandari and Pallavi Joshi were selected for the lead roles. The outdoor filming was done in the newly established Film City in Bombay. The indoor locations such as the court, the queens' chambers and bathing chambers were constructed inside the Seth Studio in Andheri. This was art director Nitin Desai's first assignment in the industry. I watched him at different stages of his life, as he went from an upcoming art director to a businessman entangled in huge financial transactions. I felt very sad later when I came to know that his journey had come to such a miserable end. We invited Sharang Dev, Pandit Jasraj's son, to do the musical score. He composed a memorable title song enriched with Pandit-ji's exquisite *alaps*. While capturing the love-making scene between the hero and the heroine, we used the song '*Kesariya balama, padhaaro mhaare des*' as the background score, sung by the Manganiyars in high-pitched tones. During the scene, the heroine is seen with a feather in her hair, which the hero gently removes, unknotting her long, silky hair; her ornaments slowly drop to the ground and then Mansingh's robes fall away too. I congratulated myself for capturing the intensity of the love scene so suggestively and delicately in the visual language of the small screen. As a matter of fact, I drew inspiration from the Salim-Anarkali love scene in *Mughal-E-Azam*, captured by the great K. Asif. The scene shows Dilip Kumar slowly caressing Madhubala's face with a white feather, looking at her with great intensity. Madhubala is eroticism personified as she blushes and the camera closes in on her lips. In the background plays '*Prem jogan ban*', the incomparable song composed in Raga Sohani, performed by the legendary Bade Ghulam Ali Khan. Every moment of that sensual encounter ignites a sense of elation in one's body. Even though I was pleased with the scene I had shot for *Mrignayani*, I was aware that I had not achieved even a hundredth of K. Asif's magic.

Ramdas Bhatkal of Popular Prakashan (the producer of *Paulkhuna*) had beautifully conceptualised the transformation in the image of women in Marathi society over the past hundred years, as reflected in literature. Thus *Paulkhuna* (1993) was born. Choosing key milestones from various time periods and revealing iconic characters through emerging artistes was a delightful experience. Amidst the warm conversations between Grandma (Aaji) and her granddaughter (Nati), Chitra skilfully crafted a beautiful portrayal of a woman in one episode. Shridhar Phadke composed a superb title song. *Paulkhuna* premiered on Bombay Doordarshan on 14 September 1993, airing Tuesday nights thereafter. It received widespread acclaim. There were some unexpected payoffs too: the demand for old, forgotten novels increased in the public libraries of the smaller towns of Maharashtra as the younger generation turned to older literature.

The officers at Doordarshan were extremely pleased with my work for their platform. They constantly demanded something new from me though I was more inclined to do full-length films. In 2005–06, I directed my last serial for Doordarshan on great demand. Based on the acclaimed Hindi novel *Krishnakali*, they desired to create a series. Upon reading the novel, I was captivated by the rebellious and free-spirited protagonist, Krishnakali, and consequently gave my consent. It wasn't difficult for us to recreate the Calcutta of the 1960s, as we decided to film at actual locations. The talented music director Anand Modak composed beautiful music for the serial. I had a novel idea for its publicity. In order to familiarise the younger generation with the contributions of a senior writer like Shivani, I proposed that we conduct short interviews with her contemporaries and televise them before every episode of the serial. The Doordarshan officers immediately took to the idea. We interviewed legendary writers like Mahasweta Devi, Krishna Sobti, Shivani's daughter Mrinal Pande and several others. However, even though the serial went on air, for some reason, none of these interviews were ever aired. I never asked anyone why.

Throughout my career as a director, I have primarily focused on adapting renowned literary works into feature films, bringing timeless stories to life either on the small screen or the silver screen. *Ankahee* (1985) *Thodasa Roomani Ho Jaayen* (1990), *Bangarwadi* (1995), *Kairee* (2000), *Anaahat* (2003) and *Paheli* (2005) were some of the milestones in that journey.

The richness that literary works from diverse languages bring to human life is immeasurable. While reading a novel, story, or even poetry, visual possibilities begin to take shape in my mind; words on paper can evoke powerful images. The image captured by the camera is far more effective than words on paper because the abstraction of words gets represented in a visual form. However, this manifestation also limits the medium in a way. Every individual's visual imagery is distinct; it is unique to them. Great literature has the capacity to transcend the silences between words and sentences, evoking powerful experiences and connections in the reader, but when I, as a director, bring the picture in my imagination before the spectator, they get trapped at the visual level and the uniqueness of their own interpretations ceases to exist.

Let's take my film *Anaahat* as an example. The original play shows that the queen selects her former lover as her sexual partner when a directive of *niyog* is issued. The playwright had plotted in some erotic scenes. For me, her choice of partner was unimportant; what was key for me, rather, was that she would experience sexual pleasure with a man for the very first time in her life, and it was this aspect that, in my opinion, needed to be highlighted. If I had shown a real man, in flesh and blood, chosen by the queen, or had given the man's role to say a Hrithik Roshan or Ajay Devgn, I would have imposed severe restrictions on the spectator's imagination. Moreover, it would have sparked an irrelevant discussion on whether the queen's choice was right or wrong, etc. In fact, while writing a screenplay, it is essential to plan which elements should be in the foreground and which in the background. These decisions are as crucial as the ones made with regard to technical aspects at the later stages. Choices such as what should be highlighted in certain scenes or whether to ruthlessly remove unnecessary elements from the visual frame need to be considered even during the scripting phase.

'Being faithful to the original literary text' is yet another wrong-headed criterion used by our critics and audiences that limits further their aesthetic appreciation of a film. If, in the original text of *Kairee*, the central character was a boy, why was it changed to a girl in the film adaptation? Why was *Bangarwadi* filmed at a location other than the author Vyankatesh Madgulkar's village, Maandesh? Some people question Kishore Kadam's casting as R.D. Karve, citing concerns about his physical resemblance with an upper-caste Brahmin character like Karve. I've been asked whether no Marathi actress was available for the role of Karve's wife, Malati Karve? Back then, I used to respond to such irrelevant questions. Today, I would simply ignore them. Sir Arthur Conan Doyle wrote fifty-six stories in 1887, introducing Sherlock Holmes to us. We have at least two hundred interpretations of Sherlock Holmes, starting from William Gillet's film in 1916 to the series starring Benedict Cumberbatch in 2010. Shakespeare's *Romeo and Juliet* has more than a hundred film versions. Questions about veracity arise from a fundamental misunderstanding of various mediums.

Why is it assumed that Romeo and Juliet cannot be portrayed as homosexual characters?

I have always been of the opinion that a film director should have the freedom to make changes to the original literary text. However, it is necessary to have the author's permission too. When there is a change of medium, the director's interpretation should be the focal point. Naturally, audiences have a right to appraise the film and say whether they liked it or not. However, comparing the film to the original literary work and criticising it for not being faithful to the text is meaningless and counterproductive.

Discussions, arguments and controversies were a recurring phenomenon during the script-writing process for many of my films. This part of the creative process is most magical. I believe that the elements of surprise, spontaneity and unpredictability that make the creative process fascinating are still unique to the human experience and cannot be fully replicated by AI, at least not yet.

One day, Jayant Dharmadhikari came to me with a proposal to make a commercial film based on C.T. Khanolkar's *Kaalaay Tasmai Namaha* (Salutation to Time). I immediately sensed the contradiction in his proposal. For commercial success, one needed a story centred on a hero who possessed all the good qualities. Khanolkar's play revolved around the girlfriend and the wife of the male lead. Moreover, the plot did not allow the regular spectator to easily identify with the dramatic situations it contained. Thus, from the outset, I had my reservations about the project; I questioned Jayant's vision. Celebrated Marathi filmmaker Datta Dharmadhikari was Jayant's uncle. Also, Jayant had worked with the famous Hindi director Raj Khosla as his assistant. Both of these people greatly influenced Jayant's working style and outlook. The notion that a film's climax should elicit tears from female viewers, thereby ensuring box-office success, was a piece of conventional wisdom widely accepted in the industry.

On the contrary, instead of visible tears, I preferred a subtler emotional trigger, one that caused the audience's eyes to well up and left a lasting impact on their mind. My approach posed a difficulty for Jayant. But in spite of these differences, we started co-producing the film, and *Ankahee* was born.

A more significant difficulty arose from my conviction that the script should not be regressive, in that it ought not to promote superstition. I believe an artiste's role is not only to create; it is that of a social catalyst, conveying progressive ideas and encouraging audiences to think critically and gain fresh perspectives. I felt compelled to include dualities such as 'science versus astrology' and 'fate versus human will' in the script of the film. Let me summarise the plot for those who have not read the original play nor seen my film.

The son of a great astrologer falls in love with a girl and wishes to marry her. The father opposes the marriage, announcing that the girl would certainly die during pregnancy in the eleventh month after their marriage. But the boy and the girl are firm in their decision to marry. One of the astrologer's friends arrives from the village with his daughter. This man has been struggling to raise a daughter all by himself, and so, right from her childhood, he has been spreading rumours about her being possessed by an evil spirit and losing her mental balance. When the astrologer's son sees this village girl, who has lost all her confidence, he decides to marry her and get her pregnant, thinking that after her death in the eleventh month, he would marry his beloved. But his lover refuses to follow through with his cruel and selfish plan. She does not want happiness at the cost of another girl's life. Eventually she commits suicide. As an atheist who does not believe in astrology and fate, I strongly disagreed with characters that had resigned themselves to destiny and had accepted astrological predictions as the absolute truth. When Kamlesh Pande started developing the screenplay, the need to make the lover an independent, rational and strong character became all the more pronounced. We tried to capture her character in the note that she leaves behind before committing suicide: 'This is not my suicide; it is my denial. I protest against all those restrictions imposed on me, in the name of love, in the name of affection, in the name of superstition! Thus, my death is not a result of any astrological foretelling. It is my own decision. I'm taking control of my own mortality to prove that every step I take is a decision I own.'

Even Khanolkar would have appreciated the effusive clarity of these lines penned by Chitra and Kamlesh. The cast of the film—Dina-ben, Dr Lagoo, Devika Mukherjee, Anil Chatterjee, Deepti Naval and I—knew one another very well. So, the shooting was swift and seamless. I used every nook and corner of Chirebandi for the shooting. Deepti felt that she was at her best in *Ankahee*—and I agreed wholeheartedly. She liked that role immensely; even now, when we meet, she talks about it with great love. I have already mentioned the music composed for it by Jaidev-ji; I am indebted to him, and to Asha-bai too. The exquisite *alaps* sung by Bhimsen-ji during the rehearsals at Chirebandi continued to resonate in the surroundings for many more years. When Jaidev-ji and Bhimsen-ji received National Awards for their work in *Ankahee* as music director and singer, respectively, I felt proud and accomplished.

And so much of this wouldn't have been possible without Mangesh Desai, who had a legendary mastery over the art of re-recording. Until his death, he worked on all my films. One memory of him has stayed with me over the years. Khanolkar's original play included a scene where the village girl is thrown into a fit of anxiety on seeing a fan start rotating at the press of a switch. I envisioned composing this scene using sound to evoke a cringing sensation similar to that evoked by a screeching noise. Vinod Mehra, a wonderful actor, created a hard-rock piece with metallic sounds to achieve this effect.

As the intense music assaults the girl's ears, she becomes terrified, starts babbling and chanting mantras in a trance. I wanted the loud music in the background and the soft conversational sounds in the foreground. However, when Mangesh-ji saw Deepti's powerful performance in this scene, he immediately stopped the reel. For about an hour or so, he did not speak and simply paced the studio, looking distraught. Finally, he sat down in his chair, tapped my head appreciatively, and said, 'Amol, you are crazy!' His eyes were shining with admiration, which reminded me of my father. In the remaining half a day, he completed the re-recording of the entire reel to my great satisfaction.

After Mangesh-ji passed away, I used the same studio for the re-recording of two more films. Each day, before beginning work, I would softly touch his chair. His magic lingered in that place. But what disturbed me was the conspicuous absence of any tribute to him. There was not even a single photograph to acknowledge and honour his presence, or the years he gave to this studio—an act of obliteration that disturbed me deeply. I have always been at odds with the unfair nature of stardom, which excessively glorifies actors while consistently undervaluing the crucial contributions of technicians behind the scenes.

Vinod Mehra had liked the story of *Ankahee*. As a guest artiste, he ably played the role of the rationalist 'doctor' in two important scenes. One day, while I was taking him to a hospital for shooting, our car stopped on a crowded road. A few young children at the traffic intersection saw the expensive Mercedes we were sitting in and approached the window, desperately trying to see who was sitting inside. I was shying away, but Vinod rolled down his window and said 'bye' to them. The children recognised us immediately and started shouting in excitement. Vinod was surprised. 'Why are you trying to hide, *yaar*? This kind of crowd is our life's breath. Tomorrow, if they are not there, I don't know what will happen to

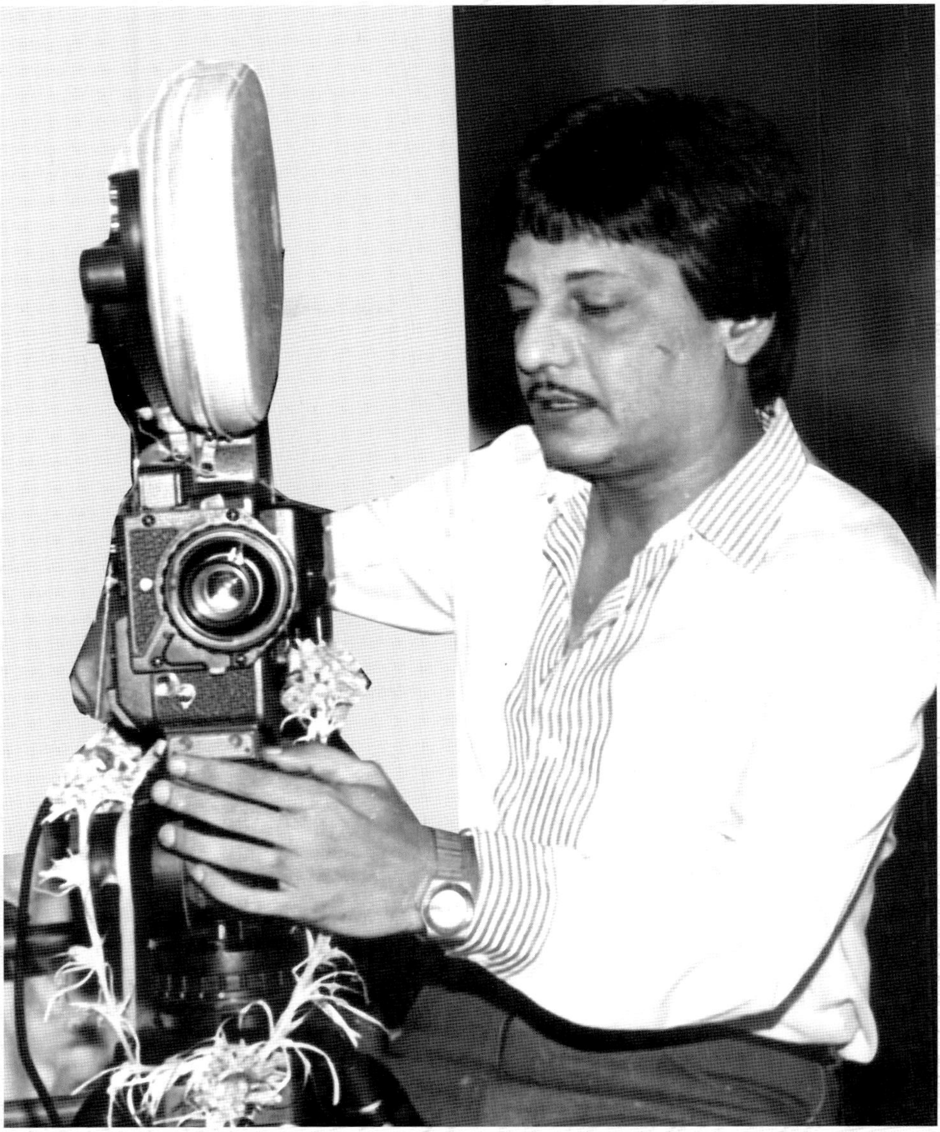

The 16 mm camera used to shoot *Ankahee* (1985)

(2000)

(2001)

(1980)

(2006)

(2011)

(2010)

(1985)

(2009)

(2006)

(2003)

(2008)

(1990)

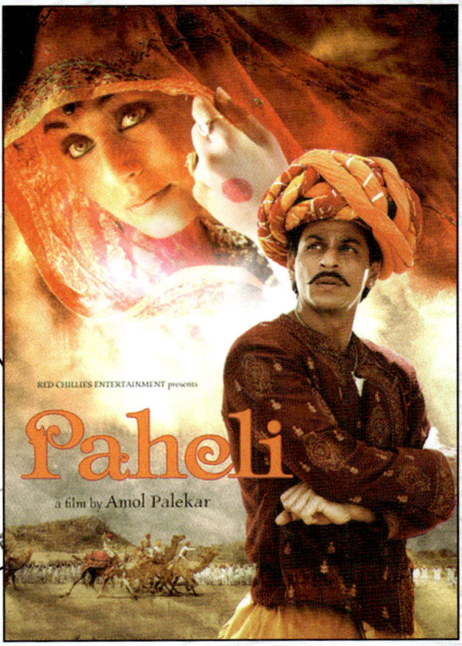

(2005)

(1995)

(1996)

(2013)

Theatre festivals in Pune (2004-08)

बादल सरकार
नाट्यमहोत्सव
पुणे – ऑगस्ट २००४

Amol Palekar presents
RANGSANGEET
MAHOTSAV
रंगसंगीत
महोत्सव २००७
Stall Rs. 150/-

With Vijay Tendulkar & Girish Karnad (2005)

With Damu Kenkre & Nana Patekar (2005)

With Satyadev Dubey, Sulabha Deshpande and Govind Nihalani (2005)

us.' His words played on my mind for a long time. Everyone in the industry would advise me to adopt all possible means of establishing and glorifying my stardom, maintaining it tirelessly and remaining in the limelight. But I never agreed; nor did I ever need it. I never believed that the measure of a person's worth is their popularity or financial success.

Ankahee marked a pivotal moment in my journey, as it ignited a deliberate commitment to questioning and challenging pervasive patriarchal attitudes and the outdated ideologies that perpetuated them—a resolve that has only intensified with time. To highlight the strengths and complexities of the two female characters in the film, I deliberately portrayed the male character (the role I was playing) as flawed, manipulative and morally weak, creating a nuanced contrast which showcased the women's characters in a more positive light. The female characters in my subsequent films became increasingly multi-layered, thoughtful, strong and self-reliant.

Anaahat (2003) was my second attempt to transform a play into a film. About thirty years ago before that, I had translated Surendra Verma's Hindi play *Surya Ki Antim Kiran Se Surya Ki Pahali Kiran Tak* to Marathi and presented it on stage. 'Although your play is tailored for the traditional stage, I believe the subject matter lends itself more naturally to the cinematic medium, and I'd love to adapt it for film,' I said to Surendra Verma and he accepted my proposal.

While presenting his play on the Marathi stage, I had already made certain changes to the original Hindi script. Verma agreed to grant me permission to make further changes to the script to suit the film's screenplay. And that's how *Anaahat* came into being. Its visual design was breathtaking, and it received stupendous international recognition. The film was commercially successful too. Of all my films, *Anaahat* holds a special place in my heart because it marked the beginning of a beautiful collaborative partnership between Sandhya and me—a joint artistic vision that brought us closer together.

Sandhya and I started our life together at the time the twentieth century was coming to an end. To move beyond the overcast skies, and also because we could not afford a house in Mumbai, we chose to relocate to the Pune residence that Sandhya had invested in while she was still based in America. In a way, Chitra and I too had started with a similar blank slate in the house at Gamdevi. But the big difference was that while the earlier beginning had been a gentle confluence of two people's paths, for Sandhya and me, it was akin to being in a ship trying to navigate a turbulent ocean battered by fierce storms. With Samiha by our side, the two of us were trying hard to steady our boat and find a sense of stability amidst the chaos. We had no compass, no sense of direction, no help from anybody, anywhere. The one priceless treasure I had was Sandhya's profound love.

For at least four or five years by then, I had been nursing the idea that Sandhya would join me in my creative journey. I also knew that this would be possible only if she left Mumbai. Otherwise, as a practising lawyer, she would find no time for a shared creative pursuit. Still, I motivated her to write the script of *Anaahat*. It was like picking many raw mangoes in a single stone!

The story of *Anaahat* is about an impotent king, who could not give a successor to the throne, and who orders his queen to be ready for *Niyog*, the custom of choosing a partner for one night of sexual intercourse. The queen is deeply fulfilled by the sexual pleasure she experiences that night. When Sandhya read the original play with its mono-dimensional depiction of a man–woman relationship, she raised a number of issues: the king and the queen could have had an intimate relationship regardless of the king's impotency; the need for the king to have an heir must be more of a political demand; as a man, the king would certainly not have liked the wife to have sexual intercourse with another man—why then did he order her to do it? Could he have opposed the ministerial authority? Did the political solution weigh on him more than his own emotions? What if there was no conception even after observing *niyog*? Or what if the queen conceived a girl? Would she be allowed to occupy the throne?

Sandhya and Dr Sameer Kulkarni jointly wrote the script for the film. Through this tale of one night, set in the 10th century BCE, they managed to convincingly depict the sexual awakening of a woman. The audience greatly appreciated this bold reinterpretation of the *niyog* tradition through a contemporary feminist lens, which offered a fresh and thought-provoking perspective. From a script of just thirty-two pages, a ninety-minute film was crafted, shot over an intense twenty-three-day shoot.

We planned to do the entire shooting in Hampi, Karnataka—its grand stone temples dating back to the 16th century BCE were the perfect setting. We decided to use the famous stepwell in one of the scenes. Official permission was required to shoot inside the temples or anywhere within the monuments as the entire area was a UNESCO World Heritage Site. This was a herculean task. We gave a detailed written declaration that we would not use oil for lamps; we would use real flowers instead of rangoli powder; we would not use nails for curtains but hang them on the pillars, and so on. Finally, we got the necessary permission. To source fresh flowers, we'd travel twenty kilometres to a market and participate in an early-morning auction. To block the natural light, we bought handloom cloth in spools from neighbouring villages. Driven by a deep respect for the ancient, majestic stone monuments and a commitment to honouring our promises, we poured our heart and soul into the project.

We chose pure silk costumes to complement the film's classic ambience and period setting, enhancing its aesthetic appeal. Real gold ornaments, also true to the period setting, were provided by a young jeweller couple who also took on the responsibility of its maintenance and security. The price of the ornaments on site was ten times more than the budget of the entire film!

Sonali Bendre played the role of the queen. It is unquestionably the best work of her entire career. With effortless grace, she became one with the queen's multifaceted personality. Conveying the queen's regal maturity and poise, and later her unfettered joy in exploring new depths of sexual pleasure, Sonali delivered a richly textured and compelling performance. As she returns to her palace, she asks herself the question 'Is this what a man is?', while slowly dropping pieces of her clothing to the ground. The audience gets deeply stirred by her candid expression of sexual pleasure. Recently, I watched her in the OTT series *Broken News* and once again admired her talent. Anant Nag and Deepti Naval too gave exemplary performances in *Anaahat*.

Sandhya had seamlessly woven some ragas in the Dhrupad style (appropriate for the period the film was set in) into the screenplay's background score. Some of the scenes became all the more intense and enchanting because of Uday Bhawalkar's powerful singing and the resonating sound of the rudraveena. The festive scene in which the queen starts preparing for the ritual of *niyog* has pieces played on the pakhawaj in the background. *Anaahat*'s music added another powerful dimension to its story.

We took the ambitious decision of releasing the film in the newly emerging multiplex theatres rather than in the older single-screen cinema halls. It was a calculated risk that we felt would do justice to the film's high-quality visualisation and aesthetic value. Though the film was in Marathi, we released all the prints with English subtitles. The tickets were Rs 100 or 150, which was considered expensive in those days. However, despite the price of the tickets, audiences came to watch the film and gave it immense love and adoration. The collections amounted to three times our expenditure on the film. The film ran for sixty weeks, after which we set yet another trend by deciding to share the profit with the entire crew, including the artistes and technicians. Upon my personal invitation, Jaya Bachchan graced the occasion to distribute mementos and the bonus to everyone.

From then onwards, we decided to use the profits from our previous films as capital for the next film. I gratefully refer to this phase as the 'post-Sandhya era', marking a liberating transition where I finally broke free from the stifling grip of financial insecurity and dependence. I had faced extreme financial stress when raising funds from the market for *Ankahee*. Similarly, the producer of *Bangarwadi* had abandoned the film and declared bankruptcy while the film was only halfway complete. Relying on external funding can severely hinder the creative process, as it introduces insecurity and undermines artistic autonomy. Those events imprinted painful memories.

As we embarked on our new journey together, Sandhya took on the responsibility of managing our finances. As a result, I have experienced a profound sense of comfort and security. Concerns such as how to secure funds, whether the film would be completed without financial hurdles, and how to recover stalled projects—such worries no longer troubled me. I experienced a surge of inspiration, as if my mind had been unlocked and unleashed. Immediately after *Anaahat*, we started working on the movie *Paheli*.

Vijaydan Detha was known as 'Bijji' in the literary world of Rajasthan. I had read a lot of his work. His stories were a treasure trove of local oral traditions. Injustice to women, social repercussions of economic inequality, manipulations and conspiracies by individuals and society, and customs endorsed by patriarchy were his favourite themes. Bijji has fearlessly critiqued and condemned the deeply ingrained, oppressive elements of traditional social hierarchy. We travelled to Jaipur to acquire rights to five or six of his stories.

Accompanied by Bijji, we explored small villages around Jaipur, Jodhpur and Udaipur. We also saw exquisite palaces that showcased Rajasthan's signature style of colourful wall murals. Our experience of the state was multi-faceted as we took in all the variety its natural surroundings had to offer. The colours, aromas and sounds of Rajasthan, its ornate designs, its marble mines, the sand of its deserts, its ornaments and attires, the magical environment full of dance and music, all had a profound impact on us. The spirit of everything we saw and experienced started to seep into our script.

Mani Kaul had already made a marvellous film that was faithful to the original story, titled *Duvidha* (The Dilemma), which depicted the plight of the village women. Sandhya was conceptualising it from an entirely different angle. She was exploring it as a woman's fantasy. She extensively discussed her approach with Bijji and acquired his permission to make changes in the form of a contract.

Paheli starts with a wedding procession passing by a village while returning home. The village has a tree in which resides a ghost who falls in love with the bride. On the same night, the bridegroom has to leave on business in some faraway place. The ghost visits the bride in the disguise of her husband. But his love for her is so true and pure that he cannot cheat her. So he tells her, 'I am a ghost, not your husband. But my love for you is genuine. I'll go away if you refuse to accept me.' The young bride has never experienced such love in her life; her desires have never before been taken into account. She has never had such freedom of decision. She is torn between the shadows of her past and the promise of true love in the present. This is her heart-wrenching dilemma. Sandhya's contribution was to give the folklore a contemporary dimension. She introduced new characters and situations into the script, made numerous changes to the original story, and altered the ending to create a compelling film script.

In the later half of the story, a shepherd poses a challenge to the real husband and the ghost to ascertain who is who. Eventually, the shepherd imprisons the ghost. What happens afterwards is different in the film than in the original story. In the original story, when the real husband returns to the bride, society and relatives console the girl, saying 'the ghost cheated you, you are not to be held guilty'. She meekly accepts this and submits to reality by hiding behind their consolation. In the end, as the ghost's child, a girl, is lying in the embrace of her mother, Bijji makes the following comment: 'May this young girl be spared the typical hardships of womanhood, so that her mother's sacrifices and pain will not have been in vain. Even animals cannot be so easily exploited in this manner; they would at least protest once in a while. But where is the woman's own will?'

On the other hand, in Sandhya's script, the young mother blesses her baby, saying, 'May you possess the strength to make your own choices and to own the consequences of your actions.' She tells her husband that the ghost did not cheat her and that she, herself, had made the choice of accepting the ghost. She is unwilling to betray the love showered upon her by the ghost by telling a lie. She tells the truth to her husband as a strong woman who is ready to face the consequences of her own decisions. Seeing this, the ghost is once again tempted to enter the real husband's body and be with the woman he loves!

Bijji immensely liked the contrasting binaries that we had woven into the script: firstly, that of the traditional woman, held back by societal constraints and expectations versus the modern woman, empowered to transform her life through her own choices; and secondly, that of the pragmatic husband, shaped by societal conventions versus the idealised lover residing in the woman's imagination. Bijji frankly admitted that 'if I had thought of it this way, I would have ended the story exactly like you have.' In that moment, I was reminded of great writers like Badal-da and Sadanand Rege, who had the generosity to embrace other interpretations of their own work. We took leave of Bijji and began to prepare for the next steps.

Recognising the script's demand for music rooted in Rajasthani folk traditions, we decided to contact Ismail Darbar who was a renowned music director at the time. But within two or three meetings, his limitations became evident. We were so disillusioned that we found it difficult to believe that he had composed memorable songs for films such as *Hum Dil De Chuke Sanam* and *Devdas*. Things became clearer when we noticed that after these two films, director Sanjay Leela Bhansali began crediting himself as the music director for his own movies.

We then turned to our favourite composer of Telegu and Tamil films, M.M. Kreem. In recent times, he has composed music for hit films like *Baahubali* and *RRR* and was even awarded an Oscar for the *Naatu Naatu* song. But even twenty years prior to these accolades, we had experienced his musical brilliance that embodied a stunning fusion of Indian and Western styles. We have shared wonderful moments with Kreem sir, creating music and singing Marathi songs. He would often hum his latest compositions and seek our feedback, making us feel like an integral part of his creative process. Even today, Sandhya and he share a close bond.

Based on her visualisation of the screenplay, Sandhya would suggest different ragas for the song situations to him, and he would compose and play two or three tunes on the harmonium. Contrary to our earlier experiences of creating music for our films, where words preceded the tunes, all compositions were ready without lyrics. Kreem sir agreed to our wish that the music would be created solely using live instrumentation, with no reliance on pre-recorded tracks or synthesised sounds. We discussed which Rajasthani instruments would be used for each song. Kreem sir masterfully composed a tune based on Raga Jogkauns for the song *Khaali hain tere bina dono akhiyan, tum gaye kahaan?*, using two instruments—the ravanhatta and the cello. We suggested the names of famous singers like Sonu Nigam, Kalapini Komkali and Shruti Sadolikar as well as the new talent from Pune, Bela Shende. He accepted our recommendations. Kreem sir graciously acknowledged Sandhya's significant contribution to the music of *Paheli*, humbly stating, 'The music is as much mine as it is yours, Bhabhi-ji.' Such artistes are a rare breed; Kreem sir is indeed a gem.

Next, we approached Gulzar saab with the ready tunes. His lyrics exemplify a rare blend of linguistic virtuosity, innovative imagery, delicacy of expression and profound sensitivity, reflecting his exceptional skill and wisdom as a poet. Kreem sir's stunning compositions were elevated by Gulzar saab's evocative lyrics, which explored the complex nuances of romance and separation. Lines such as *'Yaad hai kya tujhe raah ki beriyaan'*, *'Tere roop ki halki dhoop mein, do hi pal hain jeene hain'* or *'Ja-ja, na daal paheli, barson ke baad saheli, jagne ki raat aayi hai / dekha karti thi sapna, sapne ko aakhir apna kehne ki raat aayi hai'*, became very popular. Gulzar saab made it a point to be personally present at every recording, paying special attention to the diction of the singers.

Alongside the music arrangement, we studied the local props and costumes. Sandhya and her friend Neena Parikh were travelling frequently for meticulous research, starting at the Calico Museum of Textiles in Ahmedabad and then collecting embroidery samples from artistes in the narrow lanes of Old Delhi. Meanwhile, I was thinking of new actors for different roles. I had the handsome Bengali actor Jishu Sengupta and Sharmila Tagore's younger daughter Soha in mind. A big producer of mainstream cinema showed interest in the film, provided we roped in stars. While writing the script, Sandhya had Shah Rukh Khan and Rani Mukherjee in mind. The moment the big producer heard these names, he grabbed at the opportunity. The script was read out to Shah Rukh in his office.

When I stressed on the need for an actor who could nuance both roles with subtle variations of goodness, avoiding simplistic good-vs-evil characterisations, Shah Rukh lit another cigarette. He was well aware of the project's progress and the efforts we had invested in it, and that seemed to spark his sharp business acumen. 'Would you mind if I produce this film?' His question left me stunned and speechless. He negotiated a deal for the rights with the earlier producer, and Red Chillies Entertainment became the new producer of *Paheli*. In our second meeting, he seemed to have carefully studied the details of the script. Not only that, he agreed to the names of all the actors I suggested for the other roles, and ensured their availability.

Shah Rukh was greatly interested in special effects in movies. He started looking more deeply into the animation of puppets, the ghost's magical tricks, the shepherd's three tests that came at the end, and so on. I wanted to avoid shooting the double-role characters or the scenes in which the husband and the ghost come face to face with each other in a conventional, restrictive manner. I had prepared a storyboard for the shots of each one of these scenes. Shah Rukh tried to understand each frame. As a producer, he left no stone unturned to create the dream-like ambience that I wanted for most of the scenes. Thanks to the outstanding acting talent of every single member of the cast, the film turned out to be a visual treat. We were able to complete the shooting in just forty-six days because of Shah Rukh's complete involvement in the film.

Some sporadic discordant notes were heard during the shooting, which mainly involved the dance director's style of choreography. I became restless when, instead of using the rich base of traditional Rajasthani folk dance forms, generic Bollywood-style choreography was incorporated into some of the song sequences. Moreover, I disliked anyone behaving in an uncivilised manner with the junior artistes and assistants, or using foul language on set. Gradually, some gossip about me started circulating in the film industry. I also came to know that Shah Rukh's friend circle disapproved of his involvement in such an offbeat film; they were displeased that he wore a moustache in the film! They were convinced that the film would tank.

Certain film magazines even resorted to derisive comments. My well-wishers and the technical team suggested that I speak out against the disparagement. But I did not find it necessary. My aim was to complete the film exactly as I wanted it, without any change. Eventually, it did turn out to be the way I had envisaged it.

Throughout my career, I never engaged with the industry's unseemly power plays and gossip, consistently keeping my poise. It is this detachment that has probably resulted in an enduring rift between me and the industry. If you work in a disciplined manner, with meticulous planning, and avoid flashy, unnecessary expenditures, you can complete even a grand film like *Paheli* within a reasonable budget; our film proved that. Because we had managed to keep the budget within the projected limit, the producer was able to earn a decent profit by selling different rights even before it was released.

For the premier of the film, there was a lavish function. My friends greatly appreciated the film. Shyam Benegal and Javed Akhtar generously praised the film as a modern classic that showcased Indian culture in a captivating and alluring way, and declared it worthy of realising India's long-held aspiration for an Academy Award. The film was nominated as India's official entry for the Oscars. However, by this time, Shah Rukh had moved on from the film and made no special efforts to promote it, nor were we very keen to promote it on our own.

Like *Paheli*, I adapted two more films from renowned literary works: *Bangarwadi* (1995) from a novel and *Kairee* (2000) from a short story. I also made two more attempts which never saw the light of day.

The first one was a proposal from the gifted musician Hridaynath Mangeshkar who wanted me to do a film on *Darshan*, a story by the writer Charuta Sagar. I liked the story. We agreed that the brilliant writer Vyankatesh Madgulkar would write the script. I personally financed a trip to Saundatti with Madgulkar and Charuta Sagar. We explored the area extensively, observing a diverse range of spiritual practices and ceremonies dedicated to the worship of Goddess Yellamma. When I shared my scheduling preferences with Madgulkar, he advised me, 'First talk to Mangeshkar about the financial transactions; then we'll see.' I approached Mangeshkar with the basic layout of the film as well as the budget. 'We shall announce the film on the occasion of Lata didi's birthday' was his assurance. I was invited to an intimate function at their residence at Prabhukunj. But neither at the function nor subsequently was there any announcement of the film. When I brought this up with Madgulkar, he said, chuckling, 'That's the reason why I had asked you to talk to them first.' Even later, Mangeshkar never mentioned *Darshan* in our interactions. Neither did I bring it up.

After many years, Rajeev Patil, who was my assistant during the filming of *Anaahat*, produced a marvellous film called *Jogwa* based on the story *Darshan* by Charutha Sagar and two other novels by the eminent writer Rajan Gavas named *Chaundak* and *Bhandaryog*. Rajeev presented the film in the form of a captivating love story, coupled with wonderful music, which gained enormous popularity. My vision and outline of the film had been very different, of course. In my opinion, the tradition of *jogte* or *devadasis* is not a religious one; it is a social construct. It is essentially a form of social ostracism sanctioned as a ritual, stripping individuals of their community and dignity. Why else would children from upper-class families not be offered as *jogte* or *devadasis* to the gods. I wished to present such questions in an artistic manner in the film that I was planning. It is possible that Mangeshkar already knew that I was on the 'wrong path', deviating from making a 'successful film'!

The second unfinished project was based on a story by the accomplished writer Gauri Deshpande. The story was titled '*Dena*' (The Debt). Gauri had begun writing the script for the film herself, and during our conversations, my own vision of the story began to take shape. The story was about a Sikh family settled in Nanded. The son goes abroad against the wishes of the father and drifts apart from the family; after his death, his foreigner wife comes to India to meet the father-in-law with their child. It was a moving portrayal of how familial bonds got unexpectedly forged during a pivotal ten-day period, highlighting the emotional journeys and transformations of the characters. Sandhya elaborated on the script written by Gauri. We situated one-fourth of the scenes in a foreign country. Sandhya and her scientist friend based in the US, Girish Deshpande, contacted associates of Nicole Kidman, offering her the lead role. Nicole and her associates saw *Anaahat* and liked the film. We were advised to bring a Hollywood studio on board. For an internationally renowned actress like Nicole, we had only one name in mind for the role of her father-in-law—that of the actor par excellence Amitabh Bachchan. But we started to develop cold feet as we thought the project to be too unwieldy and unviable. If only we had been a bit more patient and persistent, the film might have become a reality. But after much deliberation, we finally wound up the project that was titled *Udhaar* (The Debt). Before her death, Gauri expressed regret, saying, 'I would have loved to see the film made by you, my friend. You should not have given up.' That regret haunts me to this day.

In1994, a Marathi producer approached us with a proposal to make a film based on Madgulkar's novel *Bangarwadi*. When we met Madgulkar, he gave me his own script, which he had written for the great actor-director V. Shantaram. But I did not like it as it was conceived within the visual framework of mainstream cinema and had songs. After a lengthy discussion, I requested him to take the lead in writing it himself, incorporating my suggestions and ideas. He agreed. But there was a caveat: I would have to sit with him while he wrote! After he finished writing a scene, he would read it out to me and proceed only if I approved. The screenplay was ready within twenty days or so. The film followed the story of a young man who was appointed as a school teacher in a small village, and depicted how he formed emotional connections in an unfamiliar environment. The story was simple yet dramatic. My discussions with Madgulkar proved to be immensely helpful as I started conceiving the film's visual language. We decided to reduce the verbal load, and develop the story through events. The new teacher arriving in the village, red dust rising from his worn-out slippers, the surrounding green trees and shrubs, the grey and soiled red hues emerging from the famine, and the rustic landscape—all began to take shape in my mind. We visited Madgul and other surrounding villages with Dhangar—a shepherd community—settlements, and decided on the locations for the shooting. The cast comprised thespian Chandrakant Mandare who was in his nineties, a number of young theatre actors and local residents from the locations.

To capture the contrasts in the schoolteacher's life in the village through the changing seasons, we planned to split the shooting into two distinct phases, each taking place in a different season. We encountered a lot of difficulties while shooting in the parched weather of May. The temperature would soar to forty-five degrees on most days, and shooting would slow down considerably under the scorching sun. A few artistes had to be hospitalised due to heat strokes, while I, myself, started suffering acutely from varicose veins. On top of all this, the producer withdrew financial assistance all of a sudden, without citing a reason.

I completed the shooting using my own funds and then approached the NFDC. After many meetings, the NFDC came on board for the film's distribution. Despite the previous producer's inflated expense claims, which allowed him to earn profits in spite of his irresponsible conduct, the NFDC reimbursed all the costs.

The film had no songs. Vanraj Bhatia had composed the background score combining Marathi folk music with Western harmony; this proved to be a special feature of the film. *Bangarwadi* won the National Award for the best feature film in Marathi in 1996, the Filmfare Award for best feature film and direction in 1997, along with the Maharashtra State Awards in five different categories. It shone brightly at seven international film festivals.

Despite all the challenges, *Bangarwadi* was made very quickly. But the film *Kairee*, based on G.A. Kulkarni's short story, took fourteen long years. Initially, we prepared the script in response to a promise made by a Pune-based Marathi realtor to finance the film. Perhaps the flamboyant realtor expected me to create the usual commercial film. Naturally, he withdrew when he heard that the film would have no songs. After that, the screenplay remained tucked away inside a drawer. After a few years, in 1985-86, I approached the NFDC. The script committee there strongly recommended the project. They also accepted the meagre budget I proposed. Only the sign-off from the chief officer was left. But at the last minute, my project was set aside and Vijaya Mehta's *Pestonjee* was cleared for financial assistance. B.K. Karanjia was the chairman of the NFDC at the time, and *Pestonjee* was based on a story written by him. Such matters of conflict of interest and unethical politics swaying financial decisions are routinely ignored. I was disheartened, but had no desire to fight for my film. Once again, I closed the drawer specially reserved for the script of *Kairee*. Within a year and a half, G.A. Kulkarni passed away. Had I challenged the NFDC's decision back then, I could have completed *Kairee* in G.A.'s lifetime. My dream to watch the film with him remained unfulfilled.

In 1996, the Ministry for Women and Child Welfare in Delhi sent an invitation to a few select directors. The ministry wanted us to make a full-length film on the theme of mother and child. I took *Kairee* to them, and the ministry liked my proposal. While revisiting the script, I thought that instead of the boy in the original story, the lead could be a girl visiting her maternal aunt's house. This shift enabled me to portray the yearning of Taani maawshi (Aunt Taani), a woman oppressed by a patriarchal society, to rescue this young girl from her distressing circumstances. In her final moments, Taani maawshi tells her niece, 'Don't confine yourself. If you don't get what you want in life, be prepared to grab it.' A story of a marginalised woman's quiet strength awakening empowerment in a young girl felt most compelling. Also, a final scene was added, where the now grown-up girl returns to her village, her roots, reflecting on the bittersweet memories of her childhood.

Fourteen years before *Kairee's* eventual release in 2000, we had selected a large house in a village called Kokisare in the Tal-Konkan area for shooting. When we restarted the film, that house was still available. We put together a cast of nuanced actors like Mohan Gokhale, Shilpa Navalkar, Atul Kulkarni, Sonali Kulkarni, Upendra Limaye and Leena Bhagwat, and in the course of the auditions, we discovered a sweet young girl called Yogita Deshmukh.

During the shooting, I made a conscious change in my directorial style. Until then, I was used to working in a disciplined manner according to a pre-planned outline with well thought-out storyboards. To capitalise on the dynamic interplay of sunlight and its shifting hues through the day, I adopted a more flexible approach to cinematography, allowing the natural environment to influence the visual narrative. I used the delicate rays of sunlight filtering through the leaves and twigs of the sprawling banyan tree in the location to shoot an almost dream-like scene between Taani maawshi and the girl. For another segment of the same scene featuring the two characters, I chose a picturesque grassy setting in Kolhapur Film City. We captured this portion when the waist-high grass had matured to a golden yellow, and was bathed in the soft, warm glow of the fading evening sun. The girl and her aunt were shown sitting on the steps of a huge old well, with light waves shimmering on the water's surface and their moving reflections dancing in the ripples. The cumulative effect of these visuals elevated the narrative beyond a purely realistic representation, creating a distinct mental realm that was both immersive and thought-provoking for the audience.

Kairee was made in Hindi. While distributing it all over India, Shyam Shroff of Shringar Films started a new trend by showing the film with English subtitles. (We followed the same trend for all my films thereafter.) The appreciation we received from audiences within the country and outside was overwhelming. The Japanese are known for their reserve and lack of emotional display, but *Kairee*'s impact was evident when it was screened at the Fukuoka Film Festival to a packed theatre. As the viewers exited the gallery, I was deeply moved to see that many of them were visibly emotional, their eyes brimming with tears. After the screening, looking up at the skies, I paid a heartfelt tribute to Mohan (Gokhale), who had left us too soon—soon after completing the dubbing for his dialogues.

I received the national Rajat Kamal (Silver Lotus) award in 2000 for *Kairee*. In my mind, I immediately dedicated it to G.A. Kulkarni for his powerful story, and to my daughter Shalmalee, who instilled in me the resilience to bounce back from defeat. Her tireless motivation taught me to let go of self-pity after a setback, to leave failure behind, and to summon the courage to rise again with renewed strength and determination. I recall a moment from her childhood when she had lost an important match and cried inconsolably, swearing

{15}

never to hold a badminton racquet in her hands again. For two days, she showed no interest in the game. But, on the third morning, she asked, 'Aren't you taking me to the court?' The strength of character and resolve she showed that day has stayed with me.

Returning to the theme of my experiments with adaptations, I must mention the film *Thodasa Roomani Ho Jaayen* (1990), which was originally a Hollywood film, and the plays *Rashomon* (1980) and *Kusur* (2019), which I adapted from films.

The then director of Doordarshan, Bhaskar Ghosh, appealed to a few directors to send proposals for some good film projects. It must have been around 1990. I had already experimented with the musical form in the tele-serial *Kachchi Dhoop*. I now wished to do a similar experiment in the film medium, and that's what I did with *Thodasa Roomani Ho Jaayen*. Chitra took up the difficult job of transforming the famous Hollywood film *The Rainmaker* into prose and verse. She wrote the screenplay with the dialogues in English. Kamlesh Pande's translation of her dialogues into Hindi was simply magical. Also, with his creative talent, he blurred the lines between dialogue and lyric, converting prose into songs and vice versa. This new narrative form was unfamiliar to the audiences. So, we advertised the film in my voice on the radio in an entirely unconventional way.

> I am here to tell you a few things about the film. What should normally happen is that when you switch on your cassette recorder, the music should play. But this film is a little different—it is a musical. Now you may ask what makes it different? In our country, isn't every film a musical? In our film, the characters don't only sing songs when they fall in love—they burst into song even when they're upset, angry, or just chatting with friends. It's here that our film diverges from the rest. We are sure you will like our new venture.

After this statement, lines from the title song were played.

No trace of clouds in the village of the sky
The jungle burns in its own shadow
This is the season, dear,
let us, You and I,
Sing songs of the rain
Let us be a little romantic

(Original Hindi poem)

बादलों का नाम ना हो अंबर के गाँव में
जलते हों जंगल ख़ुद अपनी छाँव में
यही तो है मौसम, आओ तुम और हम
बारिश के नगमे गुनगुनायें
थोड़ा सा रुमानी हो जायें।
मुश्किल है जीना उम्मीद के बिना
थोड़े से सपने सजायें,
थोड़ा सा रुमानी हो जायें।

The memory I'm going to narrate here is from the time when Nana Patekar had just become popular as 'Anna' in the film *Parinda*. Early one morning, an angry young Nana arrived at Chirebandi.

'I heard you are making a new film. Why didn't you take me?'

'Because your inherent nature is different from that of the character. This role is of a charismatic wanderer who brings hope to drought-stricken villages, showing dreams of rains to people till the rains actually arrive.'

'Why can't I play that role?'

'He is a simple, affectionate man, my dear. He doesn't get angry; no fights, no abuses.'

'Even so, I'll certainly be able to do it. I'll stand naked before you, and surrender completely. Let's try for eight days.'

From the next day onwards, Nana arrived every morning for a rehearsal. In four days' time, I saw a loving and caring man emerge from the Nana I knew, who was rough around the edges, somewhat rowdy too. This wasn't the Nana Patekar the public was familiar with. The Nana I saw in the course of our rehearsals was a genuine person. I agreed to cast him in the role of 'Baarishkar', saying, 'Doordarshan has offered me five lakhs for the production. I'll pay you five thousand.' During the entire period of shooting, Nana did not once argue with me, let alone fight with anyone else. I should have floated this news in the media. There was news that he had beaten up his director, Vidhu Vinod Chopra, on the sets of *Parinda*. Nana still cherishes memories of playing Baarishkar and often recites the long poem '*Haan mere dost wahi baarish*' with all his heart.

The cast of *Thodasa Roomani Ho Jaayen* was special. I was very pleased that the brilliant actor Vikram Gokhale was roped in.

In 1976, the veteran theatre director Damu Kenkre, on behalf of the theatre production group, Goa Hindu Association, invited me to play the central character in the play *Barrister* and sent me the script. I would have certainly liked to play that role under Damu's directorship. But I wasn't willing to perform the same role for the next many years and over hundreds of shows. Also, given my other engagements, it wasn't feasible for me to find time for rehearsals. Within a year, Vijaya Mehta staged the play with Vikram Gokhale in the lead role. After the show, I met Vikram and conveyed my compliments on his brilliant performance and very restrained style. He simply embraced me and said, 'Please do recommend my name for some roles in Hindi films.' I immediately invited him to A.V. Mohan's sets and introduced him as a very fine actor.

Vikram said to A.V., 'Give me any role, I won't mind. I'm ready to work for free as well.'

'Don't compromise your worth by accepting low-paying roles in the mainstream. Never accept marginal roles there; do keep in mind that not only are you a wonderful actor, but you are a handsome hero too,' I scolded him in private.

A few months before Vikram's sad demise, I visited his studio for some dubbing work. We revisited some old memories. I did not argue with him about his politics as he was unwell, but I countered each of his saffron-clad messages during our WhatsApp chats.

For *Thodasa Roomani Ho Jaayen*, we selected Pachmarhi in Madhya Pradesh as our location. It was suitable for the script—with its bungalows from the British period, roads going up and down, and above all, trees without a single leaf. The ultimate irony was that we were filming scenes of a sweltering summer and drought on chilly winter nights in December; we had to use a water spray on the actors' skin and clothes before each take to create the illusion of sweat. We had overlooked another important difficulty with this location; the artificial rain machine could not be carried up to Pachmarhi because of its altitude. But the script demanded heavy rains at the end of the film! Finally, the military unit present there brought their fire-fighting equipment and allowed us to capture the rains. We shot continuously for twenty-five days and finished the film. The entire crew was happy with how the production had worked out for this very sensitive film.

Thodasa Roomani Ho Jaayen holds a special place in my heart, and I often receive validation that today's younger generation appreciates the film as well. In hindsight, I have two lingering thoughts: firstly, that our innovative musical approach didn't receive the widespread recognition it deserved, largely due to the film's limited reach beyond urban audiences; secondly, I wonder if Vanraj Bhatia would have been a better choice as a music director? Perhaps he would have unlocked a richer, more diverse sonic landscape. I could have provided an opportunity to Vanraj Bhatia, until then only used as a background score director, to showcase his full range and versatility as a composer.

Our play *Kusur* granted us a great opportunity to experiment with sound. Upon reaching my seventy-fifth year, many people approached me for public interviews or paid tribute to my life's work by hosting live orchestral performances featuring my film songs. At no point in my career was I interested in such uninspiring interactions. Considering the affection showered on me by people, Sandhya was saddened that I didn't reciprocate their feelings with alacrity. 'Why don't you repay the love of all these people by acting again on the stage? In any case, the new generation hasn't seen you on stage. Your seventy-fifth birthday can be celebrated in a different way and publicly with your fans. They will get a feast and it will be a challenge for you too,' she urged me. I liked her idea, so we searched widely for good plays in different languages but failed to find something that felt right for us.

One day, Samiha got me to watch a Danish movie called *Den Skyldige*. A brave police officer who takes to the streets and confronts criminals, gets a temporary emergency service-room duty as a demotion. He sits in a chair for days on end, answering calls and recording crimes. Then, a pivotal day arrives when the officer receives a call from a woman in distress. From that moment on, he becomes more and more entangled in the case. What begins as a kidnapping case escalates into domestic violence, then murder, and eventually transforms into an even darker crime. With every call, he interprets the situation through the lens of his own biases, gradually building a map of prejudices that prompts the audience to reflect on their own deeply ingrained notions and social beliefs. When Sandhya said, 'This social thriller can be adapted into a play of an entirely different style,' I was immediately excited. But with her being a lawyer, we couldn't even start working on the play until she received formal permission in writing from the original writers of the film.

Finally, after six months, we got the consent, and within two weeks, her play with Hindi dialogues was ready. Upon understanding the demands of the part, I felt a surge of nervousness. When I looked in the mirror, I was struck by my ageing face; my voice was strained, and I sensed a significant drop in my energy levels. Taking the stage was a vital opportunity for me to gauge my physical endurance and emotional range while portraying the complex role of Dandavate, a retired police officer. Being on the stage for eighty straight minutes without any exit was a daunting proposition.

We began the rehearsals with great vigour, absorbing the energy of the script and working to shake off any rust that may have accumulated on my skills over time. But even before we did that, Mandar Kamalapurkar, a talented sound director, created tracks for all the key sounds—the intermittent phone calls, the sound of rain, an ambulance's siren, the noise of traffic and mobile ringtones. Sandhya and I were personally present when the characters were recording their dialogues. The play truly came alive in the voices of Preeta Mathur, Ashish Mehta and Neel Chapekar, who played the three main characters who aren't seen on stage and are only heard. After we performed the play at the National School of Drama in Delhi, the students inquired whether the phone calls my character Dandavate received were actual live calls made by different actors positioned offstage. This was a testament to the convincing quality and seamless integration of the pre-recorded tracks.

Sandhya's set design was unique too. The walls of the room were represented by strings of LED lights and long curtains with Google Map prints. There were six phones with six red lights on a large table with a computer, and a few chairs. A red light would turn on whenever a phone rang, indicating which phone had received the call, and I had to run from one end of the table to the other to answer each call. Throughout the play, I couldn't sit for more than five minutes. Beyond this physical movement, there was another challenge—my responses had to be perfectly timed since the callers' dialogue tracks were pre-recorded.

On the evening of 24 November 2019, I stood in the wings of NCPA stage in Mumbai for the first performance of *Kusur*. I shut my eyes tight to relieve the restlessness I felt between the three bells, and took a deep breath. I heard the announcement of the credits. When my name was announced, I heard loud applause, and my heart skipped a beat. When the moment of entry came, my trepidation reached its peak.

{17}

What if I fell short of everyone's expectations? After the third bell, the persona of Amol Palekar faded away, and only the character, ACP Dandavate, existed on stage. Way back, while performing in the play *Hayavadan*, an inexperienced Amol Palekar would develop a back pain before each show due to nervousness—Puri saab would give me a gentle back massage and say, 'All the best, son!' The journey from those formative years to the moment of performing ACP Dandavate was enriched with a deep sense of fulfilment and pleasure. And this sense of fulfilment was rekindled when I was met with thunderous applause from the audience of *Kusur* as the curtain fell. At the end of *Kusur*, Dandavate crosses the proscenium frame and leaves the stage. In the background, a moving *azaan* can be heard. He merges into his own ascending shadow.

That day, in NCPA, standing to support me in the darkness of the wing was Samiha. She held my hand and hugged me tight, and said, 'Epic, Sape!' With that, she turned me back to the stage before my eyes could well up. Co-actors Naresh Suri, Ashwini Paranjape and all the technicians were standing on the stage. At that moment, I met the adoring gaze of my beloved, brimming with pride and affection. She had tirelessly poured her heart and soul into our shared dreams for four unforgettable months, perfecting every aspect with precision and care.

Although I had initially announced only twenty-five shows, we ended up performing *Kusur* twenty-eight times across India before the COVID-19 pandemic halted our run. Every single show was sold out. Even in Ahmedabad, a city grappling with widespread anti-Muslim sentiment, the play received an extraordinary response. Sandhya and I were happy that we could spread the message of religious harmony through our art. With the bountiful profits we earned from *Kusur*, we want to produce one more play; and if not, we will donate the money to a social cause.

Through *Kusur*, we sought to hold up a mirror to some deeply entrenched prejudices in society, much like we did with the screenplays of *Daayra* and *Thaang*. But it was Shalmalee who truly gave me the opportunity to turn the mirror on myself and examine my own prejudices when she first opened up to me about her sexual orientation. My instant reaction had been one of unconditional support. But later, as a father, I was consumed by a deep-seated fear. What unknown doors had my daughter opened, and how would society respond to her homosexuality? I worried about her privacy, safety and well-being. How could I shield her from harm?

Our society's response to this issue is marred by ignorance, rejection, misguided biases and, worst of all, intolerance. Consequently, we tend to shy away from introspective discussions about our sexuality from an early age. Society tends to sanctify the biological sex assigned at birth and the normative gender roles associated with it, but it is crucial to acknowledge that human sexuality can unfold in diverse ways, and these variations are equally authentic, natural and worthy of acceptance. Over time, I came to understand the horrific abuse and humiliating treatment inflicted upon eunuchs, hijras, so-called *chhakkaas* and the transgender community at large. The traditions and rituals surrounding the third gender have such deep roots that many from the community remain impervious to psychological insights, scientific understanding and even compassion, and thus, resist change.

Similarly, do we ever truly reflect on how the man–woman relationship is stifled within the narrow and socially accepted boundaries of the matrimonial institution? Do we recognise sexual pleasure as a profound and multifaceted human experience, beyond mere necessity, habit or instinct? Do we ever attempt to revitalise and strengthen the fabric of male–female relationships by repairing the frayed and worn-out threads that bind them together? I tried to address such issues throughout my directorial journey.

In *Daayra* (1996), I explored the emotional world of two characters —a transvestite struggling to tap into the core of his femininity and a young woman disguising herself as a man to escape the clutches of male aggression. In *Anaahat* (2003), I tried to deal with intriguing aspects of female sexuality. In *Thaang* (2006), I attempted to decipher homosexuality in the context of a marital partnership. In many ways, the overarching theme of this trilogy was groundbreaking and ahead of its time.

Daayra came to me through Pravesh Sippy. Pravesh, the son of N.N. Sippy, the extremely successful producer of films like *Chor Machaye Shor* and *Sargam*, aspired to create work that diverged from his father's preferred genre of commercial films. He approached me with a screenplay written by London-based writer, Timeri N. Murari. While the story's core idea was commendable and surely appealing to international audiences, the script lacked depth and finesse. The male lead who yearns to express himself by wearing female clothing encounters a young person who appears to be a man but is actually a woman. Murari had not grounded the story and the scenes in any soil. He concurred with my suggestion that the screenplay required a complete overhaul. I felt compelled to educate the audience about what it meant to be a transvestite and to ensure that the male character was portrayed without any disabilities or handicaps. I proposed to root the story in the community of the Gotipua folk dancers of Odisha and adapted the narrative to make it uniquely Indian. As I explored the dual narrative of a man seeking self-expression through feminine attire and a woman compelled to adopt a male identity, I introduced a societal character that embodied the external forces of bias, hatred and intolerance towards those who defied conventional norms. Given the brutal treatment they would typically face from society, we felt it necessary to modify the original happy ending written by Tim to a tragic one, underscoring the devastating consequences of societal intolerance. As a result of these changes, the story transcended its original boundaries and acquired a universal humanitarian resonance, making it relatable to a broader audience.

While negotiating the terms of the agreement, Murari insisted that his name remain as the screenwriter, even for a completely revised screenplay. Chitra, my colleague Shashank Shankar and I agreed, and we were credited as additional screenwriters. In our enthusiasm to embark on a new project, we naively overlooked the importance of securing proper recognition for our contributions. To add to this, we later heard that Murari produced a play based on this theme with Rahul Bose in London. Of course, I don't know if he used our plot for the same.

We started looking for Indian actors for the two lead roles. We initially chose Milind Soman with his handsome, svelte physique, and the accomplished model Madhu Sapre. They were the talk of the town at the time. I worked hard on their dialogue delivery, their diction and expressions for over two hours every day. I invited the wonderful danseuse Jhelum Paranjape, a disciple of the great dancer Kelucharan Mohapatra, to come and teach dance-based body language to them. Barely two weeks into training, Milind stopped coming. His 'nay' came through Madhu. He might have acknowledged that he could not portray the character. Madhu, who had been passionate about playing the role, shared her disappointment with me after a few years. She had established a new life in Paris, but couldn't shake off the regret of missing a crucial chance. This episode revealed to me another facet of the complex, intriguing dynamic between a man and a woman.

We then invited Nirmal Pandey, who had recently made his mark in a small role in Shekhar Kapur's *Bandit Queen*, to meet us. He was a National School of Drama graduate with sound training in theatre. And for the role of the woman who would disguise herself as a man, we called on the then upcoming actress Sonali Kulkarni. Rehearsals started afresh. Through the simple yet powerful act of sitting, Jhelum vividly illustrated to both of them the stark contrast between masculine assertiveness and feminine reserve, as embodied in their distinct body languages. From that point on, Nirmal and Sonali's physical expressions began to align with our visualisation of their characters.

The producers entrusted the composition of songs and background music to the Anand-Milind duo. Two beautiful songs were composed and sung in the voices of Yesudas and Asha Bhosle. An old-fashioned lullaby too was to be recorded in Asha-bai's voice. Upon hearing the song's melody, Asha-bai insisted that the instrumental accompaniment be recorded live, in a traditional manner, with the entire orchestra playing together in the same room. We accepted the idea, and the next day the recording resumed. The producers agreed to my suggestion of creating two distinct edited versions of the film, catering to different audiences—a shorter ninety-minute version was prepared for international consumption, from which a song shot with Rishi Kapoor and Meenakshi Seshadri was edited out.

Our shoot began by harnessing the breathtaking natural beauty of Odisha's coastline and the rich cultural tapestry of its villages, providing a visually stunning and culturally immersive setting for our story. I envisioned the film's final shot on the very first day: the camera crane pans out, and as it rises higher, it captures the hero lying down with his head on the heroine's lap on the pristine white sand, until their existence blends seamlessly into the vast expanse of the ocean.

In the beginning, I noticed that Nirmal would consume an entire bottle of rum each evening after the shoot. I chose not to object, as his drinking was not affecting his performance the next day. However, his body would emit a strong odour of alcohol throughout the day. Three days before shooting a crucial romantic scene with Sonali, I warned Nirmal not to drink until after the scene had been shot, and he agreed. Sonali had never voiced any complaints about this issue. I have always believed that it is the director's responsibility to ensure the comfort of the actors and technicians in the unit.

The entire shooting of the film was completed in twenty-six days. During the final stages of the shoot, the four producers began fighting over money. Since one of the producers, Pravesh Sippy, was present with us every day on set, their quarrel did not reach my doorstep. But I had sensed that these people would not allow the film to be properly distributed. Their fight continued in the court of law. Tragically, despite receiving widespread international recognition, this film with a unique theme never saw a release in India. After several years, we heard that the songs of the film were available for listening on different platforms.

As soon as the film was completed, invitations came from three international festivals—Toronto, London and Valenciennes in France. Following packed shows at all three venues, engaging Q&A sessions were conducted, revealing an outpouring of appreciation and admiration for the film from enthralled audiences. Noted film critic Richard Corliss of *Time* magazine was impressed by the film's artistic presentation. The film was included in *Time* magazine's list of top ten films of 1996. When Sonali and I arrived for the Valenciennes festival, French journalists surrounded us and the organisers had to arrange a police force to escort us to the hall.

The film received the Grand Prix Award for the Best Film. The French announcer declared Sonali as the winner of the 'Best Male Actor Award', and Nirmal the winner of the 'Best Female Actor Award'. The interpreter explained that Nirmal and Sonali's outstanding performances had transcended traditional gender roles, prompting the judges to blur the conventional actor-actress distinctions and to swap the categories as a tribute to their remarkable talent. We heard the news that the producers used this opportunity to release *Daayra* in Leicester Square, London, and it ran very well. At the

national level, I received the Special Jury Award at the 44th National Film Awards. I did not leverage all this international fame for my own personal publicity, expecting the media to take cognisance of such achievements. But that wish proved to be naive. The film wasn't selected for screening at IFFI's Indian Panorama section solely because it had songs. I protested this decision, and my protest was widely publicised. Recently, a viewer referred to the film as a 'road film', and I entirely agreed. It was indeed the story of two outcast souls roaming through the wilderness.

Thaang was the third film in our trilogy about sexuality. The film had a powerful screenplay that was set in Mumbai. The story unravels the intricate threads of a marriage between an accomplished lawyer and a talented hotel chef, plunging into the depths of the emotional crisis that ensues when she confronts his concealed homosexuality. All the supporting characters—her mother, his father, their colleagues and friends—collectively decipher the subject from various angles.

During Sandhya's time in the US, a pivotal movement was gaining momentum, focusing on HIV/AIDS awareness, gay rights and advocacy for LGBTQ+ relationships. The law firm where she worked was at the forefront of this movement. On her return to India, she used her experiences to prosecute cases related to job insecurity, inequality and the physical abuse of homosexuals. In India, same-sex relationships often remain hidden, leading to forced marriages between gay men and women, perpetuating the harmful myth that marriage can alter one's sexual orientation, resulting in devastating emotional consequences. Sandhya's urge to present a sensitive perspective on this subject found expression through the screenplay of *Thaang*. The progressive and humanistic ideas expressed through the characters' dialogue in *Thaang* reveal how far ahead of its time this 2006 film was.

Immediately after *Paheli*, we started shooting *Thaang* in various locations in Mumbai and beyond, such as at a small flat near the railway tracks, a hospital, a court, a church and a picturesque beach in the Konkan region. To create a claustrophobic effect, we incorporated the sound of the sea, passing ships, local trains, a radio and the traffic as background music. The scene in which Sai visits her husband in the hospital after years of separation has no dialogue. Using the soft, mournful strains of Raga Poorvi, played on a recorder, we tried to create a stirring, immersive experience for the audience.

Since the husband hid his same-sex relationship from his wife, an argument ensues, and we chose to shoot this scene at the dining table. To add depth, Sandhya placed a large photo of Buddha's severed head on the wall behind the table, symbolising the violence and the painful separation. In 1767, the Burmese army had conducted a massacre in Ayutthaya, Thailand, and not even the giant statues of Buddha were spared from destruction. If Buddha, an abiding symbol of peace, becomes a victim of such violence, how can human beings ever hope to escape it? Although many might not have noticed this symbolism, it resonated with the young couple whose house we used for filming. They asked Sandhya if they could keep the photograph, hoping it might bring a sense of peace to their home.

A scene of physical intimacy between the two men was shown right at the beginning of the film, with the idea of giving a visual but suggestive experience to most people who have no idea about homosexual relationships. Actors Shishir Sharma and Rishi Deshpande brought the scene to life. After the screening of the film for special invitees, two senior cine-critics approached us. After whole-heartedly appreciating the film, they said, 'Why did you opt for restraint in depicting the love scene, when you were the one director who could have masterfully captured the intensity of passion in a beautiful way?' This was a peculiar criticism indeed. Even after hearing how much we had to fight with the Censor Board to retain the scene, the two critics were not willing to retreat. And now, when we see explicit erotic scenes in serials and movies on OTT platforms, we feel that we should give zero marks to our suggestive artistic shot.

With the help of accomplished actors such as Mrinal Kulkarni, Amrita Subhash, Sachin Khedekar and Vijaya Mehta, we convinced the great playwright G.P. Deshpande to perform the role of the male protagonist's father in *Thaang*. However, the production department team faced a logistical challenge due to his absent-mindedness resulting in multiple retakes, requiring them to go to great lengths to procure the necessary film stock from our office. We had given him instructions like: when 'action' is called out, take off your glasses and put the bowl on the plate in front of you; then drink water and heave a sigh; then look at the co-actor; then eat and then wear your glasses again. But he would forget half the instructions, and we would have to shoot all over again. But once the film was released, his role was widely admired. He gladly accepted the admiration because by that time he had forgotten how much he had fumbled while acting.

The soundtrack for *Thaang* was created by Anand Modak. I'm especially fond of the song '*Paandharyaa shubhra hattinchaa, raanaatoon kalap nighaalad*', written by the poet Grace and sung by Ravindra Sathe.

When we read out the screenplay to the journalist couple Radhika and Prannoy Roy, they thought that this subject should be presented to an international audience as well. They offered to finance the English version, *Quest*. Thus, two separate films were produced simultaneously in two different languages. Since the actors in both versions were the same, each shot was done first in Marathi, and immediately thereafter in English. Prabhat Company had done two such films before in the same way—*Manoos* in Marathi and *Aadmi* in Hindi and *Kunku* in Marathi and *Duniya Na Mane* in Hindi. I had also made *Dhyaasparva* and *Kal ka Aadmi* (2006-07) in a similar manner.

Upon its release, *Thaang* received a warm embrace from LGBT groups, who saw it as a powerful and rational validation of their experiences and struggles, presented through an artistic and sympathetic lens. Numerous young individuals, searching for answers, reached out to Sandhya for guidance and support. The film's influence extended far beyond its initial release, as many parents confessed that the movie's sensitive and realistic depiction of homosexuality led to a profound shift in their attitudes. It allowed them to see homosexuality as a natural and valid expression of human identity.

Despite being selected for the Best Film Award in both Marathi and English languages at the National Awards, the board decided not to give two awards to the same film; thus, only *Quest* received the National Award. After watching the film at international festivals and experiencing overwhelming appreciation for it, it was abundantly clear that the questions raised in the film were relevant to people across borders. Sadly, it could not be released on television due to the 'A' certificate issued by the Censor Board; and therefore, a large public viewership for the film wasn't possible. I'm happy that I am presenting it to global audiences through this book.

I didn't approach the question of which film to make in which language with the intention of targeting a specific audience or maximising profits. Had that been the case, a film like *Anaahat* would have been made in Hindi. Although *Quest* was produced in English, this alone is not necessarily the reason it translated to a broader viewership. However, it did expand the film's potential to reach a non-Marathi speaking audience, tapping into a new demographic. I think each subject brings with it its own language and its own audience. *Kairee* is a film I had always intended to do in Marathi. However, when I finally landed an opportunity to actually make the film in Hindi after waiting for fourteen long years, I chose not to miss it. When I worked on *Paheli* with Shah Rukh and Amitabh, some critics scoffed, saying, 'He's sold out to mainstream cinema.' But I had chosen Shah Rukh and Amitabh for their exceptional acting talent, not their commercial draw. I remained true to my artistic vision, and while many labelled it a non-mainstream film, its fan base has steadily grown over the past fifteen years, thanks to the rise of OTT platforms. My approach has always been to create films that first resonate with me, and in doing so, gradually attract their own unique audience. Also, with the advent of dubbing technology, reaching a broader audience has become possible.

Sandhya wrote a screenplay on a wonderful subject and I loved it. We felt that the film should be made in English, and so the film *And Once Again* was made. We had once spent many days in a peaceful place in the western part of Sikkim, overlooking the Kanchenjunga. The only crowd that could be seen there was that of young girls, freshly initiated into monastic life, and elderly Buddhist monks. One could also see many Buddhist nuns, with shaved heads, dressed in maroon robes, sitting in meditation for hours in the monastery—although I found the place a little dark and gloomy, if I'm to be honest.

Sandhya used to linger in the monastery for hours, talking to everyone. She found herself grappling with existential questions: what if the monks' pursuits proved futile? What if their sacrifices didn't yield the desired outcome? The sight of a young nun, barely eight years old, with her life stretching out before her like an endless canvas, filled Sandhya with a sense of hopelessness. Even after returning from there, she could not abandon these thoughts. The screenplay of *And Once Again* unfolded out of this restlessness.

In the beautiful landscapes of Sikkim, we secured official permission to shoot in prohibited areas. We even managed to shoot inside a Buddhist monastery, respectfully adhering to sacred protocols at all times. We did encounter some unexpected hurdles during this time though. As there was only one bank in the capital city of Gangtok, we were unable to withdraw money by cheque for our daily needs. Naturally, it wasn't possible to carry the lakhs of rupees in cash that would be required for twenty-six days. Also, we were not paying people in our unit in cash to ensure that our transactions remained clean and transparent. Finally, we approached the chief minister to arrange a mobile bank for us, and now the facility is permanently available there for all residents.

The location's unusual daylight pattern required us to reschedule our shoot. With dawn arriving at 5 a.m. in February, we'd embark on a two-hour journey to the site at 2 a.m. to capitalise on the early morning light. Following a swift rehearsal, the camera would start rolling at 5 a.m. As darkness fell by 2 p.m., we would conclude the day's shoot and return to the hotel for some sound sleep.

Initially, we planned to capture sync sound on location, recording the actors' dialogues in the serene environment. However, the omnipresent chirping of night insects, even during the day, posed a challenge, as it would have been jarring to hear their trilling in daytime scenes. To maintain authenticity and avoid confusion, we dubbed all dialogues in the studio instead, ensuring a more controlled and immersive audio experience for the viewers.

All these difficulties were overcome due to the cooperation of our crew and actors. Wonderful actors like Antara Mali, Rajat Kapoor and Rituparna Sengupta delivered amazing performances. The Buddhist community at the monastery praised Antara Mali's nuanced portrayal of a nun, finding it authentic. Presenting *And Once Again* through this book is a deeply fulfilling experience.

Dhyaasparva was yet another attempt to deal with the issue of women's sexuality. I feel extremely proud to have made a film on Raghunath Dhondo Karve, a solitary crusader who openly advocated and pursued the issue of birth control throughout his life. Since I never wished to join in the trend of making biopics on political figures, I consciously selected an unsung non-political hero who had been overlooked even within Maharashtra's reformist circles, despite his immense contribution. He was ostracised in 1921 for making the revolutionary statement, 'It is the woman who should have the right to decide whether she wants a child, and to decide when to have it, and with whom to have it', in a public meeting. Spreading sex education through his self-funded magazine called *Samaaj Swaasthya* (Health of the Society) from 1927 to 1953 was a groundbreaking initiative. There were many dramatic events in the life of this man who risked his life to build a healthy and well-informed society.

Karve's friend, the doyen of the Kirana tradition of classical singing, Ustad Abdul Karim Khan, attended his wedding. As the latter sat down to eat along with Brahmins, there was a huge commotion. R.D.'s father, Maharshi Karve, apologised to all and settled the matter.

The father and son had a bitter argument over this. Ironically, that prejudice continued even after the completion of the film. Following the state award, Doordarshan invited me for an interview at their studio. They requested some footage from the film to play in the background, and it was this dining scene. But Doordarshan asked for another footage, pointing out that a particular scene showing a Muslim sharing space with Brahmins while eating was already in its possession but was deemed too provocative for broadcast. Doordarshan, a government-run organisation, was raising this objection even though the film had already received clearance from the Censor Board. I firmly refused to provide additional content. Eventually, my interview was aired without any part of the film in the background.

R.D. Karve's wife Malati-bai had died on the first day of Diwali. Karve had brought a handcart belonging to the Arya Samaj and took her body to the crematorium in it. He had a fight there. He strongly objected to the Brahmins present there insisting that the body could be cremated only after performing the last rites since Malati-bai had been a Brahmin. Further, two law suits were filed against him for alleged obscene writings. He had Barrister Bhimrao Ambedkar as his advocate. Their logical arguments demolished the very definition of obscenity.

Despite the dramatic nature of these events in his life, Chitra's screenplay approached the subject with remarkable restraint, maturity and objectivity, with a commitment to authenticity, and grounding it in thorough research. The wonderful actors Kishor Kadam and Seema Biswas virtually lived the roles of R.D. Karve and Malati-bai. Both of them and Chitra, in my opinion, deserved National Awards for their attempts to portray this couple's lonesome crusade.

I have been fortunate to receive unwavering support from numerous celebrated actors, who graciously accepted small but significant roles in my projects. Their exceptional performances have left a lasting impact. I will forever be grateful to Dr Lagoo, Hemu Adhikari, Sachin Khedekar, Atul Kulkarni and Sanjay Mone, among others for their contribution to *Dhyaasparva*.

The first part of the film showing R.D. Karve's childhood was made in black and white. It served as a prologue. Since we could not afford to shoot on the expensive black-and-white film, we first shot on colour film, then did colour-correction and printed it in greyscale. Oscar-winning costume designer Bhanu Athaiya, working on a shoestring budget, created an authentic wardrobe to evoke the era. Seema Biswas worked very hard to look natural in a nine-yard traditional saree. Kishor too changed his gait for the suit-and-boot dress code. Nitin Desai designed the sets to suit the times. The background music composed by Anjan Biswas lingers in the mind long after the film ends.

Dhyaasparva in Marathi for the Maharashtra government and *Kal ka Aadmi* in Hindi for the union government—two separate negatives for two films on the same screenplay were produced in 2001 in two languages. To maximise the films' reach, I adopted a grassroots approach, personally carrying the film print to villages throughout Maharashtra. I organised screenings for various groups, including bank employees, educators, students, factory workers and community members. Interactive Q&A sessions after the screenings enabled thought-provoking dialogues on critical issues like sexual health, birth control and gender equality. I did this religiously for a year. Both the films won national and state-level awards. The anti-hero in the film was so compelling that even the most puritanical minds couldn't ignore him.

Receiving accolades for *Dhyaasparva* was a triumph, but exploring that subject matter weighed heavily on my heart. I had similar mixed feelings after making two more films.

I made *Dhoosar* in 2011 on Alzheimer's disease. On the one hand, it was satisfying to make this kind of a film for the first time in an Indian language, but on the other, delving into the complexities of this illness, I realised that death seemed a gentler reality than the unrelenting suffering of living with an incurable condition that strips away one's independence.

Despite tackling different subjects, *Dhoosar* and *Samaantar* are linked by a shared ideological underpinning. Sandhya and I not only believe in euthanasia, but also in the concept of 'voluntary death'—a thread that runs through both these films.

Both *Samaantar* and *Dhoosar* were written by Sandhya. In *Samaantar*, a sixty-year-old industrialist, having lived a fulfilling life, applies to the Swiss government for assisted suicide. In *Dhoosar*, a mother with Alzheimer's hides her diagnosis, articulating her fears of death through poetry. While unravelling life's unresolved questions of mortality, Sandhya explored the complex layers of human relationships and emotional bonds through her screenplays for these two films.

Initially, Sandhya had Girish Karnad in mind for the lead role in *Samaantar*, but I loved the character so much that I grabbed the role for myself using my veto. I also declared to her that my portrayal of the character would outshine Girish's. Since Sharmila Tagore liked the subject a lot, she agreed to act as my co-star even though the film was in Marathi. The entire shoot was done in Pune and Kolkata.

Dhoosar was shot entirely in Goa. Shefali Shah was signed on for the lead role. Although she initially showed enthusiasm by attending the song-recording sessions, she ultimately left the project two weeks prior to our scheduled shooting. Recently, she has been acting in OTT serials, but decades ago, she might have faced challenges working in Marathi cinema, particularly playing an older woman's role.

{22}

But it happened for the best—Reema Lagoo's performance was unparalleled. Anand Modak and Avinash Chandrachud composed unforgettable music for both the films which went on to win the state awards in the best music and the best film categories.

I especially liked the sensitive songs written by Kishor Kadam aka Soumitra for both the films. They were sung beautifully by Shreya Ghoshal, Shankar Mahadevan and Sudesh Bhosle. The lyrics, the tunes, the instrumentation were all excellent. Anand Modak's eyes had filled with happiness when he heard Shankar say, 'Amol-ji, these are terrific compositions, almost like those of Pancham [R.D. Burman].'

Once, while browsing through an in-flight magazine, Sandhya and I came across a striking image of an unusual temple in Bardhaman district, about 102 kilometres from Kolkata. The temple had 108 alternating black and white *pindis*—Shaivaite lingams. It was there that we decided to shoot the song '*Nusate Nusate*'. After wrapping up the shoot successfully, our convoy set off for Kolkata. Along the way, we passed fields of tall white hay, neatly stacked against a dusky sky, just before sunset. Seizing the moment, Sandhya quickly directed Sharmila and me on our movements while the camera crew readied themselves. We managed to capture some stunning footage for the song's finale.

{23}

Being a Reliance production, *Samaantar* became available for in-flight viewing and on the Prime Video OTT platform, and reached a much broader audience. Even now I receive emails of appreciation from distant corners of the world. I would love to see all my films on OTT platforms so that they can be enjoyed by a wider audience. However, the truth is that not just my films but even acclaimed Marathi movies by new-age directors are being overlooked by OTT platforms. They refuse to acquire them or offer fair compensation for them. As a result, outstanding award-winning content remains unnoticed due to inadequate publicity. I've been informed that

Samaantar (2009), with
Sharmila Tagore,
Sandhya Gokhale

some platforms are unwilling to accept older or regional content even if it is offered at no cost. When monetisation options have been exhausted, I think filmmakers should make their content universally accessible freely through the web.

At the end of *Dhyaasparva*, a statement is heard in the voice of Nana Patekar in the Marathi version, and in Gulzar saab's voice in the Hindi one, against the backdrop of a huge crowd:

'On October 14, 1953, Raghunath Karve died.
His voice did not reach his countrymen in his lifetime.
Will it reach them at least today?'

Throughout his life, Karve demonstrated an extraordinary ability to defy convention and swim against the tide. What was the source of his strength and conviction? Where did he get the strength to swim against the tide throughout his life? Why did society treat him with such disrespect? Why did we, as a society, ignore his visionary perspective? Even after completing the film, these questions continued to haunt me. Though I felt proud as a director, I felt ashamed as a human being and regret as a member of this society that rejected him.

In 1920, he boldly predicted that 'human reproduction and copulation will soon be decoupled. Consequently, the grip of religion will weaken, and the twentieth century will usher in an era of science and rational thinking'. A century later, we find ourselves in a world where scientific progress is at its peak, yet religion's influence persists, defying his forecast.

Today, with so many heinous incidents happening around us globally, it feels like our senses have become numb. Migrant workers, forced to flee their homes and states in search of livelihoods, could be seen trekking back hundreds of miles in massive numbers during COVID-19, but we were powerless to halt their exodus. Purveyors of falsehoods and toxic hatred continue to spew their venom 24/7, and we seem unable to muzzle them. Perpetrators of heinous crimes roam free, and we cannot bring them to justice; orphaned girls are being exploited, and we are unable to protect them. Leaders prioritise political gains over secular values, and we are not able to hold them accountable.

Then what have we achieved so far?

Today, I have one fear that I have never experienced before—is the surrounding darkness strangling me? Is my ultramarine blue essence fading?

I agree with Antonio Gramsci when he says, 'I'm a pessimist because of intelligence, but an optimist because of will.'

In ultramarine hues,
my essence unfurls;
A drop of blue
dispersing far and wide,

Alas, those days are long gone,
when I stood watching
the resplendent rising sun,
emanating luminous rays
that lit up the environs.

All I am able to see now
is the path winding down;
Spanning eight long decades
with twists and turns,
laden with obstacles, strewn with pitfalls.

The path has culminated,
next to the same drop,
although by now, it's a dense condensate.

Spiralling downwards,
perhaps all the way, into the gently diminishing future;
perhaps till it becomes tranquil and cold.

Oxygen has gone down to fifty.
My eyes are weak.
Fleeting fragments of a life once aglow
Now whispers of memories, in winds that blow.
But still, my viewfinder captures the 'Hyacinth',
Gripping my umbilical cord, tightly, in one hand
and in the other, holding a kite;
trying utmost to fly it into the glowing sun.

I'll voice my depths,
Till this ultramarine essence gleams.

Filmography

Year	Title	Language	Acting/ Direction	Direction
1971	Shantata! Court Chalu Aahe	Marathi	Acting	Satyadev Dubey
1971	Bajiravcha Beta	Marathi	Acting	Raja Thakur
1974	Rajnigandha	Hindi	Acting	Basu Chatterjee
1976	Chhoti Si Baat	Hindi	Acting	Basu Chatterjee
1976	Chitchor	Hindi	Acting	Basu Chatterjee
1977	Bhumika	Hindi	Acting	Shyam Benegal
1977	Taxi-Taxie	Hindi	Acting	Irshad
1977	Tuch Mazi Rani	Marathi	Acting	R. Tipnis
1977	Agar	Hindi	Acting	Ismail Shroff
1977	Gharaonda	Hindi	Acting	Bhim Sain
1977	Kanneshwara Rama	Kannada	Acting	M.S. Sathyu
1977	Kanneshwara Rama	Kannada	Acting	M.S. Sathyu
1977	Safed Jhooth	Hindi	Guest Actor	Basu Chatterjee
1977	Wohi Baat/Sameera (Unreleased)	Hindi	Guest Actor	Vinay Shukla
1978	Damaad	Hindi	Acting	Rajat Rakshit
1978	Footpath (Incomplete)	Hindi	Acting	Amol Palekar
1978	Shringaramas Paper Boats (Both unreleased)	Kannada English	Acting	Pattabhi Rama Reddy
1978	Bin Baap Ka Beta (Incomplete)	Hindi	Acting	Mukul Dutt

1978	Agantuk (Incomplete)	Kannada	Acting	Amol Palekar
1979	Ankush (Incomplete)	Hindi	Acting	Mukul Dutt
1979	Amar Milan (Incomplete)	Hindi	Acting	M. Hanif
1979	Solva Sawan	Hindi	Acting	Bharathiraja
1979	Gol Maal	Hindi	Acting	Hrishikesh Mukherjee
1979	Baton Baton Mein	Hindi	Acting	Basu Chatterjee
1979	Mother	Bengali	Acting	Narayan Chakraborty
1979	Jeena Yahan	Hindi	Guest Actor	Basu Chatterjee
1979	Do Ladke Dono Kadke	Hindi	Acting	Basu Chatterjee
1979	Meri Biwi Ki Shaadi	Hindi	Acting	Rajat Rakshit
1980	Apne Paraye	Hindi	Acting	Basu Chatterjee
1980	Akriet	Marathi	Acting	Amol Palekar
1980	Aanchal	Hindi	Acting	Anil Ganguly
1981	Kalankini	Bengali	Acting	Dinen Gupta
1981	Yun Bhi Hota Hai (Incomplete)	Hindi	Acting	Mohan Kavia
1981	Ashwamedher Ghoda (Incomplete)	Bengali	Acting	Shankar Bhattacharya
1981	Chehre Pe Chehra	Hindi	Guest Actor	Raj Tilak
1981	Agni Pareeksha	Hindi	Acting	Kamal Majumdar
1981	Naram Garam	Hindi	Acting	Hrishikesh Mukherjee
1981	Plot No. 5	Hindi	Acting	Yogesh Saxena
1981-82	Britta (Incomplete)	Bengali	Acting	Pijush Ganguly
1982	Shriman Shrimati	Hindi	Acting	Vijay Reddy
1982	Jeevan Dhaara	Hindi	Acting	T. Rama Rao
1982	Olangal	Malayalam	Acting	Balu Mahendra

1982	Spandan	Hindi	Acting	Biplab Roy Chowdhury
1982	Ram Nagari	Hindi	Acting	Kantilal Rathod
1983	Nirvaan (Unreleased)	Hindi	Acting	Jalal Agha
1983	Chena Achena	Bengali	Acting	Pinaki Chaudhuri
1983	Pyaassi Ankhen	Hindi	Acting	Ram Kelkar
1983	Ashray	Hindi	Acting	Biplab Roy Chowdhury
1983	Rang Birangi	Hindi	Acting	Hrishikesh Mukherjee
1984	Prarthana	Bengali	Acting	Asit Sen
1984	Aadmi Aur Aurat	Hindi	Acting	Tapan Sinha
1984	Ados Pados	Hindi (TV series)	Acting	Sai Paranjpye
1984	Tarang	Hindi	Acting	Kumar Shahani
1985	Ankahee	Hindi	Acting	Amol Palekar
1985	Jhoothi	Hindi	Acting	Hrishikesh Mukherjee
1985	Brahman, Kshatriya, Vaishya, Shudra (Incomplete)	Marathi	Acting	Haider Ali
1986	Baat Ban Jaye	Hindi	Acting	Bharat Rangachary
1986	Khamosh	Hindi	Acting	Vidhu Vinod Chopra
1986-87	Satyajit Ray Presents	Hindi (TV series)	Acting	Sandip Ray
1987	Kal (Unreleased)	Hindi	Acting	Dilip Dhawan, Haider Ali
1987	Kachchi Dhoop	Hindi (TV series)	Acting	Amol Palekar
1987-88	Aa Bail Mujhe Maar	Hindi (TV series)	Acting	Jyoti Swaroop
1988	Naqab	Hindi (TV series)	----	Amol Palekar
1990	Thodasa Roomani Ho Jaayen	Hindi	----	Amol Palekar
1991	Mrignayani	Hindi (TV series)	----	Amol Palekar
1993	Paulkhuna	Marathi (TV series)	----	Amol Palekar
1994	Teesra Kaun	Hindi	Acting	Partha Ghosh

1995	Bangarwadi	Marathi	---	Amol Palekar
1996	Daayra	Hindi	---	Amol Palekar
2000	Kairee	Hindi	----	Amol Palekar
2001	Dhyaasparva & Kal ka Aadmi	Marathi Hindi	----	Amol Palekar
2003	Anaahat	Marathi	----	Amol Palekar
2005	Paheli	Hindi	----	Amol Palekar
2006	Thaang Quest	Marathi English	----	Amol Palekar
2007	Dumkata	Hindi	----	Amol Palekar
2007	Krishnakali	Hindi (TV series)	----	Amol Palekar
2009	Samaantar	Marathi	Acting	Amol Palekar, Sandhya Gokhale
2010	And Once Again	English	----	Amol Palekar
2011	Dhoosar	Marathi	----	Amol Palekar
2011	Bhinna Shadja	Documentary		Amol Palekar, Sandhya Gokhale
2013	We Are On, Houn Jau Dya	Marathi	-----	Amol Palekar, Sandhya Gokhale
2015	Ek Nayi Ummeed: Roshni	Hindi (TV series)	Acting	Sanjay Tripathi
2020	Gormint (Unreleased)	Hindi (OTT series)	Acting	Ayyappa K.M.
2021	200: Halla Ho	Hindi (OTT film)	Acting	Sarthak Dasgupta
2023	Gulmohar	Hindi (OTT film)	Acting	Rahul V. Chittella
2023	Farzi	Hindi (OTT series)	Acting	Raj & DK

List of Plays

Year	Title	Language	Acting / Direction	Theatre Company	Direction / Production
1967	Chup! Court Chalu Hai	Hindi	Acting	Theatre Unit	Dir.: Satyadev Dubey
1967-68	Suno, Janmejay	Hindi	Acting	Theatre Unit	Dir.: Satyadev Dubey
1968	Aadhe Adhure	Hindi	Acting	Theatre Unit	Dir.: Satyadev Dubey
	Aadhe Adhure	Marathi	Acting		
1969	Vallabhpurchi Dantkatha	Marathi	Direction and Acting	Theatre Unit	Co-directed with Satyadev Dubey
1970	Pagla Ghoda	Hindi & Marathi	Direction and Acting	Theatre Unit	Co-directed with Satyadev Dubey
1971	Draupadi	Marathi	Direction	India Culture League	----
10/11/1971	Avadhya	Marathi	Direction and Acting	India Culture League	----
1971	Tumchi Aamchi Goshta	Marathi	Direction and Acting	Bank of India	Inter-bank Competition
1972	Hayavadan	Hindi	Acting	Theatre Unit	Dir.: Satyadev Dubey
1972	Punascha Hari Om	Marathi	Acting	First production by Aniket	Dir.: Satyadev Dubey

1972 1973	Suryastachya Antim Kiranapasun Suryodayachya Pratham Kiranaparayant	Marathi	Direction	Aniket	(Edited version) Collected plays at Inter-bank Competition
1972	Rao Jagdev Martanda (First commercial play)	Marathi	Direction	Kalavaibhav	Co-directed with Dr Lagoo
1972	Chal Re Bhoplya Tunuk Tunuk	Marathi	Direction	Unmesh	----
1973	Aajacha Karyakram Yashasvi Karanyasathi Aaplya Sahakaryachi Garaj Aahe	Marathi	Acting	Bahuroopi	Dir.: Achyut Deshingkar
1973	Gochi	Marathi	Direction	Aniket	----
1973	Chal Mere Kaddu Thummak Thummak	Hindi	Direction and Acting	Agradoot, New Delhi	----
1973	Ek Ande Phutle	Marathi	Set Design and Lights	Amal Theatre	Dir.: Dilip Kolhatkar
19/08/1974	Vasanakand	Marathi	Direction and Acting	Aniket	----
1974	Pratima	Marathi	Acting	Avishkaar	Inaugural play of Chabildas Theatre
1974	Anamika Natya Mahotsav Bayaan Ek Buddhu Ka (A silent one-act play)	Hindi	Direction	Anamika, Kolkata	----
1975 1980	Aprakaashit Divakar	Marathi	Direction	Aniket	----
1975	Julus	Marathi	Direction	Bahuroopi	----
1976	Party	Marathi	Direction and Acting	Aniket	----
26/04/1977	Nakshatranche Dene	Marathi	Poetry Presentation	----	Produced by Bhaskar Chandavarkar

1978	Garbo	Marathi	Acting	Roopvedh	Dir.: Dr Shreeram Lagoo
1978	Aapla Buwa Asa Aahe	Marathi	Acting	Aniket	Dir.: Damu Kenkre
1979	Ani Mhanun Konihi	Marathi	Producer	Aniket	Dir.: Dilip Kulkarni
1980	Rashomon	Marathi	Direction and Acting	Aniket	----
1983	Mukhavate	Marathi	Direction and Acting	Rangayatri	Produced by Madhukar Naik
1985-86	Sambhogapsun Sanyasaparyanta	Marathi	Producer	Aniket	Dir.: Satyadev Dubey
1990	Nagamandala	Marathi	Producer	Aniket	Dir.: Dilip Kulkarni
1992	Pagla Ghoda	Marathi	Direction and Acting	Aniket + NCPA	Did not act in the initial shows
1992	Kaala Vajeer, Pandhara Raja	Marathi	Acting	NCPA	Dir.: Vaman Kendre
2007	Pagla Ghoda	Bengali	Direction	Epic Theatre	New Jersey
2011	Aadhe Adhure	Hindi	Direction	Natyabharati	Washington D.C.
2019	Kusur	Hindi	Direction and Acting	Anaan Nirmitee	Co-directed with Sandhya Gokhale